WE CLAIMED THIS LAND:

Portland's Pioneer Settlers

By Eugene E. Snyder

Binford & Mort Publishing
Portland, Oregon

We Claimed This Land:
Portland's Pioneer Settlers

Copyright © 1989 by Binford & Mort Publishing
All rights reserved. No part of this book may be reproduced in any form or by any electronic or mechanical means including information storage and retrieval systems without permission in writing from the publisher, except by a reviewer who may quote brief passages in a review.

Printed in the United States of America
Library of Congress Catalog Card Number: 89-60948
ISBN: 0-8323-0471-9 (hardcover)
ISBN: 0-8323-0468-9 (paperback)

First Edition 1989

Contents

Preface v
Introduction ix
    Free Land Out West ix
    The First Survey xi
    Some Characteristics of Our Pioneers xx
The Pioneers' Stories 1
Index 279
Acknowledgments 288

BY THE SAME AUTHOR

Early Portland: Stump-Town Triumphant
   Rival townsites on the Willamette River, 1831-1854, and the dramatic story of Portland's victory in the battle to become Oregon's metropolis.

Skidmore's Portland: His Fountain and Its Sculptor
   Victorian Portland, from the 1850s to the 1880s, as seen through the life of Stephen Skidmore. Includes a biography of Olin Warner, the sculptor of Portland's famous Skidmore Fountain.

Portland Names and Neighborhoods: Their Historic Origins
   More than 950 street, school, and park names, with biographical information about the persons for whom they are namesakes. Detailed accounts of the development of several noteworthy neighborhoods.

About the cover:
The cover illustration is a reproduction of a painting by Clive Davies, an Oregon artist.

Preface

"Pioneers, O Pioneers" is the theme of a well-known poem glorifying our forefathers. The word evokes some stereotyped images: covered wagons, ox teams, log cabins. And, in the case of Oregon, some historic names come to mind: McLoughlin, Jason Lee, Joe Meek...But the great mass of immigrants remain rather faceless, unless one of them happens to be your great grandfather. Except for such relatives or those who became politically or economically prominent, the pioneers are an impersonal multitude.

In the following pages, we meet a cross-section of our earliest arrivals, chosen not because they because famous, or infamous, but on the basis of one criterion only: they were the first to settle on the land that is now occupied by the city of Portland, Oregon.

These 212 pioneers typify the Western immigrants of the 1840s-1860s, but most of them will not be found in your conventional history books. They were, and have heretofore remained, quite obscure, as individual characters. However, significant information about them is available from records of early land claims, real estate transactions, old newspapers, and other archival material, giving us insight into their personalities and circumstances. Taken all together, these 212 biographies provide an intimate acquaintance with "The Pioneers" as they really were.

These first settlers are also interesting because their names are in daily use in purchases of real estate. The title to every lot in Portland is traced back to one or another of them, as original owner.

Among those who fall within the city limits of our sample, the space allotted to each pioneer varies widely. There is no correlation whatever between the length of a subject's biographical sketch and his social importance, creativity, or moral worth. Some, who left no monument either physical or intangible, are portrayed in detail, because their activities illustrate interesting aspects of frontier life. Others, whose lives would seem to offer intriguing potentials, are discussed only briefly, because no more information was available.

A Note on Illiteracy

A substantial number of our first settlers (perhaps one out of ten) could not write, as shown by the use of "X," his (or her) mark on deeds or wills. But illiteracy in the 1850s was not an indication of a person's intelligence or abilities. These were frontier people, many of whom grew up where there were no schools, who began working on farms as children, and who led migratory lives. Despite a lack of literary skills, they often did very well in an unstructured and expanding frontier community. But the signature by "X," his mark needs to be mentioned because it is one ingredient, though a minor one, in a lifelike portrait of "The Pioneer."

Prices and Inflation

To appreciate the significance of the amounts of money mentioned in these biographies, one needs to keep in mind the greater value of the dollar in those days. It's difficult to construct a "consumers' price index" that would relate the price level of the mid-nineteenth century to that of today because the items to be included in a "typical household budget" are so very different. As random samples, we note that advertisements in Portland in 1862 offered a "good meal" at a hotel for 25¢. A week's board and lodging in a hotel cost $9. To arrive at a general impression of the values involved, we can multiply the dollar amounts of the 1850s-1860s by fifteen to get a rough equivalent in 1989 dollars.

Street Boundaries Only Approximate

We have used the names of present-day streets to indicate the boundaries of the pioneers' claims. These perimeters are only approximate. The boundaries of the original claims often followed section lines (or half-section or quarter-section lines). But streets, as laid out by developers platting subdivisions, do not always follow such boundaries. As a result, the boundaries of original claims often run through the middle of city blocks. But the streets cited will, in most cases, enable you to identify the original claimant who first owned your property.

Sources and References

The materials for this book were drawn from many sources. If a source has some special significance, it is indicated. But I have not burdened you with the elaborate references and footnotes which might be appropriate to an academic treatise. It is my aim to produce readable narratives, unencumbered with pedantic technicalities, yet scholarly in the sense of being accurate.

Anyone who has delved into local history archives knows there often are inconsistencies among the various sources, particularly as to dates of birth, dates of settlement, etc. Dates of death are usually reliable, not only because the event is so incontrovertible, but also because it generally happened later in the century when reporting was more methodical. Where there are inconsistencies, I have used the date that seems most probable.

Some of the archival references to our early settlers are advertisements they placed in newspapers. These give us clues to their place of residence and occupation as of that date. Many small advertisements appeared in newspapers of the 1850s and 1860s stating that "the undersigned" had found a stray horse or cow. One reason, of course, was that there were many animals around — in that rustic setting, most households had livestock of some sort. And perhaps people were helpful and neighborly to a praiseworthy degree in those pioneer days. But another reason for all those ads was that livestock is personal property and, according to common law, the person who found a stray animal could claim it as his own, provided he made a reasonable effort to notify the owner. A newspaper advertisement describing the animal constituted such a reasonable effort. As to such ads mentioned in the following biographies, we will not presume to appraise the balance between neighborly love and acquisitiveness. After the 1860s, those ads became less numerous. There were more fences, there was more branding, and as the free and open society gave way to organization and statistics, there was registration of animals with government agencies.

A Point of View

The great historian, Edward Gibbon, once wrote: "History is generally only the register of the crimes, the follies, and the mistakes of mankind." Perhaps that is true of traditional history — concerned with rulers, great conflicts, and the rise and fall of nations, and politicians. But the stories of most of our humble and obscure pioneers may contradict Gibbon by registering not defeat, but, on the contrary, adventurous triumphs and successes, even if they did take place in the relatively small cosmos of Portland. Perhaps Gibbon would disagree, but not one of our original settlers seems to me to have been, if understood fully, a truly unlovely character.

To capture the flavor of life in the mid-nineteenth century, I have used many quotations from newspapers of the day. These remnants from their contemporary environment will, I hope, help you to know these pioneers as human beings, and to share their life experiences in a palpable and personal way.

Eugene E. Snyder
February 14, 1989

Introduction

Free Land Out West

If you own real estate, the title to your land goes back, through a chain of buyers and sellers, to some original first owner who got it from "the United States." But where, you may ask, did "the United States" get *its* title? That depends on the part of the country we are considering. The great mid-section, now comprising 13 states in the Missouri-Mississippi valley, was acquired in 1803 by the "Louisiana Purchase" from France. (You are not to ask where France got *its* title.) As for the Pacific Northwest, a treaty with Great Britain in 1846 allocated it to the U.S. Before that, both countries had claimed it. The compromise of 1846 established the boundary between Canada and the United States at the 49th parallel of latitude. This gave to the U.S. the title to all lands in Idaho, Washington, and Oregon — a rough approximation of the Columbia River Basin.

Much of this area is still owned by the Federal Government — the National Forests, for example. But most of it was sold or given to "settlers." The history of this distribution of the public domain is chaotic, and not entirely free from incidents of fraud and violence. Land Offices were established at which ownership was transferred from the Federal Government to private individuals by means of deeds such as "United States to George W. Smith." Those offices were deluged by such a rush of applicants that a new expression was added to the American vocabulary: ". . .doing a Land Office business" — idiomatic for crowded, clamoring, frenzied action. For our purposes, we can summarize it all by saying that private ownership of the land that is now Portland, Oregon came about in one of four ways:

1. Free land grants, as provided by the Donation Land Act, which Congress passed on September 27, 1850. It applied specifically to the Oregon Territory, which then included what is now the State of Washington. That Act granted free land to settlers who would agree to live upon and cultivate their claims for four consecutive years. After four years, the applicant made final "proof" (that he had, indeed, lived upon and cultivated the land as required), and the Land Office issued a "patent" (title to the land). The Act granted 320 acres (½ section) to every male citizen over 21 years of age who arrived in Oregon before December 1, 1850, and to a married couple 640 acres (1 section). The Act's provisions led to a great scurrying to get to Oregon before December 1st, and also precipitated some rather hasty marriages. For arrivals after December 1st, grants were reduced to 160 acres for single men and 320 acres for a couple. December 1855 was the expiration date for this offer of Free Land.

2. Homesteads. Congress passed several "Homestead Acts," which generally provided for the sale of public land at $1.25 per acre.

3. Purchase of School Land. The Federal Government granted such land to States to help finance public education. The State of Oregon sold off some "school land" in what is now Portland. These tracts are identified by the names of the individuals who bought them from the State.

4. Grants to veterans ("Military Bounty" land warrants). A warrant, for a specified number of acres, was negotiable, and could be sold by the veteran who received it to someone who was then entitled to acquire the acreage anywhere in the public domain. Prices paid for such warrants were usually in the range of 70 cents to $1 per acre.

The following table shows how the 212 original claimants within our Portland boundaries acquired their land:

    Donation Land Claim ("DLC") 152
    Homestead 26
    Purchase of School Land 19
    "Military Bounty" Warrant 17

These add up to 214 because two settlers who had homesteads also used "Military Bounty" warrants to get additional acreage.

The size of the 152 DLCs varied widely:

More than 400 acres (mostly
about 640 acres) 52
About 320 acres 77
About 160 acres 19
Small parcels 4

The acreages offered in the Donation Land Act were, of course, maximums. Settlers often selected claims which were less than that because they liked a certain location but claims of surrounding previous settlers left only smaller tracts still available. Or the course of a river or slough might restrict acreage but, even so, the site was desirable because of the convenience of water transportation. After about 1850, remaining unclaimed tracts of 640 acres could be found only by going rather far out from the Portland village townsite. A smaller tract close in might be more appealing than a whole section out in the wilderness. That depended partly on whether the settler intended actively to farm his claim for many years, or to hold it only for a few years as a speculation.

The First Survey

If you are flying over the western United States, you may look down and see that where the hand of Man has fallen upon nature, it is a rectilinear hand. Nature is curvaceous, but Man — at least in matters of real estate — seems to prefer squares. The undulating countryside is covered with rectangular ranches, farms, and other property holdings. It is a checkerboard landscape.

The reason for this appearance is that property lines in the West were all laid out by rectangular survey. The lines for such a survey are analogous to the lines of longitude and latitude that determine location on the world's surface. From a "starting point," a north-south "meridian" is laid out (corresponding to a meridian of longitude) and also an east-west "base line" (corresponding to a parallel of latitude).

A good example is the survey that began at Portland, Oregon, by which every lot in Portland and, indeed, in all of Oregon and Washington, is located and identified. It is called the "Willamette Survey." On June 4, 1851, a stake was driven at the starting point and from there the initial survey lines were measured off northward to Canada, southward to California, and eastward to Idaho. The stake was later replaced by a stone marker. That starting point is now memorialized by a bronze plaque in the little "Willamette Stone State Park," located in the hills west of Portland near Skyline Boulevard. (Idaho was surveyed later, with its own starting point for a "Boise Meridian" and "Boise Base Line".)

The "Willamette Survey" was ordered by the Donation Land Act and was an essential part of that Act. Without the survey, there would be no way to locate and identify the boundaries of the settlers' claims. The Act required appointment by the President of a Surveyor-General for the Oregon Territory. He was to set up a Land Office at Oregon City (then the capital of the Oregon Territory), establish his starting point "at or near the mouth of the Willamette River," and hire survey crews to survey a "Willamette Meridian" and "Willamette Base Line."

President Fillmore appointed John B. Preston to be the Oregon Surveyor-General. Fillmore was a Whig, and he saw to it that his appointee was also a Whig. In those days, many Federal offices were filled by the so-called "spoils system," whereby the President appointed people of his party to Federal jobs. "To the victor shall go the spoils" was an ancient slogan applying to military combat, but it also applied to victories in an election. The spoils system had, of course, many abuses, but it did mean that there was less opportunity for the build-up of an entrenched bureaucracy. When the party in power lost an election and the President had to leave, many Federal employees left with him. In any case, there is no reason to doubt that "General" Preston, as he was sometimes called, was a competent surveyor.

When Preston was preparing for his trip, he agreed to escort five young ladies to Oregon City — an interesting assignment which came about in this way. There was, at Oregon City, a Congregational minister, George Atkinson, who had come to Oregon by ship in 1848. He established a Clackamas Female Seminary and also helped to start the Tualatin Academy, at Forest Grove. He needed teachers for these and other schools, and he requested his sponsoring Congregational Society "back East" to send out teachers. Five devout young ladies had answered the call, and the Church Society arranged for the girls to come West under the care of Preston. Thus, Preston had not only to convey considerable impedimenta for surveying, but also to shepherd five young ladies, his wife (Lucy Ann), and his young daughter (Clara). From this, we can deduce something about General Preston's character. We see him as a kindly and patient man.

Meanwhile, out in Oregon, settlers were complaining about the slowness of the survey. People had preceded government, and settlement had run far ahead of surveying. Thousands of pioneers were living on land they claimed but to which they had no clear title because the boundaries of their "claims" were vague. Some claims had been registered informally with a "Provisional" Government that functioned at Oregon City from about 1845 to 1848. A more official registration of claims was possible with the Territorial Government created in August 1848. But the claims were marked only by stakes driven rather casually into the ground or by blazes on tree trunks, which could have no legal standing until the boundaries were described and located by a general survey of the Territory. Hence, the impatient clamor for the Willamette Survey to be hurried along.

The Preston party arrived at Oregon City April 20, 1851. That seems quite expeditious for those days. The Donation Land Act was not passed by Congress until September 27, 1850. President Fillmore had to find and appoint a good man (a Whig). Preston had to collect surveying gear, travel (with his entourage) by ship to Panama, cross the Isthmus on mule-back, take another ship to get to San Francisco, and then await a ship for the trip to the Willamette River. All this was accomplished in just seven months.

In preparing for his survey, General Preston could refer to several maps prepared by early settlers and explorers. One, called the "Clark Map" and based on observations by the Lewis and Clark expedition, was published in 1810. It showed good detail along the Columbia River, but the hinterland was blank and the compass directions of the mountains and rivers were slightly askew. The "Chapin Map" published in 1839 was accurate as to large features such as the location and contours of the Columbia River and Puget Sound. Captain (later General) John Fremont explored the area in 1842 and maps were prepared from his observations. The "Smith Map" published in 1843 showed quite good detail for Oregon and Washington. And the General Land Office in Washington, D.C. was making surveys and maps which would have been available.

Preston wanted his Base Line to lie entirely on the south side of the Columbia River and not to criss-cross the river, because such crossings would be very troublesome for the survey crews. Fortunately, the Base Line did not go up and over Mt. Hood, which would also have been a bit awkward. For his north-south meridian, Preston wanted a line which would cross the Columbia River only once and also pass west of Puget Sound, for convenience in surveying. Having thus determined roughly where his Base Line and Willamette Meridian should be, Preston knew, from the intersection of those lines, where to drive the stake for his starting point.

The survey crews were composed of at least four men: a surveyor (armed with a compass, a telescopic transit, and, hopefully, some knowledge of trigonometry); two chainmen (one on each end of a chain measuring exactly 66 feet in length); and one or more axe-men (whose job it was to cut a straight path through the underbrush).

The surveyor would aim his transit, the axe-men would hack away and the chainmen would stretch their 66-foot chain. The lead chainman would drive in a stake, the rear chainman would come forward and place his end of the chain at the stake,

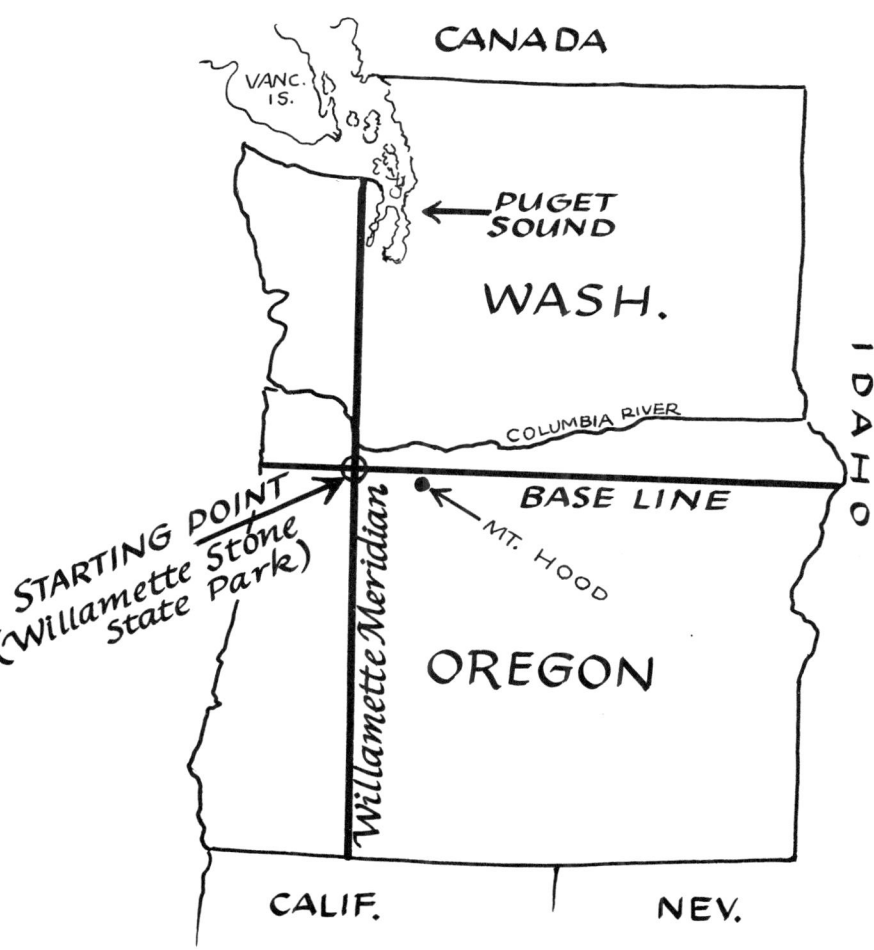

and the lead chainman would trudge on another 66 feet and drive in another stake. When they had repeated that operation 80 times, they would have advanced exactly one mile. At that point, they would drive in a marked stake which would later become the starting point for surveying a section line. And at six miles (480 chain-lengths and perhaps several days of weary work — the crews would camp out in the wilderness at night), they would drive in a bigger stake, which would mark the corner of a Township.

Out in the field, real-life surveying can become much more complicated — detouring around lakes, or going up and down a hill. Our purpose here is simply to show how Townships and Sections are created. The system was devised by Thomas Jefferson, when Virginians were pushing settlement westward over the Appalachian Mountains into the Ohio Valley. Townships are large squares six miles on a side, and thus containing 36 square miles, each called a Section. The survey lines east and west from the starting Meridian measure off "Ranges." The map titled "Numbering of Townships" shows how they are identified. In giving a location, it is customary to state the north-south number first and then the east-west (Range) number. For example, Ross Island, shown on the map, is located in Township "1 South, 1 East."

The next map shows "Divisions of a Township into Sections." We have used Township "1 South, 1 East" for our illustration. Continuing our example, we see that Ross Island is not only in that Township but, more specifically, in Sections 10, 11, 14, and 15 of that Township.

Each Section (i.e., one square mile) contains 640 acres, and many settlers qualified for that large a Donation Land Claim. But most settlers received only parts of Sections. Sections are divided into four smaller squares ("quarter-sections"), each containing 160 acres. And those quarter-sections are further divided into four smaller squares, each containing 40 acres. To understand the system, find "Council Crest" on the map, in Section 8. Its precise location would be stated as being "in the S.W. ¼ of the N.E. ¼, Section 8, Township 1 South, 1 East, Willamette

Introduction xvii

Numbering of Townships

Range 2 West	Range 1 West	Range 1 East	Range 2 East
Township 3 North	3N, 1W	3N, 1E	3N, 2E
Township 2 North	2N, 1W	2N, 1E	2N, 2E
Township 1 North	Starting Point of Willamette Survey →	1N, 1E	1N, 2E
		Base Line	Stark Street
Township 1 South	1S, 1W	1S, 1E	1S, 2E
Township 2 South	2S, 1W	2S, 1E	2S, 2E

Sauvie Island · COLUMBIA · WILLAMETTE · Willamette Meridian · RIVER · Ross Island · Ca. 41st Ave. · 162nd Ave.

xviii Introduction

Division of a Township into Sections
Example: Township 1 South, 1 East

Survey." To a person familiar with the system, that description would give as exact a location as an airplane navigator would need to find the landing strip on Guam.

Principal survey lines often became the alignments for arterial streets. Thus, Stark Street is on the Base Line and was originally called Base Line Road. Division Street is on a section line in Township "1 South, 1 East" and was originally called Section Line Road. Section lines became the alignments for several other major steets on the East Side: 62nd, 72nd, 82nd, 92nd, 102nd, and 122nd.

As for Surveyor-General Preston who came into office as a political appointee, he also went out in the same way. The Whigs lost the election in November 1852. A Democrat, Pierce, was elected President. He took office March 4, 1853, and soon appointed a Democrat to replace our General Preston.

Mr. Preston's tour of duty had not been altogether joyful. Besides the constant nagging to hasten the surveying, he also had to endure a personal tragedy. It is mentioned in the diary of Mrs. Atkinson, wife of Rev. George Atkinson. They also lived at Oregon City and were friends of the Prestons. This is her entry for November 25, 1853:

- Last night at 11:00 Clara Preston, only daughter of J. B. Preston, died of croup and congestion of the lungs. It was a house of grief. This is the last of three children.

Her entry for November 28 added:

I attended the funeral of Clara. The parents are bowed down with grief, yet they feel that God has done it for wise reasons...

Thus, we now see Surveyor-General Preston not only as a patient man, but also a man of devout faith.

Some Characteristics of Our Pioneers

Readers will not have gone far into this volume before they discover there was great diversity among these 212 first settlers of the Portland area. But within that diversity are some general characteristics, some common denominators, which enable us to visualize a prototype of "The Pioneer" as an individual. The tables below will help us to identify some of those characteristics.

These 212 first settlers also represent, collectively, a certain mix of individuals, which we believe is typical of the pioneers of the 1840s-1860s. At least, our 212 typify, both individually and collectively, those pioneers who were interested in an agricultural, small-town environment. Our settlers are not, of course, representative of those who went to the California gold fields.

Our Portland sample does omit one small component in the over-all westward migration, those who came not for economic but for religious reasons. There are no groups of Christian Separatists in our Portland sample, though we do have one or two saint-like recluses and a few quirky hermits.

Among our 212 are many who had already been pioneers — by migrating earlier from New England, New York, Pennsylvania, or Virginia to Illinois, Missouri, or Iowa, for example. Apparently, Oregon sounded even better — the field just a bit farther on seems greener to people with a nomadic bent.

Oregon's reputation as a land of opportunity appealed also to those still in the eastern states, particularly the less well-established citizens — it is not your successful bourgeois who pulls up his tent stakes, so to speak, and emigrates. If the emigrant was *very* adventurous, of free-wheeling style and speculative disposition, he probably went to California. But some of the early arrivals in Portland were young men from the East who sensed that their ambitions might find greater scope out on the frontier. Of these, some became rather large frogs in our small pond, whereas, had they remained in the more developed and structured societies of their birthplace, they might have created scarcely a ripple.

Not all of our settlers were successful. Four were suicides, and not in the passive sense Benjamin Franklin had in mind when he wrote, "Eight out of ten men are suicides." Ben was thinking of ill-advised habits of living. But one of our pioneers drowned himself deliberately, one put a bullet through his head, and one purposely drank poison. The fourth took a long sharp knife and cut his own throat. Also, one of our pioneer settlers was hanged, legally and publicly, on a street corner in early-day Portland.

Some other information about our 212 original settlers can be arrayed in tables. Place of birth is known for 181 of them. One was born in Oregon. Obviously, he was not a Donation Land claimant (the cut-off date for DLCs was 1855). He acquired a homestead in 1880. Here is the Place of Birth for the remaining 180:

East	(37%)	South	(10%)
New England	26	Virginia	8
New York	16	No. Carolina	3
New Jersey	3	So. Carolina	1
Pennsylvania	15	Georgia	1
Delaware	2	Tennessee	3
Maryland	4	Louisiana	1
	66	Arkansas	1
			18

Old West	(38%)	Foreign	(15%)
West Virginia	5	Ireland	11
Kentucky	17	Germany	8
Ohio	30	England	7
Indiana	3	Scotland	1
Illinois	7	Norway	1
Missouri	6		28
	68		

xxii   Introduction

The place of birth frequently was not the place where these people grew up. Many, when still children, came with their parents from the East or South to the Old West, which included, of course, not only the states listed above as places of birth but also Iowa, Kansas, the Dakotas, etc. On that basis we estimate that between one-half and two-thirds of our first settlers came actually from the Old West.

For the foreign born, it is surprising how many came from such a small country as Ireland, until we remember that this was the time of the "Potato Famine."

We also know, for most of our 212 original settlers, the year when they arrived at Portland and their age at that time.

Year of Arrival		Age at Arrival	
Before 1845 . . . 8	1851 9	0 - 16 11	
1845 . . 13	1852 47	17 - 24 34	
1846 . . . 3	1853 14	25 - 35 64	
1847 . . 22	1854 1	36 - 50 56	
1848 . . 10	1855 1	Over 50 11	
1849 . . 15	1856-60 8	Not known . . . 36	
1850 . . 21	After 1860 . . 11		
	Not known 29		

Many members of one large wagon train of 1852 came to Portland. As for the 19 who came after 1855, they were too late for the Donation Land Act; their claims were by Homestead or by Military Bounty warrant.

The records show that our 212 settlers were about equally divided between married and single at the time of their arrival at Portland:

Single 98
Married 104
Not known 10

Church affiliation is known for 71 of our 212 settlers. Not surprisingly, most of them were Methodists, because the Methodist Church had been first in the field with missionaries and circuit-riding preachers. But other denominations were represented. Besides the settlers shown in the following table, others no doubt had some church connection, even if not mentioned in surviving records.

Methodist	36	"Christian" Church	2
Baptist	9	Lutheran	1
Roman Catholic	9	Church of the Brethren	1
Congregational	4	Presbyterian	1
Unitarian	4	Episcopalian	1
Jewish	2	United Evangelical	1

As for our settlers' claims, what did they do with their land after they acquired it? Did they keep it, live on it, and farm it? Or, as soon as they received the title, did they sell it and move on? Were they land developers or land speculators? This is another way of asking whether the Donation Land Act was a success, because it was the intention of the Congressional majority who passed that Act that it should promote the small family farm. That institution was believed, and still is believed by many, to be the Soul and Foundation of the American Way of Life! Opposed to this in Congress in the 1840s were the representatives of the Southern Plantation system. The Donation Land Act was a victory for those advocating the family farm. But Free Land can also be merely a speculative windfall. To assess the effectiveness of the Donation Land Act, we have divided our original settlers into two groups:

(1) those who died at Portland still owning their claim, or most of it.

(2) those who, within a few years after their arrival, sold their land or left Portland.

The allocation between these two groups is far from precise. And, for 16 of our settlers, the information is too scanty to permit even a judgment call. In the following table, those who used military warrants or who bought "school land" are shown separately, because the objectives in those programs were quite different. One would expect the interest in such land to be more speculative, and the figures show that to have been so. The Homestead acts were intended, like the Donation Land Act, to promote settlement and cultivation, and the results seem to have been similar. The entries in the table add up to 214 because, as explained earlier, two of the 212 settlers acquired land both by homesteading and with a military bounty warrant.

	DLC	Homestead	"School Land"	Military Warrant	Total
Retained their claim	96	12	6	7	121
Sold their claim or left Portland	51	9	8	9	77
Not known	5	5	5	1	16
Total	152	26	19	17	214

Of our 212 individuals, nearly all started life here as farmers. Certainly, the 178 who took up DLCs or Homesteads did so because they were required to live upon and cultivate their land for a certain number of years. Some of the others also began as farmers. But, as we saw, at least 77 quickly sold their land. Also, for most of those who retained their claims, agriculture eventually became a side-line. The list which follows shows the principal lifetime occupation of the 143 settlers for whom such information is available. We see a diverse assortment which includes just those skills and professions which would make possible the existence of a small town based on horse transportation. Our pioneer land settlers were also our pioneer townsmen.

Accountant 1	Herbalist 1	Real Estate 3
Baker 1	Hotel owner 2	Riverboatman 4
Blacksmith 3	Investments 1	Salmon packer 1
Boardinghouse owner 1	Laborer 3	Saloon owner 4
Carpenter 1	Land developer 6	Sawmill owner 1
Clerk (office) 1	Lawyer 5	Shipping 3
Contractor 1	Merchant 2	Speculator 1
Cooper 1	Miller 1	Stock-raising 2
Dairyman 5	Minister 9	Stonemason 2
Farmer 49	Nurseryman (fruit) 3	Surveyor 1
Financier 1	Photographer 1	Tanner 1
Florist 1	Physician 2	Teacher 1
Grocer 1	Plasterer 1	Tinsmith 1
Harnessmaker 1	Printer 2	Wagonmaker 2
		Woodcutter 9

Besides the 49 farmers, those engaged in dairying, land development, fruit-growing, real estate, stock raising, and wood cutting show the uses they could find for their land claims.

But these are generalities. Now, in the following pages, let us become better acquainted with our pioneer settlers as individuals, as friends.

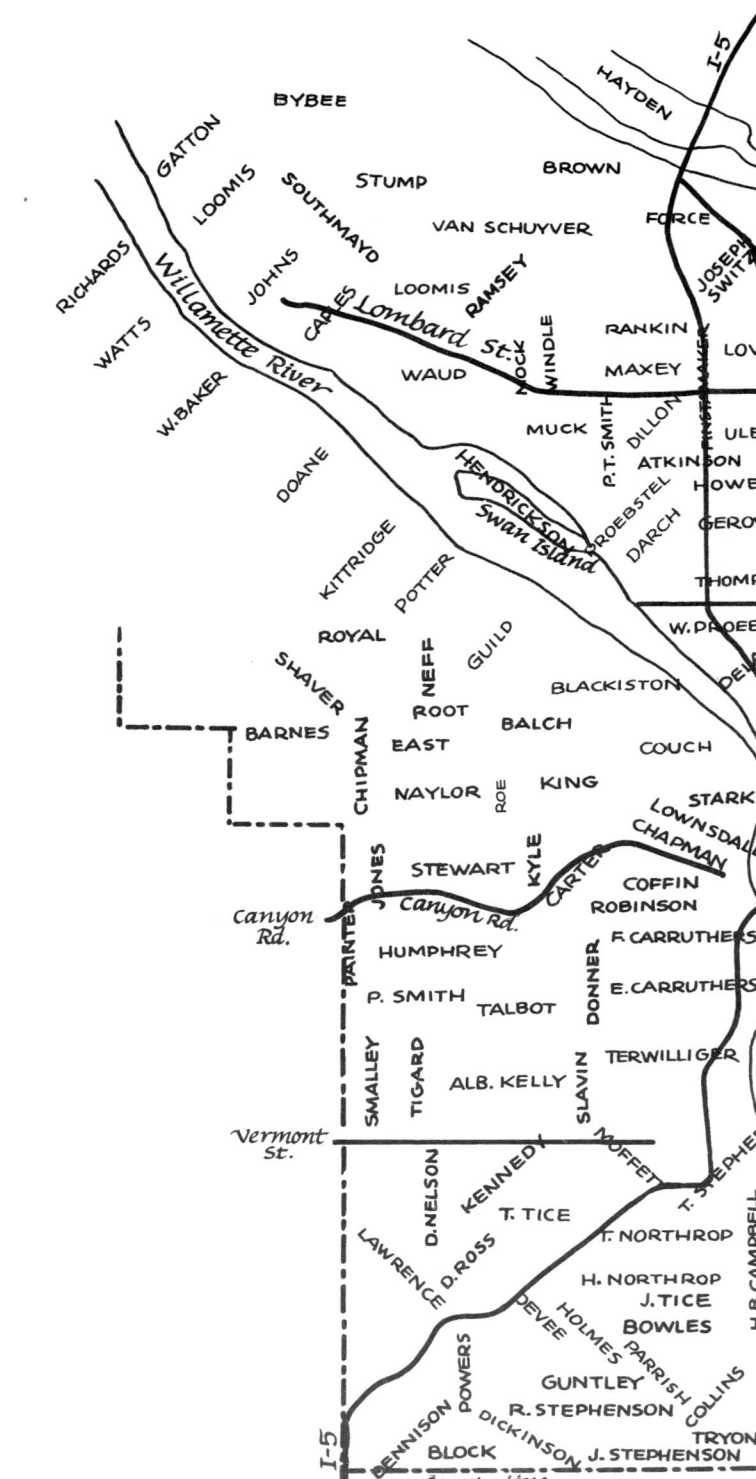

Columbia River

- JOHN SWITZLER
- WITTENBERG
- Y. SMITH
- McCLUNG
- BURRAGE
- P. BAKER
- WILSON
- A. SUNDERLAND
- 42nd
- MILLARD
- JEHU SWITZLER
- HOLTGRIEVE
- J. WILLIAMS
- STEVENSON
- I-205
- PAYNE
- B. SUNDERLAND
- DUVALL
- HALL
- WHITAKER
- CULLY
- G. LONG
- McENTIRE
- RENNISON
- CRIMMINS
- HOLLAND
- EMERSON
- LEMMON
- I. HILL
- MONAGHAN
- TOOHILL
- SWIFT
- HOLMES
- L. HILL
- PULLEN
- SCHRAMM
- QUIMBY
- McKEOWN
- ALLARD
- BOWERING
- T. KELLY
- CLARK
- BURRAGE
- HILDBURGH
- GILFRY
- BARNARD
- MAYNARD
- LUTHER STREET
- WATT STREET
- I-84
- Fremont St.
- Union Ave.
- IRVING
- BACKENSTOS
- LOWENBERG
- STREIBIG
- PRETTYMAN STREET
- J. QUINN
- HAY
- BURRAGE
- CANN
- GILHAM
- G.W. SMITH
- BARR
- WHEELER
- SULLIVAN
- T. QUINN
- DAVIDSON
- SCHMEER
- G. GRAY
- H. CASON
- GILFRY
- CLARY
- KERNS
- G.W. SMITH
- Stark St.
- P. PRETTYMAN
- S. NELSON
- GRADON
- STARR
- J. STEPHENS
- MURRAY
- CORWIN
- D. PRETTYMAN
- WITTEN
- R. GRAY
- P. KELLY
- Powell Blvd.
- TIBBETS
- C. KELLY
- H. KELLY
- ABRAHAM
- MARQUAM
- LENT
- KERN
- GATES
- B.P. SMITH
- ROSS Is.
- E. LONG
- J. KELLY
- H.T. CAMPBELL
- CASON
- A. LUELLING
- 39th
- WARREN
- FITCH
- McLEAN
- I. WILLIAMS
- W.J. CAMPBELL
- Foster Rd.
- J. WILLS
- MILLER
- YATES
- BATTIN
- McMAHAN
- JOHNSON
- H. LUELLING
- CREEK
- G. WILLS
- County Line
- TORRENCE

Abraham

When James Abraham left England for America in 1821, he was only ten years old and Portland was not yet even an idea. Its site was inhabited by beaver, enjoying the clear streams then flowing down from the west hills. But the young Englishman was destined to be a pioneer Portlander and an important figure in the city's development during the last half of the nineteenth century.

The transatlantic voyage by sailing ship must have been an exciting one for the boy. He was traveling with his parents, and the family settled on a farm in Ohio, where James grew up. He and his father began operating a sawmill there in 1834, an enterprise they carried on profitably for several years. In 1849, James, then 38 years old, married Jane, and in 1852, he and his wife and son William came to Oregon by ox-team.

Under the provisions of the Donation Land Act, the Abrahams were entitled to claim 320 acres. The tract they selected is bounded today by these southeast streets: on the west, 42nd; on the north, Holgate-52nd-Powell; on the east, 62nd; and on the south, Raymond. There, Mr. Abraham put up a small cabin, which was the family home while he began to lay a foundation for future wealth. His first job was with Luelling & Meek, pioneer nurserymen (and also DLC settlers) whose orchards were near the present-day Sellwood district. Later, Mr. Abraham went into the nursery business on his own. He invested his profits in real estate and became a land developer in East Portland. He was promoter of the Mt. Tabor Railway, which ran from the Willamette riverfront to 69th Avenue until replaced by streetcars.

Mr. Abraham's financial success enabled him to make some important gifts to the Methodist Church, of which he was a devoted member. He contributed $25,000 to the Portland Hospital, operated in the 1890s by the Methodists, and $45,000 towards construction of Centenary Methodist Church in East Portland. Those were gifts of lavish dimensions in terms of the prices of those days. In the 1890 City Directory, James Abraham is listed as a resident of East Portland, residing on 7th Street, and his occupation is given as "capitalist."

The one child of the Abrahams died in an accident at the age of 14. The *Oregonian* September 1864 noted:

> Fatal Accident — We are pained to learn of an accident that happened yesterday, resulting in the death of William Abraham, son of James Abraham, living at Mt. Tabor, in this county. [Mt. Tabor was then a rural area lying well outside the city.] The youth had taken a shot gun and was proceeding to the country, when he stumbled and fell, discharging the contents of the gun into his abdomen, death ensuing in a very short time. Willie was aged about 14 years. We shall miss him; he worked at our office on Saturdays, an apt and sprightly lad. But today he is gone.

In 1893, Mr. Abraham died and his wife came into possession of the entire estate. It was valued at $100,000 and consisted principally of 11,000 acres of timber land. The widow, also a faithful Methodist, outdid even her husband's generosity, and gave *everything* to the church. She made over the entire estate in trust for the use of the School of Theology at "Portland University," which the Methodists operated during the 1890s at the site where the University of Portland is today. The Abraham's adventureful lives thus appear in retrospect to have been the means through which a large fund of frontier capital was diverted from secular to sacred uses.

Allard

Alvin Allard was born in Vermont and was 36 years old when he arrived in Oregon in 1852. Being unmarried, he could claim only 160 acres under the Donation Land Act. He selected a tract bounded today by N.E. 15th, 24th, Fremont, and Prescott streets. He had an eye for the future; his tract included part of today's Alameda Heights, valuable view property. But he did not hold it long enough to reap substantial profits himself. In 1865, he sold the 160 acres for $600 to William Irving, the sea captain who owned a large claim just to the south. What restlessness or urgency prompted Alvin to sell so prematurely, we can only imagine. With his $600, he seems to have disappeared from the Portland scene.

Atkinson

The 1849 gold rush brought several men to California who eventually came north to Portland — either because they had found their fortunes and were looking for a place to invest the money or because they had *not* been successful there. One was Josiah Little Atkinson. Born in Massachusects in 1823, he helped his father on the family farm until he was 26, and then sailed around Cape Horn with other "49-ers" to try his luck in the gold fields.

His brother George had already set a example for the younger Josiah by coming to the Pacific Coast two years earlier, also sailing 'round the Horn. Brother George, however, came to work in quite different fields. He was a pioneer Congregational Church minister, who served at Oregon City beginning in 1848. He moved to Portland in 1863, became pastor of the First Congregational Church, and had a distinguished career in church work and also in promoting public education in Oregon.

Josiah, in his more earthly endeavor, dug for gold in California for three years, then invested his mining profits in a sawmill. In 1856, he married Isabelle. He was doing very well financially when a fire destroyed his entire investment. In 1866, he and his wife came to Portland. Letters from his brother George, describing the opportunites in Oregon, probably brought Josiah north to these greener pastures. Here, he entered the real estate business, in which he was active for the rest of his life.

Josiah L. Atkinson

The land which bears the name of Josiah Atkinson as first individual owner is a 160-acre tract that had been "school land." The Donation Land Act allocated some land in each township to the State, the proceeds from the sale of which should help pay for the establishment of schools in the new Territory. The State was gradually selling off this land, and in 1870 Josiah bought a quarter-section for $400. It is bounded today by N. Interstate, Delaware, and Killingsworth streets, and Portland Boulevard. The purchase was a windfall for the Atkinsons. Within seven months, Josiah and Isabelle had sold 108 of those acres for $2675, and the remainder continued to appreciate in value.

Josiah Atkinson died in 1902, aged 78. He was an active member of the First Congregational Church and of the Masonic Lodge.

Colonel Jacob Backentos

Backenstos

Colonel Jacob Backenstos was a turbulent spirit whose active life, full of adventure and controversy, ended in suicide. Born in Pennsylvania in 1811, he spent his early manhood in Illinois, where, in 1836, he married Sarah L. Lee, a niece of General Robert E. Lee. In 1844, he was a sheriff in Illinois when persecution of the Mormons was causing violence and disorder. Sheriff Backenstos, at the head of a posse, gave an order to fire upon a body of men resisting his authority — whether he was acting against the Mormons or against their persecutors is not recorded. As a result of the shooting, in which one person was killed, the sheriff was tried for murder, but was fully acquitted.

Shortly thereafter, he enlisted in the army to serve in the Mexican War. During that conflict, he was made a Lieutenant Colonel "for gallant and meritorious conduct." After the war, his regiment, a cavalry unit known as the "Mounted Rifles," was assigned to Fort Vancouver. They rode horseback across the plains, arriving in Oregon in October 1849. Three years later, partly because of a controversy with another officer, Colonel Backenstos resigned from the Army.

Jacob and Sarah settled on a 402-acre Donation Land Claim in November 1855, one month before the DLC law expired. They qualified for 640 acres, but by 1855 unclaimed land close to town was harder to find. Their claim is bounded today by N.E. 36th, 57th, Brazee, and Fremont streets.

The Colonel engaged in the business of loaning money and buying land claims, and "amassed considerable wealth." Just as things seemed to be going smoothly for him, a quarrel with a neighbor over some real estate led to the Colonel's downfall. A newspaper report gave this account:

> During the argument, Col. Backenstos snapped a revolver several times at the neighbor, it missing fire; the neighbor, Col. Backenstos alleged, meanwhile pursuing him with an axe, and nearly severing his thumb from his hand with a blow of it.

As a result of this ugly misunderstanding, the Colonel was indicted for assault with intent to kill. He asked to have the trial transferred from Multnomah to Clackamas County. The people of Multnomah County, he said, were prejudiced against him. A few days before the trial was to begin, he told a friend that even in Clackamas County he had so many enemies he would not get a fair trial. Nevertheless, he added with significant emphasis, he would never go to the penitentiary — he would die first. Later that day (September 26, 1857), he settled all his debts and, with a neat attention to detail, "told his wife where his watch was." That night, he drowned himself in the Willamette River opposite the village of Portland. The editor of the *Oregon Statesman* gave this character vignette:

> There was much feeling against him in the community, growing out of his business transactions. He was an intelligent and personally agreeable man, we believe, but his business transactions had rendered him odious to many. He leaves a widow and several small children.

That autumn was, indeed, a tragic time for the Backenstos family. About a month after the suicide, the *Oregonian* printed this item:

> Accident — The eldest son of Mrs. Backenstos accidentally shot himself through the hand while out gunning on Wednesday last. The hand was amputated by Dr. Wilson, of this city. The unfortunate boy is doing well.

Sarah Backenstos was named "administratrix" of the affairs of her husband, according to a newspaper advertisement concerning claims against the estate. The Colonel's adventurous and sensational frontier life ended, like many controversial careers, in the probate court.

Baker
Perry G.
William W.

A pair of brothers whose names are attached to two of Portland's original land claims were William Wells Baker and Perry G. Baker. They came from Virginia, where their father was a blacksmith.

William, born in 1828, left the family home first, moving to Iowa, where he married "Isabell" in 1849. The following year the young couple came across the plains to Oregon, arriving at Portland in September. William must have been well-favored and somewhat distinguished; after only three months in town, and though he was only 22 years old, he was called a "prominent Portlander" in an account of a ceremony in which he participated on the occasion of the first issue of the *Oregonian*. By April 1851, the Bakers had selected a 615-acre Donation Land

Claim on the west bank of the Willamette River opposite the St. Johns townsite. During the 1850s, they lived on their claim, and William operated a store and warehouse on the riverbank, at what came to be called "Baker's Landing." It was about six miles below the early Portland townsite. Early in the 1860s, the Bakers moved, from what then would have been a rather remote location, into Portland. In the City Directory of 1863, W.W.Baker is listed as a fruit merchant. The family lived at Ninth and Oak streets. The "W. W. Baker & Co." store was at First and Morrison streets, and the young proprietor did so well that he later built, at that location, the Occidental Hotel.

Another William Baker, owner of the Oyster Saloon in the 1860s and later a wagon-driver for the F. Opitz German Bakery, is not to be confused with our DLC pioneer.

About 1866, the William W. Bakers left Portland. They returned about 1875. Where or how they spent the interlude is not recorded, but it is possible they returned to the East Coast. On his return to Portland, Mr. Baker became editor and publisher of the *Thoroughbred Stock Journal*. The family residence was now at S.W. Front and Grant streets. In 1880, W.W.Baker began publishing a periodical called *Rural Spirit & Resources of Oregon*. The enterprise evidently thrived; by 1886, the firm had become "William W. Baker & Sons," and the magazine was being aimed at a larger market, its title having been broadened to *North Pacific Rural Spirit*.

Meanwhile, William's younger brother, Perry, had come to Portland and made a successful career for himself. He had remained in Virginia for several years as a helper in his father's blacksmith shop. In 1854, motivated by letters from brother William, he came to Oregon. The following year, he married Maria Loomis. She was the daughter of Donation Land Claim settler James Loomis. The marriage was performed in St. Johns by Solomon Richards, Justice of the Peace. Richards, too, was an original Donation Land claimant. These relationships show the interwoven closeness of the small community.

Perry worked first as a teamster, driving a wagon and team of horses out of a livery stable at S.W. Front and Salmon streets.

During this period, he acquired the claim which bears his name — 131 acres near Columbia Slough between N.E. Levee and Sunderland roads. He used a "Military Bounty" land warrant which he bought for about $160 from a volunteer who served during the "California Indian disturbances." Perry and his wife received title to that land in 1864 and the next year they sold it to Jehu Switzler for $200. Maria could not write; she signed the deed with "X," her mark.

In 1870, Perry went into business on his own, as a building contractor. Later, he took many contracts for street work in the city. He was also, during the 1870s, a member of the Portland Volunteer Fire Department. The Perry Bakers had nine children. Mr. Baker, who died in 1903, invested extensively and profitably in real estate. Migration to Portland by these two young Virginians opened up for both of them careers not only prosperous but rich in variety.

Balch

In a statement made just before he was hanged, Danford Balch said he was born in 1811 in Massachusetts and "My opportunities for education were very limited." As a young man, he came out to Iowa where, in 1842, he married a girl named Mary Jane. He and his wife and young family were among Portland's earliest pioneers, crossing the plains to Oregon in 1847, when he was 36 and Mary Jane 29.

In October 1850, the Balch family settled on their Donation Land Claim. Their tract extended from present-day Lovejoy Street to about Thurman Street and from 23rd Avenue to Macleay Park. Balch Creek, which runs in the deep canyon down through that park, is named for this pioneer. The small stream, now only a trickle, was the source for the municipal water supply during Portland's early days. Mr. Balch's claim contained 346 acres. Since he was clearly entitled to claim 640 acres, he evidently preferred to sacrifice some acreage in order to get a location close to town. He had delayed taking up a claim for three years after his arrival in Oregon. By October 1850, he would have had to go farther out to find an unclaimed tract as large as 640 acres.

Living on their DLC farm, the Balch family grew to nine children. The only memorial record of Mr. Balch during those years is an advertisement he placed in the newspapers in May 1858 about a cow he had found wandering on his farm:

> TAKEN UP by the undersigned, living in Multnomah County 2 mi. N.W. of Portland, one white cow with some red on her sides and head; crop off the right ear. Nine years old.
> D. Balch

An amiable, easy-going, and peaceful citizen, one would have said. Yet, the very next year, it was Mr. Balch's fate to be hanged publicly on a street corner in the center of Portland.

The trouble began, as it so often does, over a woman. In the fall of 1858, Mr. Balch had working for him on his farm a young man called Mortimer Stump. Mortimer was the son of Cuthbert Stump, another of Portland's pioneer Donation Land Claim settlers. Mortimer, the hired man, was living *en famille*, taking his meals and residing in the Balch home amidst the nine Balch children. In this captivating environment, Mortimer developed a truly fatal infatuation for the oldest Balch daughter, Anna, aged 15. Mortimer disclosed his passion to Mr. Balch and asked consent to marry her, but the father, so far from giving his blessing, ordered Mortimer off the premises. Anna, however, viewed Mortimer's proposal quite differently; a few days later she ran away from the farm and eloped with him. They crossed the Columbia River on the Switzler ferry (operated by another Donation Land Claim family) and were married clandestinely at Fort Vancouver, Washington Territory, by a Justice of the Peace.

For about a week, Mortimer and his young wife lived with his parents on the Stump Donation Land Claim, located in what is now east St. Johns. Then, on Thursday, November 18, the whole family (Mortimer, his parents, and Anna) came in to Portland by wagon, to purchase furniture and supplies so that the newlyweds could set up housekeeping on their own. They crossed the Willamette River by the Stark Street ferry, which was operated by a Donation Land Claim settler known affectionately as "Uncle Jimmy" Stephens. The ferry was large enough to transport wagons and teams of horses.

During the afternoon in Portland, Mr. Stump senior happened to meet Mr. Balch in Starr's Store, where they had an angry verbal exchange. Mr. Balch later alleged that Mortimer's father said during the encounter that he couldn't understand why Balch was making such a fuss about his daughter, that she was "just an ordinary little b----." Whether those were his exact words, or merely the sense of his statement as recalled by Balch, is uncertain, since there is no testimony by witnesses to substantiate it. In any case, the argument infuriated Mr. Balch. He got on his horse, rode out to his farm, found his double-barreled shotgun, loaded it with a heavy charge of buckshot, and appeared at the Stark Street Ferry just as the Stump party were getting aboard for their return trip. In the presence of the family and a dozen other passengers, he shot both barrels into his unwanted son-in-law, who "fell dead upon the spot."

Thereupon, the ferryman came up to Mr. Balch and said, rather quaintly, "I don't allow such work aboard my ferry." Mr. Balch replied that he "could not help it, it was an accident." He maintained throughout his trial that he had come simply to re-possess his daughter and had brought the gun only to defend himself, since, he alleged, Mortimer had threatened "to pound me within an inch of my life if I ever came after my girl." The gun, he affirmed under oath., had gone off accidentally.

Editor T. J. Dryer, of the *Oregonian*, commenting on the shooting, wrote: "There are several rumors afloat in relation to this horrible affair which we refrain from mentioning, as the whole thing will undergo a legal, and we hope a proper, investigation. Balch has always been regarded as an honest, industrious man, and heretofore sustained a good character, as far as we know. The deceased had numerous relatives living near here, and is said to have been a respectable young man. Thus," added the editor, showing the compassionate side of his character, rather than the vinegary cynicism he often revealed, "Thus have two large families been clothed in mourning by the commission of this 'murder most foul.'"

Mr. Balch was lodged in the county jail from November until the following spring, awaiting trial. By then, he had discovered that the jail was such a flimsy building that he could break out of it, which he did. For several months, he remained at liberty, at least a liberty of sorts. He hid out in the forest (what is now Forest Park) near his farm, taking many of his meals in his own farmhouse kitchen. His other needs were supplied by friends, for the community was by no means united in condemning him.

During the spring and early summer weeks which he spent in his forest hideout, Mr. Balch tried to sell his farm, acting through the friends who came to see him. Had he been able to do so, he planned to leave town on a sailing ship for South America. There were always ships at anchor in the river, and even at that early day, there was trade between Portland and the longer-established cities of Spanish America. The escape might have been easy — there were then no troublesome details such as passports, visas, or vaccinations. However, potential buyers of his farm were wary. They knew the land was valuable and would certainly become more so, but they were afraid the seller might not be able to convey to them a proper legal title before he was caught and hanged.

At the end of July 1859, Mr. Balch was re-arrested. The secret of his hiding place was betrayed by some meddling Judas, and the sheriff, accompanied by a party of armed men, hid in ambush in a wood near his farmhouse and seized him when he came in for breakfast. Late in August, he was tried and sentenced to be executed on October 17th.

There was much sympathy for him in the community. Extra guards were placed at the jail because, as the *Oregon Statesman* expressed it, "An attempt by local citizens to break into the jail for the release of Balch is apprehended." Such a storming of Portland's Bastille, if it was ever really contemplated, never occurred, and Mr. Balch was hanged on schedule, stoutly maintaining until the end that Mortimer's death was an accident.

Shortly before his execution, he received spiritual ministration from the Rev. Thomas H. Pearne, editor of the *Pacific Christian Advocate*, a Methodist periodical published at Portland. A written statement was prepared, signed jointly by both men, in which Mr. Balch recounted the whole sad episode, though the words and style of the document are clearly those of the learned Methodist divine. Rev. Pearne did not miss the opportunity to strike a blow against liquor, the condemned man admitting in the statement that he had, for several years, been indulging somewhat freely in intoxicating beverages and that, on the day of the fatal shooting, he had had two drinks.

The account of the execution, as reported in the *Oregonian*, contained these details:

> Danford Balch expiated his crime on the gallows on Monday last. There were about 5 or 6 hundred people present to witness the death of this unfortunate man, who, under the excitement of intoxicating drink, ignorance of the law, and evil advice, slew his fellow man. Among those who witnessed the hanging were the whole Stump family and also the daughter of Balch, that is, the widow of the murdered man.

A pioneer Portland resident who was a spectator at the hanging recalled in later years that the execution took place at Front and Salmon streets. Recollecting the event, he said, "I passed a saloon just across the street from the gallows, and in the reception room of the saloon, I saw, sitting in the window, Mrs. Balch and Anna [Balch] Stump. They had come to witness the hanging."

Editor Dryer, of the *Oregonian*, found the fact that a daughter had voluntarily witnessed her father's hanging almost unbearably revolting. His indignation burst forth in an especially flowery passage, in which he characterized the daughter's behavior as "a disgrace to the age and to every principle of filial affection exhibited by every species of brute creation, in the sea, or upon the earth." For some reason, the presence of Danford's wife at the spectacle did not seem to surprise the angry editor.

The *Oregon Statesman* correspondent was aghast at some other aspects of the execution. He wrote:

> Danford Balch was executed near the jail in Portland. [The jail was at Second and Taylor streets.] The awful spectacle was witnessed by an immense concourse of people, among whom I was pained and surprised to observe a large number of women and children. The wretched victim of the law was attended to the scaffold by the Reverends Pearne and Lewis, of the Methodist Church. Some individual, a speculator, had erected some seats near the gallows, intending to turn an honest penny by leasing them to spectators of Balch's dying agonies. But during the night preceding the hanging, some persons threw the seats into the river, thereby spoiling a very mean speculation.

To what extent Rev. Pearne was able to bring comfort to Danford Balch is hidden in the silence of the confessional. However, the following excerpts from the statement Mr. Balch signed just before his death give us some grounds for believing those ministrations were not in vain:

> I have great solicitude for my children. I suppose the married one will not return home. As to the children that are at home, I would like my wife to put them out at good homes, where they will be well trained and educated. I never before had any difficulty with the law. I never had occasion to strike a man in anger in my life. I trust it will be well with me in another world. My reasons for feeling and hoping so are my reading of the Scriptures and my hope in the mercy of God.

Following Danford Balch's execution, his land claim was divided into two parts, the west half (186 acres) being allotted to Danford's estate and the east half (160 acres) being assigned to his wife, Mary Jane. Danford's half lay in the rugged terrain around Balch Canyon, and it was sold by the court-appointed administrator for $700, to pay for charges against the estate. Mary Jane's east half, which included the present-day residential area around Chapman School and view property along Westover Road, became the subject of some complex transactions. In 1862, Mary Jane Balch sold her land to one John Confer for "five thousand dollars." How much of that purely nominal value she ever received is a moot question, since she took payment in the form of a mortgage from Confer and then, in a few months, became the wife of that same John Confer!

In 1869, John and Mary Jane Confer sold all their interest in the east half of the Balch DLC to John H. Mitchell, an attorney (and later U.S. Senator) who was looking after the Balch affairs, for $550. Evidently, Mary Jane could not write; she signed legal documents with "X," her mark. In September 1870, attorney Mitchell bought the interests of the Balch children in the Balch claim for $5550. Two weeks later, he sold the east half of the Balch DLC, and all interests therein, to Bernard Goldsmith (mayor of Portland at that time!) for $15,000. From then on, houses and streets began to appear, small tracts were sold off for subdivisions, and it was not long before the landscape bore little resemblance to the rustic hillside where, in 1858, Danford Balch had found a stray cow wandering on his farm.

Barnard

During an uprising of the Cayuse Indians in 1847-48, a regiment of "Oregon Volunteers" was recruited. Among those answering the call to arms was Joel Welch, who later received, under the Military Bounty Land law, an affidavit for 160 acres of government land. Such affidavits could be used by the soldier himself to acquire free land, or could be sold to someone else. Welch sold his to Obed M. Barnard, a harnessmaker who was living in East Portland in the early 1870s. Barnard found a 160-acre parcel of land (bounded today by N.E. Brazee, Fremont, 82nd, and 92nd) and used the affidavit to become the first person to have his name attached to those acres.

There is no record of what Barnard paid Welch, but the market price for military affidavits was usually about $1 per acre. If Barnard paid about $160 for the affidavit, it was not a bad investment because, in 1878, he sold the 160 acres to Henry Buckman for $900.

Barnes

    Charles
    Isaac
    William

Three parcels of land near Skyline Boulevard and Cornell Road first came into private ownership when Isaac Barnes and his sons, Charles and William, bought some "school land" from the State in 1870. Isaac and Charles each bought 40 acres and William bought 320 acres. The price was $2 per acre.

Surviving records give little information about this family. Isaac's wife was Esther or Hester — the uncertainty is probably related to the fact that she signed legal documents with "X," her mark. William, who was born in 1835, married Elizabeth. Charles, born in 1836, married Lydia. In 1888, Isaac and William sold 238 acres to a real estate company for $32,000.

This William Barnes was not the William T. Barnes for whom Barnes Road is named, though it seems probable that the two families were related. William T. Barnes was born in 1829, came to Oregon in 1852, and, with his wife Sarah Ann, took up a Donation Land Claim of 305 acres near Beaverton.

Barr

Two quite different life threads touched momentarily in 1869, with the result that the family name "Barr" became attached to a tract of land in northeast Portland. One of the actors in this story was Samuel E. Barr, a Pennsylvanian who came to Portland in 1852. The other was one Edward Hamilton, captain of a company of "Ohio Volunteers" in the Mexican War.

Samuel Barr had married a "Margaret" in Pennsylvania, where their first child, named Margaret Ann but known as "Annie," was born in 1844. Within the next year or two, the family moved to Iowa, where a son was born in 1847. Just as the daughter had been given the mother's first name, the son was christened Samuel M. Barr.

Mrs. Barr died in December 1847, following the birth of her son. On the 4th of July, 1849, Mr. Barr remarried. His second wife was a 22-year old girl named Margaret Jane Waterman. The work of the genealogist is not made easy by the fact that both Mr. Barr's wives and his daughter were all named Margaret.

In 1852, Mr. Barr, leaving his two children with their young stepmother, came across the plains to Portland "with a band of hardy pioneers," as a biographer expressed it. He planned to build a career and a home in Oregon and then return for his family. After four years at Portland, Mr. Barr had achieved sufficient status to be elected a representative to the Territorial Legislature. In the election of June 1856, he received 48 votes to 36 for his opponent, George Menill. In 1859, after seven years of separation, Mr Barr returned to Iowa to collect his wife and children. They boarded a sailing vessel on the East Coast and came 'round Cape Horn to Portland. It was a memorable trip for daughter Annie, aged 15, and young Samuel, aged 12.

Back in Portland, Mr. Barr, a Republican, again sought public office and in June 1860 was elected Justice of the Peace for the "north Portland district." In the election, he received 265 votes to 46 for W.M. King, his Democrat opponent. During the next few years, Mr. Barr's name appeared frequently in newspaper announcements of marriages he had performed. In such items, he was referred to as "S.E. Barr, Esq.," from which we visualize him as a man of some dignity and bearing. Squire Barr was also a genial and friendly man. When his daughter Annie was married in April 1861, at the age of 16, to Lyman Chittenden, the announcement in the *Oregonian* concluded with this sentence: "The printers were bountifully remembered." Mr. Barr evidently celebrated the occasion with unusually lavish largess. But joy was short-lived; only four months later, Annie died.

Meanwhile, back in Ohio, Captain Hamilton had received a "Military Bounty" warrant good for 160 acres, free, from the public domain. The Captain didn't want to come west, where unclaimed land was still available, so he sold his warrant. Mr Barr bought it and, in 1869, used it to acquire a 160-acre parcel of land bounded today by these N.E. streets: 92nd, 102nd, Halsey, and Brazee. He paid about $160 for the warrant, and it was a good investment; two years later, in May 1871, he sold the 160 acres for $1600.

Mr. Barr used his profit to move his growing family — he had seven children by his second Margaret — to a homestead near Astoria. There, he died in 1880. His wife lived until 1917, reaching the age of 90. The son, Samuel M. Barr, continued to live at Portland, where he owned a shoe store and later the Barr Hotel. The other children scattered over the Northwest, but the name remains on that original claim.

Battin

Thomas E. Battin owned his pioneer land claim for only two weeks. But it was long enough to get his name attached to it forever, and also to turn a rather neat profit.

Tom, who was born in Pennsylvania, was a young man of 19 when he came west, in 1864. He came without family, and joined a wagon train as a hired cattle drover, employed by one of the migrating families. When they reached Boise that fall, he stopped and spent the winter there. During those months, he met and married Caroline. She could not read or write, but that was a trivial detail which then, especially on the frontier, did not have the uncomplimentary implications it might have a century later. Tom did not let her lack of literary skills blind him to her good qualities, and there is nothing in the record to suggest that she did not make him a good wife.

In the spring, the young couple came on to Portland, where Tom worked at cutting cord wood, He saved his money and invested astutely in real estate. Most of his purchases were lots from earlier claims, whose pioneer owners were now beginning to sell some of their land. In the case of one tract, however, he was the first individual owner. It was a 160-acre parcel of "school land" which he bought from the State of Oregon in February 1871 for $200. Two weeks later, Thomas Battin and wife Caroline sold the 160 acres for $1000. The tract is bounded today by these S.E. streets: 62nd, 72nd, Flavel, and Clatsop.

The Battins then acquired a farm about a mile to the south, where they made their home for the remainder of their lives. The neighborhood near 82nd Avenue and Johnson Creek is still known as "Battin," an echo of the old family farm. Mr. Battin was a charter member of the first Grange in Oregon.

Blackiston

William Blackiston was born in Ohio and settled on his claim in April 1850, when he was 22 years old. The tract he selected is bounded today by N.W. 28th, Thurman, and Reed streets, extending to the river. Blackiston, unmarried in 1850, was entitled to claim 320 acres under the Donation Land Act. His tract, as surveyed, contained only 200 acres. He rightly assumed that the location, with its valuable riverfront and wharf sites, more than compensated for the sacrifice of some acreage. But none of this potential value ever benefitted "Billy" Blackiston, as he was familiarly known by everyone in the community.

Billy was a convivial sort, bibulous and sociable. Gradually, however, his appetite for strong drink "gained complete ascendancy," as an obituary writer expressed it, until he was unable to manage his affairs. His name became especially well-known in the Courts, where, in extensive and intricate litigation, he eventually lost his claim. The drink must also have aged him remarkably because, even in his 30s and early 40s (he died at 45), he came to be known as "Old Billy" Blackiston.

"Old Billy" died very suddenly one summer day in 1873 at his home, which was located on the riverbank of his claim. According to a newspaper report, "He was standing on the porch of his house, apparently in the enjoyment of good health, when he was observed to drop suddenly as if shot through the heart." He had married in the 1850s and was survived by two children.

His obituary, written in a day when newspaper writers gave their evaluations quite openly, concluded with these comments:

> Few men in the vicinity of Portland were better known. Mr. Blackiston might have been among the wealthy men of the county. His interests in valuable lands contiguous to the city were allowed to slip from his grasp by degrees, through want of attention to business and in yielding to the demon of drink, until he was reduced to a condition of absolute poverty and want.

The writer then suggested that we forget his weaknesses and remember "his many generous traits of character."

Bloch

Portland's first Jewish community was Congregation Beth Israel, organized in 1858. One of its founders was H.F. Bloch. Mr. and Mrs. Bloch came to Portland about 1857. With them came their daughter Flora, who had been born in New York City. By 1865, according to that year's City Directory, there were 65 members of Congregation Beth Israel. The synagogue was then at 5th and Oak Street.

Mr. Bloch was employed at A. Cahn & Co., wholesale grocers, whose store was on Front Street. The Bloch family home was for several years at what is now W. Burnside and Park Avenue.

Mr. Bloch's name is attached, as first owner, to a 160-acre tract in S.W. Portland near Mt. Sylvania. It had been "school land" and was sold by the State in 1871, when Mr. Bloch bought it for $240. The following year, he sold it to Robert Irving for $400. Today, Kerr Road runs through the tract, which includes part of the "Mountain Park" development.

Mr. Bloch was also a contractor, and had business interests in Union County. He died at Portland in 1884.

Bowering

William C. Bowering was born in England in 1812 and, when just a boy, emigrated with his parents to the U.S. He became a citizen as a result of his father's obtaining citizenship while William was still a minor.

In 1838 in New York, William married Isabel, and in 1852, when he was 40 years old, the couple came to Oregon. In June 1854, they settled on a 320-acre Donation Land Claim. Their L-shaped tract is bounded today by these N.E. streets: 24th, 29th-Fremont-33rd, Halsey, and Prescott. It includes the residential view property Alameda Heights, suggesting that Mr. Bowering could visualize future value. But in 1859, on a trip to California, he died. Mrs. Bowering held onto the property until 1870, when she and her two children sold it to Owen Wade for $1250. Only a few months later, as the price of this property began its rapid rise, Wade sold just half of the tract for $2400.

Bowles

Jesse T. Bowles lived in the vicinity of Portland from 1852 until at least 1870. He was born in Missouri and was 22 years old when he came to Oregon in 1852. As an unmarried man, he could claim only 160 acres under the Donation Land Act. He selected a tract in what is now S.W. Portland, near Boones Ferry Road and Maplecrest Drive.

He subsequently married Minerva and, in 1864, they sold 80 of their acres for $1000. In 1870, they sold the remaining 80 acres for $600. It probably did not concern them that they were leaving in the archives no other records whatsoever for future historians to dig out and ponder.

Brown

Alexander M. Brown and his wife Rebecca came to Oregon before December 1850 and, under the Donation Land Act, took up a claim of 626 acres. Today, it includes the "Vanport" area, West Delta Park, and the Delta Park Golf Course. Mr. Brown died in 1856, and Rebecca was named "administratrix" of the estate. Other than the fact that, in 1861, she sold 160 acres to Joseph and William Switzler for $1200, the files hold no further information about this family. The rest is silence.

Burrage

Perhaps because he was a professional surveyor, Charles W. Burrage's name is attached, as first owner of record, to several small parcels of land in Portland. In the course of surveying, he seems to have discovered pieces of land that had been overlooked. And he was on hand when "school land" was offered for sale. One tract (160 acres bounded today by N.E. 57th, 62nd,

Halsey, and Fremont streets) he acquired under a Homestead Act, so he must have lived on it for the minimum residence period required by that law. And he was the first owner of a 40-acre tract bounded today by N.E. 15th, 19th, Killingsworth, and Holman streets, also acquired under a Homestead Act.

Mr. Burrage was born in Massachusetts in 1830 and graduated from Yale University in engineering. While still in New England, he married Sarah. His health was delicate, and, seeking the therapy of a fresh frontier environment, he and his wife and two children came to Oregon. They travelled from New York City to Panama by steamship, crossed the Isthmus, and then came up the west coast by steamship, arriving at Portland in September 1861.

Within a year of his arrival here, Mr. Burrage was elected County Surveyor, and in 1865 he was elected City Surveyor. Later, he surveyed the line for what is today the Southern Pacific Railroad, from Portland to Roseburg. In 1887, seeking a drier climate for reasons of health, the Burrages moved to Colorado, where Mr. Burrage died in 1899, aged 69. While in Portland, he was a member and trustee of the Unitarian Church.

Bybee

William Bybee was born in Kentucky in 1824 and arrived in Oregon in 1850, where, as a single man, he could claim 320 acres free. He selected a tract of that size north of St. Johns where he settled in 1852. Bybee Lake, in the Rivergate Industrial Area, is named for him. He and Mary Ann Thomas, "both of Multnomah County," were married in 1858.

William Bybee was a cousin of James F. Bybee, who came to Oregon three years before William and took up a 640-acre claim on Sauvie Island. James, who signed documents with "X," his mark, made a considerable amount of money in the California gold fields. Returning to his claim, he built, during the years 1856-1858, the residence which is now known as the Bybee-Howell House, a museum maintained by the Oregon Historical Society.

Campbell
Hector B.
Hiram T.
William J.

The patriarch of this family was Hector P. Campbell, who brought his family across the plains to Milwaukie in 1849, at a time when most immigrants were heading for the supposedly easy wealth of the California gold fields. Mr. Campbell became one of Clackamas County's first school teachers. He was born in Massachusetts in 1793, his obituary noting that he and his wife had, throughout their lives, been Baptists "of an unwavering faith." Mr. Campbell was a member of the Legislature. "In fact," wrote his biographer, "he has, since his majority, with the single exception of the year that he crossed the plains, filled continuously positions of public trust, with integrity and to the perfect satisfaction of all."

One of his sons, Hector B. Campbell, was 20 years old when the family came to Oregon in 1849. Within a year, he had married Sarah Lambert. In March 1851, Hector and Sarah settled on a Donation Land Claim of 644 acres, on the west bank of the Willamette River where Riverview Cemetery and Lewis and Clark College are located today.

In 1869, Hector and Sarah were divorced. Hector returned to New England where, in 1871, he married Mary Emma Sherman. He was then 42; she was 22. Hector and Mary Emma came out to Oregon in 1891. He died in 1911 and was buried in an old cemetery between Sellwood and Milwaukie.

Two other Campbells had original Portland claims. They seem to have been related to Hector B. Campbell, but we have not been able to establish the exact relationship. They were:

Hiram T. Campbell. In the 1860s, he took up a Homestead claim of 160 acres. He sold the property in 1871 to Milton Hosford for $1200. He was not married. The tract lies north of S.E. Harold Street between 52nd and 72nd avenues.

William J. Campbell. In the 1880s, he acquired a 160-acre Homestead, bounded today by S.E. 82nd, 92nd, Woodstock, and Flavel Street. In 1887, he gave 20 acres to Hiram T. Campbell for a token amount of $1.

Cann

Thomas Hart Cann was an early Portlander who later moved to Seattle, where he died in 1915 by suicide. A newspaper account of his death stated:

> Despondency over ill-health is assigned as the reason which impelled Thomas H. Cann, well-known pioneer and former police judge of Seattle, to end his earthly life by drinking poison. He was 82. His body was found a short distance from his home by friends who had been searching for him.

Thomas H. Cann

The dark and unnatural act of suicide seems difficult to explain on the grounds of ill-health alone — so many people carry on against all the ills that flesh is heir to. But, while we can never know the contents of the secret chamber of his soul, the sketchy public records of his biography contain no hint of actions that might have been a burden on his conscience.

Mr. Cann had a long, active, and adventurous life. He was born in Illinois in 1833 and came west by ox-team to California in 1854. After a year or two, he moved to Oregon. In 1860, he joined many others in a "gold rush" to the Clearwater River valley, in what was then Washington Territory. He soon became an express messenger, travelling via the Columbia River between the mining camps and Portland. Later, he was Land Commissioner for Oregon and then Oregon's Assistant Secretary of State. In 1871, he acquired from the State 80 acres of what had been "school land." He paid $400 for the tract, which today is the first nine holes of Rose City Golf Course. Mr. Cann was active and highly advanced in the Masonic order.

In 1880, Mr. Cann moved to Seattle, where he practiced law. From 1894 to 1904, he was police judge in that city. In 1915, his wife was still living and he had two daughters and also a son who was captain of a steamship on the Pacific Coast. Yet in that year, for Mr. Cann, a spoonful of prussic acid made all the difference between discovering what joys or at least surprises the morrow might bring, and never knowing.

Caples

William Caples was a country doctor who lived in the rural community of St. Johns. He was born in 1806 in Maryland. His first wife, by whom he had a daughter named Ailcy, died, and in 1848 in Missouri he married Nancy. William, Nancy, and Ailcy crossed the plains to Oregon in 1849, and in November 1850 they took up a Donation Land Claim of 640 acres. It is bounded today by North Charleston, Fessenden, and Westanna streets, and extends to the riverfront. In 1851, Ailcy married Daniel S. Southmayd, who became the owner of an adjoining DLC.

During the years 1855 to 1882, Dr. Caples gradually sold most of his claim. The rise in the price per acre which he got for his land shows how real estate values were increasing under the combined pressures of monetary inflation, growing population, and industrial development. In 1855, the price was $5 per acre. It was $8 in 1865, $10 in 1867, $30 in 1872, and $65 in 1882.

In 1887, Dr. Caples still owned 40 of his original acres and, at the mature age of 81, was still practicing medicine.

Carter

Thomas Carter and his wife Minerva came to Oregon in 1848. He was born in Pennsylvania in 1804 and they were married in Ohio in 1826. In 1851, they took up a Donation Land

Thomas Carter and his wife Minerva

Claim of 529 acres just west of the original Portland townsite. The Carter DLC extends westward from 18th Avenue into what is now Washington Park and from Jefferson Street southward to Broadway Drive. Their farmhouse was at S.W. 19th and Jefferson Street, where the First Methodist Church is today. The Carters were, in fact, devoted members of the city's earliest Methodist Church, whose building was then at Second and Taylor streets.

With the growth of the city, Mr. Carter prospered, and he was able to help pay for construction of Canyon Road, which, conveniently, ran through his property. He also contributed money for building the first telegraph line into Portland.

The valuable Carter land claim was eventually divided among his sons, daughters, and sons-in-law. The daughters seem to have married "well." At least, the neighbors whom they married became politically prominent. One son-in-law was Joseph Smith, Oregon's Congressman from 1869 to 1871, and another was Lafayette Grover, Governor of Oregon from 1870 to 1877. Both men built homes near the Carters on what was becoming, socially as well as topographically, "Portland Heights."

Caruthers

An unusual household, even among those staking out Donation Land Claims in Portland, was that of Elizabeth Caruthers and her son, Finice. Though the title to their claim became the target of a protracted legal battle — perhaps the most complex controversy among the many lawsuits over land titles in early Portland — information about them is obscure. Such records as do exist are far from consistent. It would appear that Elizabeth Caruthers was born in North Carolina in 1792 and that she married one Joseph Thomas in Tennessee in 1816. They moved into Kentucky, where Finice was born in 1818.

(The name "Finice" is encountered in Southern Appalachia. It is pronounced FYEniss.) Mr. Thomas, it seemed, died in 1823. After his death, "for personal reasons of her own," as the record puts it, Elizabeth refused to be called Mrs. Thomas, and was known thenceforth as Mrs. Elizabeth Caruthers.

Elizabeth and Finice came across the plains to Oregon in 1847 and took up a claim on the square mile just south of the original Portland townsite. Their property thus was directly in the line of the city's future expansion southward. When the Donation Land Act was passed in 1850, Elizabeth and Finice duly recorded their claim, each taking half, or 320 acres, of their total area. The DLC law required claimants to reside on their claims, so the Caruthers built a house straddling the line between their two claims, and each lived in the half of the house situated on his or her property.

Judging by the scarcity of references to them in contemporary newspapers, Elizabeth and Finice led quiet, unremarkable lives. In 1853, Finice was nominated, as a Democrat, for County Coroner, but he was not elected. In real estate archives, there is evidence that Finice was an active speculator in land. He acquired several tracts in Multnomah and nearby counties. In 1859, according to a list published by the County Assessor, Finice Caruthers' property in Multnomah County was valued at $24,000, making him one of the wealthiest men in town. But the wealth was only on paper; he had little cash and much of his real estate was mortgaged.

Elizabeth died in 1857, aged about 65, and Finice, who had not married, died in 1860, aged about 41. Neither left a will nor had they any relatives or heirs in Oregon. Since their property was becoming valuable, the temptation was irresistible, for some people, to jump into this legal vacuum. It was not long before Mrs. Caruthers' 320 acres were simply taken over by covetous pre-emptors, on the legal pretext that she had not resided upon or cultivated the land as the law required. One enterprising fellow travelled to Tennessee and Kentucky, and returned to say that he had found the lawful heirs and purchased all their rights for himself. He started legal action against those who had preempted Mrs. Caruthers' land. Her property, in 1860, was valued at $12,000, but the title to it was unclear.

As for Finice's acreage, since he had incontrovertibly lived upon and cultivated it, a more subtle legal attack was needed. Some alleged that Finice was not Mrs. Caruthers' son. Others hinted that Finice's coat-of-arms, if he had had such a thing, should bear the "bend sinister" (a diagonal stripe supposedly meaning that one is related to his father only biologically, not legally). Hence, it was argued, there were no legal heirs. The State was urged to take over all 640 acres and sell them at auction.

About this time, there appeared upon the scene an individual named Joe Thomas (alias "Wrestling Joe") who claimed that he was Mrs. Caruthers' long-lost husband. He undertook legal action for title to the property, and the shrewdness of his legal advisor was such that he won the suit. But shortly thereafter, for reasons about which the records are tantalizingly vague, he denied the whole story, implying that he had been used by persons desiring to perpetrate a fraud.

Stephen Coffin, one of Portland's most prominent citizens and owner of the valuable property adjoining the Caruthers claim on the north, was named administrator of Finice's estate. Some surprisingly large fees and charges were allowed against the estate. In December 1861, most of Finice's claim was sold off at auction, seventeen city blocks being purchased at from $280 to $700 per block. Some of the property was bought by Jewish residents, and the area became the center of a Jewish community whose members could walk to their synagogue.

The legal skirmishing — complex, artful, and sometimes humorous — went on for many more months. It was a battle which, as long as the resources of the estate could pay the costs, continued to interest various claimants and their learned counsel.

Cason
William
Hillery

About six o'clock on a wintry Saturday evening in December 1865, Captain William A. Cason left the conviviality and warmth of a tavern in East Portland to return home. He had had several drinks to fortify himself against the cold, and was seen to be unsteady on his feet. With some difficulty, he mounted the old bay mare and trotted off towards his house, located a few miles away in what is now the Lents district of southeast Portland. The next morning, his body was found about half a mile from his home. He had fallen off the mare and died from exposure.

Captain Cason (his title probably was acquired during service in the local militia) must have come to Oregon before December 1850, because, though unmarried, he qualified for a Donation Land Claim of 320 acres. The boundaries of his claim today are S.E. 97th, 117th, Harold, and Duke streets. By 1861, he had sold 240 acres for $2350. Probate records show that he left no will, wife, or child. His brother, A.J. Cason, also a resident of Multnomah County, was named administrator of the estate, which included, besides the 80 acres still remaining from the original DLC, 1 cow, 1 calf, 1 bay mare, 1 roan mare, 1 colt, and a wagon and harness. The administrator sold the 80 acres in 1867 to E.L. Quimby for $3500.

Hillery Cason, who may have been a cousin of the William Cason portrayed above, was another Portland pioneer landowner. He was born in Illinois in 1818, where he married Delilah Ensminger in 1842. They crossed the plains to Oregon in 1853 and took up a 320-acre Donation Land Claim in the Montavilla district. The tract is bounded today by 72nd, 82nd, Halsey, and Stark streets. In 1859, their daughter was married to William Nicholson. The ceremony was performed by Clinton Kelly, an early Methodist minister and another pioneer landowner.

In 1867, the Hillery Casons sold their 320 acres to Lois Kerns for $1000, and moved to a house on 6th Street in East Portland. Hillery was a stonemason, but by 1880, when he was 32 years old, he had taken a less strenuous job; he is listed in the City Directory of that year as janitor of the Custom House. His son, W.W. Cason, continued the family trade as a brickmason. Hillery died in the early 1880s and his body is in Lone Fir Cemetery.

Chapman

The valuable business property in the city center bearing the name of William W. Chapman as first owner was part of the square mile originally claimed, in a rather informal way, by William Overton in 1843. In 1844, Overton sold it to Asa Lovejoy and Francis Pettygrove. The next year, Lovejoy sold his half-interest to Benjamin Stark, who is discussed later in this book. In 1848, Pettygrove sold his half-interest to Daniel Lownsdale. In March 1849, Lownsdale sold half of his half-interest to Stephen Coffin. In December 1849, Lownsdale and Coffin each sold one-third of his interest to William Chapman. The result was that Lownsdale, Coffin, and Chapman each had a one-sixth interest and Stark had a one-half interest in the undivided "Portland" claim. Finally, in 1852, that joint ownership was divided into four specific parcels, so that each person could receive an individual title to his tract as a Donation Land Claim. The approximate boundaries, today, of the land assigned to Mr. Chapman are S.W. Mill on the south, 18th on the west, Burnside-15th-Salmon-4th-Madison on the north, and the river-front on the east.

William Williams Chapman was born in 1808 in that portion of Virginia which, during the Civil War, broke away to form West Virginia in order to remain loyal to the Union. Mr. Chapman, however, did not share such "Yankee" views; in politics, he was a steadfast Southern Democrat. Perhaps because of his loyalty to the South, he was appointed in 1836 by President Jackson to be U.S. Attorney for Iowa Territory. In Iowa, he was elected Colonel of the militia "by a most flattering majority," especially so considering that he was only 28 years old. In 1838, he was elected to Congress from Iowa Territory and in 1844 he was a member of the convention which drafted Iowa's state constitution. In May 1847, the Colonel, his wife, and their seven children crossed the plains in two ox-drawn covered wagons, reaching Oregon that November. In 1848, though he had been in Oregon only a few months, he was named chairman of a committee formed to devise ways to protect the early settlers' land claims. The immediate recognition Colonel Chapman received as he moved to new locations suggests that his bearing, personality, and abilities were impressive.

Colonel Chapman was among the first to go to the California gold mines, where he was quite successful. He worked there from fall 1848 to spring 1849. Later in 1849, he practiced law at Oregon City, in partnership first with Asa L. Lovejoy and then with Aaron E. Wait.

In December 1849, he bought his interest in the Portland townsite, becoming a partner with Lownsdale and Coffin. He and his family and possessions were transported down the Willamette River from Oregon City to Portland by an Indian-powered "bateau" (a large canoe) in January 1850, and he had a house built where the County Courthouse is today. In Oregon, four more children were born to the Chapmans, for a total of eleven.

During the critical period of Portland's growth and ascendancy over its rival townsites, 1850-53, Colonel Chapman was active in developing imaginative promotional schemes. (This period is discussed in detail in the author's book, *Early Portland: Stump-Town Triumphant*.) But he was still open to attractive new possibilities, and in 1853, when Hudson's Bay Company was disposing of its properties in Oregon, Colonel Chapman leased "Fort Umpqua." He and his family moved to the Umpqua Valley, intending to use the old trading post as center for a vast cattle empire he envisioned. During the Indian "wars" in southern

Oregon, 1855-56, he again became an officer of militia, first Captain, then Lieutenant-Colonel. In 1856, the Democrat administration in Washington, D.C. appointed him Surveyor-General for Oregon. He moved to Eugene, where his home and the office of Surveyor-General were from 1857-1861. In 1861, he resigned his federal office, refusing to serve under a president (Lincoln) whose election he had opposed. In 1861, the Chapmans returned to Portland, where the Colonel practiced law for the rest of his life.

Colonel Chapman appears to have had even more than the usual restless energy of the pioneers. He also had the strong-willed independence one associates with his mountainous West Virginia homeland. On at least one occasion, however, that unconstrained spirit got him into difficulties. In a trial where he was attorney for a defendant, he grew impatient with the judge and asked for a change of venue. Because of the "unusually strong language" in which he expressed his opinion of the judge, he was sentenced to 20 days in jail for contempt of court. Research does not disclose what effect his outburst had on the fate of his client's case.

Chipman

Marshall (sometimes spelled Marshel) Chipman in 1855 acquired 160 hilly acres between today's Skyline Boulevard and N.W. Cornell Road, just west of Mount Calvary Cemetery. Chipman, born in New York state, arrived in Oregon in 1852, an unmarried man 30 years old. He claimed the 160 acres under the Donation Land Act, and, in 1859, sold them to Thomas Sperry for $650. He seems, from the absence of any later references, to have left Portland shortly thereafter.

Clark

Charles Clark and his wife Sarah in 1871 bought 164 acres bounded today by these N.E. streets: 37th, 47th, Prescott, and Fremont. They took title under the Homestead Act, paying $1.25 per acre, and farmed the land, which was then far out in the rural countryside. During 1881 to 1889, they sold most of their acreage, at prices increasing from $35 to $360 per acre. In 1889, Charles Clark was still farming 22 acres remaining from his original homestead.

Clary

Captain John V. Clary received a "Military Bounty" land warrant for his military service, and in the late 1850s he used it to acquire 160 acres bounded today by N.E. 82nd, 92nd, Glisan, and Halsey streets. Shortly before that, in November 1854, he had married Barbara Stevenson. The ceremony took place at Canemah, a river landing just south of Oregon City, and was performed by Harvey Hines, a pioneer Methodist minister.

In February 1860, the Clarys mortgaged their 160 acres to the Ladd & Tilton Bank for $300. Captain Clary died later that year, survived by his widow and three young daughters. Mrs. Clary, either from ignorance of the law or in the belief that the 160 acres were not worth more than the $300 they had already received for them on the mortgage, let the mortgage lapse. She also omitted having an administrator appointed for her husband's estate, which evidently included little of value aside from the mortgaged real estate

During the 1860s, the widow Clary married a Mr. Bailey, who died a few years later. Meanwhile, title to the 160 acres lay in a legal limbo. In 1869, Barbara Clary Bailey, the double widow, was approached by one Lewis Rosenthal, a grocer who was a neighbor of hers and who lived not far from the neglected 160 acres. For $135 cash, Barbara sold to Rosenthal any remaining rights or interest she may have had in the 160 acres.

Rosenthal asked the Court to name him administrator of the estate of John Clary, pointing out that neither the widow nor any other person had applied to be administrator. The Court granted his request, the widow making no objection. In 1871, acting under Court permission, Rosenthal sold the 160-acre Clary claim to Bernard Goldsmith for $2600. By then, claims and charges against the estate, as submitted by Rosenthal and allowed by the Court, had swelled to about $1800, including the mortgage, eleven years' interest, legal fees, and other expenses. The $800 balance evidently accrued to Rosenthal, since he had earlier bought from the widow her rights in the property. Then, in 1876, Rosenthal reacquired for himself, from Goldsmith, the title to the 160 acres, and he and his heirs held it thenceforth, gradually selling off parcels of it. Even though he was not a lawyer, Mr. Rosenthal seems to have handled the legal intricacies of the affair with some finesse, and apparently to everyone's satisfaction.

Coffin

Stephen Coffin was the first individual owner of 223 acres of the original Portland townsite. He was a partner with Chapman and Lownsdale, owning the property jointly until 1852. In that year, the townsite was divided into individual claims. The portion allocated to Mr. Coffin is bounded today, approximately, by these S.W. streets: Mill, 18th, and Lincoln, and extending to the riverfront. The transactions by which he and his partners acquired their individual titles were explained in an earlier paragraph under the name Chapman.

Stephen Coffin was born in Maine in 1807 and brought his family across the plains in 1847, settling at Oregon City. He was not a wealthy man when he arrived, but he was not ashamed to turn his hand to any work he could find. False pride, after all, had no place on the frontier. Working at hand labor, construction, contracting, and merchandising, he did so well that in March 1849 he was able to pay $6000 cash for half of Lownsdale's interest in the Portland townsite. That summer, he and his family moved to Portland.

Mr. Coffin was an energetic and resourceful leader — perhaps the most important participant in the various ventures that enabled Portland to outgrow its rivals. For example, he financed the town's first steam sawmill and provided capital for a steamship built for the Portland-San Francisco service. He played a leading role in construction of the Great Plank Road, which connected Portland to the farmlands of the Tualatin Valley.

One of his ventures was a disastrous failure, but it at least served to show his steady disposition. By his investment in the steamship *Gold Hunter*, Coffin lost a large amount of money and was nearly made bankrupt. That misadventure is described in the later entry dealing with another pioneer landowner, A. P. Dennison. Mr. Coffin appears to have been a man to whom reverses did not bring bitterness. He accepted the event with patience and set about to remedy his position. By 1859, his real estate holdings were valued by the Multnomah County Assessor at $20,000, equivalent to at least 15 times that amount in terms of today's level of wages and prices.

In 1862, Governor Gibbs appointed Stephen Coffin "Brigadier General of the Oregon Militia," and thereafter he was usually addressed as "General Coffin." Another aspect of his character was his opposition to alcoholic beverages. He participated in a Temperance Convention in 1854, and was one of a committee who drafted a letter advocating "temperance." The letter was sent to candidates for election to the State Senate, asking them to declare their position on that controversial issue.

Mr. Coffin's first wife died about 1850 and he married a widow, Mrs. Lucinda Pickering Hill, in March 1852. General Coffin died in 1882, aged 75. A biographer called him "a born leader of men." In politics, he was first a Whig, later making the transition along with most other Whigs to the Republican Party, of which he became an active leader. However, the only public office he held, other than that of General of the Militia, was one to which he was elected in 1851. In that year (perhaps someone had entered his name as a rather macabre joke), Mr. Coffin was elected Portland's coroner.

Collins

William Collins was born in Ireland and he first arrived in Oregon in November 1851, when he was 38 years old. He returned to the East Coast during the next year or two and married Mary in Massachusetts early in 1854. Mr. Collins was evidently a widower, as he already had a daughter. William and Mary must have set out almost immediately after the wedding for Oregon; they settled on a claim of 320 acres in August 1854. Their Donation Land Claim, today, is part of Tryon Creek State Park and adjacent residential areas. In 1859, their daughter Lucy was married to George W. Hoyt, of Portland. The ceremony was performed by Thomas Pearne, a pioneer Methodist minister.

Cornell

William Cornell was born in 1812 in Ohio, where he married Emily in 1838. They came to Oregon in 1852, and, in 1855, claimed 320 acres under the Donation Land Act. The tract is in the vicinity of N.W. Cornell Road (named for them) and Thompson Road. The Cornells sold parts of their claim in 1875 and 1877 and then, in 1882, sold their remaining 217 acres for $10,000. With the freedom provided by that sizeable profit, they seem to have left Portland, but their destination and fate have eluded our inquiries. The only other reference to Mr. Cornell is a newspaper item of September 1863, noting that W.F. Cornell (probably our William) had been elected, at a meeting in Portland, Sergeant of the Washington Guards, one of the bodies of militia organized against such possibilities as Indian uprisings during the time the regular army was withdrawn to fight in the Civil War.

Corwin

William Corwin was born in Pennsylvania in 1814. He came to Oregon in 1852 and, that December settled, as a bachelor farmer, on a 52-acre tract bounded today by S.E. 38th, 41st, Stark, and Division streets. He was entitled to claim 160 acres under the Donation Land Act, but he evidently preferred to sacrifice some area in order to find a location closer to the Portland townsite. During the years 1865 to 1878, he sold most of his land, at prices increasing from $30 to $200 per acre, realizing a total of more than $4000.

Couch

Few men can have had more adventurous, full lives than Captain John H. Couch (pronounced "kooch"), and few played a more decisive role in the genesis and early growth of Portland. It was Captain Couch who brought the brig *Maryland* up the Willamette, the first vessel ever to enter the river. And it was he who told his many seafaring friends that Portland was the "head of navigation." In 1845, he demonstrated his conviction by taking up, as his land claim, the 640 acres just north of the Portland townsite. The boundary of his claim runs westward from the river up Burnside Street to 18th, then diagonally to 20th and Lovejoy Street, west along Lovejoy to 23rd, north to Thurman Street, and east to the river. The diagonal line was determined after a boundary dispute discussed in the later entry for Amos King.

John Couch was born in 1811 in what was then a flourishing port for a great sailing fleet, Newburyport, Mass. He first went to sea at the age of 15, on a voyage to India. In 1831, aged 20,

Captain John H. Couch

he married Caroline Flanders. In the fall of 1839, then only 28 but already having seen most of the principal seaports of the world, he was given command of the *Maryland*. He took that vessel 'round Cape Horn, entered the Columbia River in June 1840 and, without benefit of any charts, sailed up to the site of Oregon City. On two successive voyages, in the brig *Chenamus* in 1842 and 1844, he came up the Willamette River. After the latter voyage, he remained in Oregon. He turned his vessel over to another captain, and at Oregon City he began a successful career as a landsman. He was then 33 years old. Besides operating a store, he was a director of the company organized to publish Oregon's first newspaper, the *Spectator*, and he was also Oregon's Treasurer under the Provisional Government. Meanwhile, his wife and children remained at Newburyport. But New England seafaring families accepted the idea — unavoidable in those pre-radio days — of living in uncertainty for years at a time.

In 1847, after three years at Oregon City, Captain Couch made a voyage back to New England. The *Spectator*, in September 1847, printed this tribute to the Captain:

☞ We learn that our worthy townsman and fellow citizen, Capt. John H. Couch, is on the eve of his departure for the States, on the bark *Toulon*. He intends returning to Oregon as soon as his business arrangements will permit. Capt. Couch was among the first of the settlers who established themselves at the Falls of the Willamette, when a dense forest covered the spot which is now pretty well known to the world as Oregon City. His gentlemanly deportment has won him a host of friends, who esteem him for his high moral worth. We cannot afford to lose such citizens even for a short period, and therefore he must hasten back with all convenient dispatch.

A year later, when Captain Couch was in New England, he was given command of the bark *Madonna*. With his brother-in-law, George H. Flanders, as Chief Mate, Captain Couch sailed out of New York harbor in January 1849, with a cargo of goods for San Francisco and Oregon. Arriving in San Francisco in July 1849 at the height of the gold rush excitement, they sold their goods at a fabulous profit and reached Portland early in August.

To the chagrin of his friends at Oregon City, Captain Couch now decided to live at Portland, where he perceived the commercial future to be. In August 1849, he began living on the claim he had astutely selected four years earlier, the square mile joining the original Portland townsite on the north. He remained for the rest of his life at Portland, devoting his energies to importing merchandise, operating a line of sailing vessels, constructing a wharf in partnership with Captain Flanders, and contributing in many other ways to the development of the town. His wife and children came out from Newburyport to join him in 1852, making the trip via the Isthmus of Panama. Captain Couch died in January 1870. Surviving were his widow and four daughters. Two of the daughters became the wives of early Portland physicians, Caroline marrying Dr. Robert Wilson and Elizabeth marrying Dr. Rodney Glisan. Clementine Couch married a prominent pioneer businessman, Cicero H. Lewis. The fourth daughter remained Miss Mary H. Couch.

Captain Couch was among the earliest members of Portland's first Masonic lodge. His brother-in-law, Captain George Flanders, was one of 16 Masons who organized the lodge in 1850. Both Captain Couch and Captain Flanders had first joined the Masons in New England. The first meetings of the Portland lodge were held in the warehouse of Couch & Co., located on Front Avenue between streets now known as Burnside and Couch. Also among the early members of Portland's first Masonic lodge were two of Captain Couch's sons-in-law, Dr. Wilson and Cicero Lewis.

When Portland was first incorporated, with a charter granted by the Legislature in 1851, Captain Couch saw to it that most of his claim, as far north as what is now Pettygrove Street, was included as part of the city. In 1865, he laid out that portion of his claim in streets and blocks, and "Nineteenth Street" became the center of Portland's most elite neighborhood. Many prominent Portlanders, including Captain Couch's sons-in-law, lived there, in stately Victorian mansions, each standing in the center of its own park-like city block.

Later, following the normal life-cycle of neighborhoods, the mantle of aristocracy passed from that part of town to "Portland Heights." The ornate wooden mansions grew shabby and as wistful as sailing ships in the age of steam. But, for many years, into the first decade of the twentieth century, those magnificent and imposing manor houses rested comfortably and with apparent permanence on their spacious grounds, exuding something more than mere respectability.

Crimmins

Timothy Crimmins was an illiterate Irish bachelor, born in the Old Sod in 1795, whose wanderings brought him to Oregon about 1860. He arrived here too late to qualify for free land, but he became the first owner of record of 160 acres which he acquired by using a "Military Bounty" land warrant. Crimmins bought the warrant from one John Rigney, "late a private in Company M, 1st Regiment, U.S. Artillery" in the War with Mexico. Crimmins paid about $160 for the warrant, which turned out to have been a wise investment. The land Crimmins selected is bounded today by N.E. Union Avenue, 15th, Prescott, and Killingsworth streets. Title was issued to him in 1866.

Tim Crimmins would seem to have been on the ragged edge of poverty during the next few years, though with temporary bursts of prosperity. From 1866 to 1872, he mortgaged his 160 acres at least four times, though managing to pay off the debt each time. The first mortgage was to the Catholic Archbishop, Father F.N. Blanchet, for $120. In all these transactions, Crimmins signed with "X," his mark. Since his name was written in by different clerks, spelling it phonetically, it appears variously as Crimmins, Crimmons, and Crimmon.

In 1872, growth and development in the community having inflated land prices, Crimmins was able to sell his 160 acres for $6400. To what use Crimmins put this great windfall, or how it may have changed his style of living, we do not know. He apparently continued to reside in the Portland area for the rest of his life, but he was the subject of no document, news item, or, let it be said, any police record. Finally, he was mentioned one more time, in the *Oregonian* of 1890, when there appeared his two-line obituary.

Cully

Thomas Cully, when he arrived in Oregon at the age of 32, had already had an adventureful life. He was born in England, crossed the Atlantic in a sailing vessel about 1840, and went to Texas, where he was a Ranger under Sam Houston. Coming over the plains to Oregon in 1845, he was among the earliest pioneers. He was also a stonemason — he had been apprenticed to that trade in England — and put up Portland's first brick chimney. It was for the village's first frame building, the house of F.W. Pettygrove, built in 1846 near Front and Washington streets. That year, Tom Cully settled on 640 acres near N.E. Cully Boulevard, named for him. His claim is bounded today by N.E. 65th and 85th, and extends northward from Killingsworth Street to the Airport. It includes Colwood Golf Course.

During 1849-50, Tom worked in the California gold fields, with such satisfactory results that, upon his return to Oregon, he married. The marriage took place in Yamhill County in September 1850 and, a few days later, Tom and Rebecca Cully filed an application, under the Donation Land Act, for the 640 acres he had held since 1846 under Oregon's Provisional Government. Romance arrived at a convenient moment; if Tom had remained single, he would have been able to retain only 320 acres as a Donation Land Claim.

For the rest of his life, Mr. Cully lived on his farm and, in the course of things, his family grew to 12 children. One ten-year old son drowned in Columbia Slough in 1861. Later, twins were born to the Cullys — "when one week old, they weighed ten pounds each," according to a news report in the *Oregonian* of 1877. Their last child, making an even dozen, was born when Mr. Cully was 66 years old.

Mr. Cully died in 1891, at the age of 78, from injuries received when he was thrown from his buggy. A newspaper gave this account of the accident:

> As Mr Cully was coming to town last Saturday, in ascending Gravelly Hill, the king-pin [the bolt holding the front axle in place] on his buggy broke, the forewheels passed from under the vehicle, and he was pitched violently over the dashboard. He was taken home and a doctor summoned, who found one of Mr. Cully's shoulders dislocated, and put it in place.

Unfortunately, the diagnosis had not embraced all of the old gentleman's injuries; two days later, he was dead.

Mr. Cully owned, besides "his fine farm of 640 acres," a brick building covering an entire block in East Portland and other city property. His obituary concluded with this tribute: "He was an honest and industrious man."

Darch

In Portland in the 1860s and 1870s, George W. Darch worked in the Stimson & Co. sawmill, which was on the riverbank at Madison Street. He was a lathmaker. George and his wife Sarah lived in a house on S.W. Park Street (then called 8th) between Market and Mill streets, from which he had a leisurely walk down what were then tree-lined residential steets to the sawmill.

In 1864, Mr. Darch became the first owner of a 160-acre tract bounded today by N. Delaware, Interstate, Prescott, and Killingsworth streets. He used a "Military Bounty" land warrant to acquire his acres. The antecedents of that warrant are curious. During an uprising of the Creek Indians, a company of militia was recruited to control them, one of the volunteers being an individual named Watty Choff. Mr. Choff had died before he received the land warrant to which his military service entitled him. However, that right was later claimed for his minor child, Charley Choff, by the youth's guardian, a man called Chilly McIntosh. The guardian sold the warrant to Portland's Mr. Darch, probably for about $160.

The Darchs held their real estate speculation for only two years, but even in that brief period they were able to realize a worthwhile profit. In 1866, George and Sarah (she signing with "X," her mark) deeded the land to Levi Estes and David Stimson for $1600. Estes and Stimson were Mr. Darch's employers, owning the sawmill where he worked.

Mr. Darch may have congratulated himself on selling for $10 an acre that which he had bought for $1 an acre. Five years later, he must have felt less pleased: in 1871, Messrs. Estes and Stimson sold the 160 acres for $4000, that is, $25 per acre. Mr. Darch continued, however, to work at their sawmill until

1874, when they closed their mill and left town. They seem to have been less lucky in the lumber business than they were in real estate speculation: Mr. Estes, at least, was declared bankrupt.

From 1874 to 1876, Mr. Darch worked as a drayman, and then he, too, like the other actors in this little drama, disappeared from the Portland scene. Perhaps it was as well; if they had been around for a few more years, they would all have been disgruntled. By 1883, the land they had owned was selling for $650 per acre.

Davidson

It was a desire to found a Christian college on this rustic and unlettered frontier that brought Elijah Davidson and his son, Elijah B. Davidson, to Oregon. They and their families, along with several other members of a church called "Disciples of Christ," came across the plains in 1850. That migration was only one in a long series of moves they made, nor was it their last.

Elijah Davidson, the father, had been born in North Carolina in 1783, and was already preaching, probably in a Baptist church, when he was 21. After serving in the War of 1812, he and his wife Margaret moved to Kentucky, where Elijah B. Davidson was born in 1819. There, the father came under the influence of Alexander Campbell, an evangelist trained at the University of Glasgow who broke away from the Presbyterian Church to preach "simple evangelical Christianity." By the 1830s, various groups and families, including the Davidsons, had joined with Campbell to form the "Disciples of Christ" (nicknamed "Campbellites"), which later became the "Christian Church." The Disciples of Christ were strong on education, and established several colleges as they moved westward with the frontier. By 1840, the Davidsons had reached Illinois, where Elijah B. Davidson, aged 21, married Saloma Jones. During the 1840s, the Davidsons, as farmer-ministers, were active in church

Rev. Elijah B. Davidson

work in Monmouth, Illinois. It was from there that they came on to Oregon.

The Davidsons spent their first winter in Oregon, 1850-51, at Milwaukie. In 1851, Elijah B., the son, settled on a 640-acre Donation Land Claim bounded today by S.E. Stark, N.E. Halsey, 39th, and 60th. The father moved to Polk County, where he and other "Disciples" took up land claims, established the town of Monmouth (named for their town in Illinois), and founded "Monmouth University," to which they all contributed part of their acreage to create the school's endowment. In 1855, Elijah B. Davidson, then aged 36, left Multnomah County and joined the group at Monmouth, leaving behind only his name, attached to his claim, as a souvenir of his passage through Portland.

Their college at Monmouth flourished for about thirty years, and several buildings were constructed. Its name was changed, about 1882, to "Christian University." By 1890, finances were becoming difficult, and, in 1892, the institution was turned over to the State, to be used as a school for teachers.

Elijah B. Davidson, like so many pioneers, still found irresistible the attractions of "moving on," and, in 1866, he migrated to Josephine County. There he lived the rest of his life as a farmer-minister. He had 13 children. Elijah senior had had 12 children, of whom, by a whimsical dispensation of nature, six had black hair and six red hair, "the two colors alternating regularly from oldest to youngest!"

Rev. Elijah B. Davidson is famous in the annals of Southern Oregon for a historic "first" in discovery and exploration. One day in August 1874 when he was hunting bear, he chanced to find, and entered, the Oregon Caves, theretofore unknown.

The elder Elijah, remaining at Monmouth, lived 87 years, hale and hearty and preaching till the end. In 1870, when he died, he had 136 living descendants. A biographer, attempting perhaps to account for his healthful longevity and abundant, varied career, noted that "During his whole life, Mr. Davidson practiced temperance and was an early riser."

Delay

During the 1850s, when steamboats in increasing numbers began running on the Willamette River, Joshua Delay went into the business of selling cordwood for their use. He cut the wood from his claim, 289 acres bounded by N. Hancock and Russell streets and extending from 17th Avenue to the river. His waterfront location, where the Fremont Bridge is today, was convenient for steamboats taking aboard their wood fuel.

Joshua Delay was born in Ohio in 1814, and married Sarah in Illinois when he was 19. The couple came across the plains to Oregon in 1852, when Joshua was 38. With them were two sons, William, born in 1840, and Joseph, born in 1845. The family settled on their Donation Land Claim in January 1853. Prior to that, the tract had been claimed by one J.L. Loring, but he had not lived on it for the four years required by the law to establish the title to the land in his own name. Loring sold his rights and interest in the claim to Delay.

During the mid-1850s, Sarah died and in January 1859, Joshua followed her. His brief obituary noted that he died "from bleeding of the lungs." His estate, valued at $1125, included 1 yoke of oxen, 2 cows, 1 mare and colt, 3 hogs, 1 wagon, 50 cords of firewood, $30 worth of "war script" for service during the Yakima Indian war, an "account receivable" of $108 due from the Oregon Steam Navigation Company for firewood furnished to their boats, and real estate valued at $750.

Meanwhile, William W. Chapman, another pioneer landowner whose career was described in earlier pages, had become administrator of the estate of Loring, who had died in 1856. Mr. Chapman, an astute lawyer intimately acquainted with the intricacies of real estate titles, brought suit to recover a share in the ownership of the land, asserting that Loring had not sold all his interest to Delay. The suit dragged on until 1871, when, despite Mr. Chapman's energetic advocacy, the issue was decided in favor of the Delay sons and heirs, William and Joseph. With their title now clear, they promptly sold all their interest in the land for $1500. William, who had married a girl named Zorilda, died at Vancouver, Washington in 1887, aged 47. His younger brother, Joseph, moved to Eugene, Oregon. But the "Joshua Delay DLC" remains forever.

Dennison

When news of the California gold discovery reached the Eastern states, in 1848, it aroused an urgent restlessness, particularly among young men whose economic prospects were somewhat obscure. In the increasingly structured society of the East Coast, a young man without special endowments could look forward to a lifetime of work which might or might not pay off in fortune and status at the end. Now, suddenly, there was a short-cut: gold.

On Christmas day, 1848, sixteen young men met in a Boston office where one of them was employed as a clerk, to consider how they might take advantage of the opportunities California offered. They came from diverse backgrounds, but they had these things in common: worldly ambition, courage, love of adventure and a feeling they might do well in the more freewheeling milieu of a frontier boom. They decided to buy a ship, load her with goods to sell in San Francisco, and go to the land of promise. By January 1849, the group had grown to 33. For $3500, they purchased a yacht-sized vessel (the brig *Randolph*, 123 tons) and hired a captain. Then, on February 8, 1849, they sailed out of Boston harbor on a seven-month voyage around Cape Horn to the Golden Gate.

Among these 33 soldiers-of-fortune was Ami Prince Dennison. He was 24 years old and, at the time of planning for the voyage, was working in a carpet factory at Lowell, Mass. His life, so far, had been undistinguished. He was born in April 1824 in Maine, and moved several times as his father changed places of employment. Ami attended schools until he was about 17, when he became an apprentice to a cabinet-maker. At the age of 22, by which time both his parents had died, Ami went into cabinet-making on his own, at Bath, Maine. The venture was not profitable and, after one year, he sold it and became an employee in the factory at Lowell. He had been there for a year when the opportunity came to sail for "El Dorado."

At San Francisco, the *Randolph* and her cargo were sold. The proceeds were divided among the ship's company, most of whom headed immediately for the mines. Ami, however, decided that a more agreeable way to acquire gold would be to live in the city and sell merchandise to the miners. He joined two San Franciscans in opening a store on the waterfront. But on Christmas day 1849, exactly one year after the adventurers' initial meeting in Boston, the store and its contents were destroyed by fire. For reasons which no records reveal, Ami decided to leave San Francisco. He came to Portland, where he arrived in February 1850. He was 25 years old.

In July 1850, young Dennison entered into a partnership with Captain Zachariah Norton, who, in his brig *Sequin*, was engaged in the coastal trade between Portland and San Francisco. That trade was highly profitable. On one round trip, in 1849, Captain Norton had made a net profit of $18,000, equivalent to more than $250,000 at today's wage-price level. In the partnership, Dennison was to conduct the buying and selling business in Portland, while the captain brought in the goods and took Oregon produce to California. After four months, however, the partnership broke up in a flurry of law suits, Norton suing Dennison and Dennison countering with a suit against Norton. The business remained in the hands of Norton, who, in November 1850, put his vessel in the command of another captain, and thenceforth remained on shore, to manage the trading himself. Nevertheless, Dennison later told a biographer that, during those four months, he had made "a neat little sum" for himself.

Despite the misunderstanding with Norton, Dennison seems to have won a friendly acceptance, even some status, among Portland's 800 inhabitants. On December 5, 1850, he participated in a ceremony of historic importance. On that day, the first issue of the *Oregonian* was printed, on a small hand press. Four of the village's "prominent" citizens were present. Each held a corner of the first page and lifted it off the type in a stately gesture. Among the four were Stephen Coffin and W.W. Chapman, two of the principal landowners and promoters of Portland. The third participant was W.W. Baker, a 22-year old Virginian who had arrived in Portland only three months before, and who was also one of our pioneer landowners. The careers of these three men were discussed earlier in this volume. Holding the fourth corner of the ceremonial sheet was A.P. Dennison. Thus, Dennison had attained within a few months a social prominence in the frontier town which, given his relatively modest background, he might not have reached in a lifetime had he remained in Boston.

With the "neat little sum" he had made for himself during his brief partnership with Norton, Dennison was now able to participate in another shipping venture. In December 1850, the *Gold Hunter*, one of the first steamships to come to the

Pacific Coast, arrived at Portland on a trip from San Francisco. The Portland townsite owners — Coffin, Chapman, and Lownsdale — were eager to have a steamship running regularly between Portland and San Francisco. When they were offered a majority interest in the *Gold Hunter* for $60,000, they jumped at the opportunity. Apparently not all of the owners of the steamship wanted to sell — ownership of the *Gold Hunter* was divided among numerous stockholders — but enough of them were in favor of selling to give the Portlanders control. The Portlanders were able to raise $21,000 in gold and currency, and the San Francisco owners accepted a personal note, signed jointly by Coffin, Chapman, and Lownsdale, for the remaining $39,000. Nearly all of the $21,000 cash was put up by the same Portland trio, but two other men — Captain T.A. Hall and A.P. Dennison — purchased small shares. Together with the shares owned by Hall and Dennison, the Portlanders had just over half of the ownership of the *Gold Hunter*, and they announced that the vessel would run regularly between Portland and San Francisco. The two minor stockholders were both given official duties aboard the vessel, Hall being made captain and Dennison purser. The *Gold Hunter* made five trips between Portland and San Francisco from December 1850 to March 1851.

Coffin, Chapman, Lownsdale believed there was an understanding that, if any of the shares held by Portlanders were sold, they would only be sold to other Portland owners, thus assuring their continued majority control. However, in March 1851, the minority stockholders in San Francisco induced Hall and Dennison to sell out to them, thereby giving *them* just over 50 per cent of the ownership. The San Franciscans then took the *Gold Hunter* off the run to Portland and diverted her to Mexican ports. It was disastrous for Coffin, Chapman, and Lownsdale. The vessel was eventually seized and sold to pay debts accumulated against her, and the three Portlanders lost their investment in the venture.

In June 1851, Dennison returned to Portland. After the sell-out in San Francisco, his first encounter with Coffin, Chapman, and Lownsdale must have been lively, but unfortunately no

Boswell was present to record it. That sort of memoir is too rarely deposited in the archives. Evidently, Dennison was able to throw a justifying light upon his action, since, the very next year, he was elected to the Portland City Council. This was the beginning of a long career in politics and remunerative public office. Dennison had not been attracted to "work," in the sense of manual labor, but he began to find a vocation in "merchandising," as selling commodities was called, and especially in local politics, where it is oneself that is promoted and, indeed, sometimes sold.

Dennison was that unusual phenomenon, a New England Yankee who was, politically, a Southern Democrat. It was later alleged, rather unkindly, that Dennison originally had other convictions, but had embraced the viewpoint of the Southern Democrats because they were in control of Oregon politics and national patronage. Certainly it was true that, from 1853 to 1861, national job patronage was in the hands of Presidents who were not only Democrats but sympathetic to the Southern point of view. In Oregon, from 1853 to 1862, politics were dominated by Democrats of a similar outlook — Oregon's U.S. Senator Joseph Lane, and Governors George Curry and John Whiteaker. Thus, it was convenient for Dennison to be a supporter of Southern Democrat policies. As for the electorate, the overwhelming majority of Oregonians during the 1850s were Democrats, partly because the opposition Whig Party was disintegrating as it sought unsuccessfully to find a consensus on the slavery question, and also because the Republican Party had not yet taken hold in Oregon.

In 1853, Dennison participated in the Washington County Democratic Convention at "Hillsborough," the county seat. (Portland was then in Washington County, out of which Multnomah County was created in 1854.) Dennison was elected Secretary of the convention and was also appointed to draft "resolutions expressive of the feeling of the convention." Though Dennison's formal education was not extensive, he seems to have had a natural flair for the oratorical style popular in nineteenth-century local politics.

Meanwhile, Dennison was not neglecting other opportunities. He was entitled, under the Donation Land Act, to claim free land, and he was not one to forego such a windfall. He found a tract of 49 acres, on the west bank of the Willamette, adjoining the Couch claim, and "settled" on it in January 1854. The law's requirement that claimants had to "cultivate the land" did not appeal to Dennison, so he filed an affidavit stating that, on the day he "settled" there, the ground was frozen so hard that he was unable to dig into it. Dennison did not hold the land long enough to establish his title, but sold what rights he had in the claim to others, who fulfilled the obligation to live on and cultivate the land. Therefore, the "patent" to that land was never issued in Dennison's name. It is another tract, aoquired later and by different means, that perpetuates the name "Dennison."

By 1853, Dennison had accumulated enough capital to finance construction of a three-story wooden building on Front Street, at the foot of Stark Street. The "Dennison Building," located at the center of the "business district" of that day, projected out over the river bank. It provided lodgings on the upper floor, office space, a large dining room, and stores on the ground floor. A side entrance led to Mr. Dennison's office, where he sold real estate, conducted an import business, and acted as a "Notary Public." Advertisements in the *Oregonian* in 1853 show that among Mr. Dennison's tenants were a lawyer, a drug store, and a wholesale drug firm. One of Mr. Dennison's interests is described in a notice he published at this time:

> Real Estate for Sale
> TWENTY valuable city lots situated in the central part of this city, and well adapted to business purposes. Title undisputed. For terms apply to
> A.P. Dennison

In December 1853, Portland's New Englanders decided to honor the anniversary of the landing of the Pilgrims with a "Celebration and Procession." Such was Mr. Dennison's status in the community — he was now 29 years old — that he was chosen "Marshal of the Day." Despite some ridicule from the town's non-Yankees, the festival was a glorious success according to this newspaper account:

> The 233rd Anniversary of the landing of the Pilgrim Fathers was celebrated in this city on Thursday last in a becoming manner. The Day was ushered in by a national salute of *thirteen* guns, fired by Capt. Ainsworth, of the steamer *Lot Whitcomb*, from the deck of his steamer.
>
> The sun arose with the splendor of a May morning, betokening as it were the smiles of a beneficent Providence upon the Day.
>
> At one o'clock in the afternoon, the procession was formed, under the direction of the Marshal of the Day — A.P. Dennison, Esq. — and proceeded to the Methodist Church, where the ceremony took place. At the conclusion of the exercises in the church, the procession was re-formed and proceeded to march down Taylor Street to Front, and thence north on Front to the dinner-room in Dennison's Building, where a banquet, fit to conclude a New England festival, was amply discussed and fully enjoyed. The company separated at an early hour, and the day closed without a single occurence to occasion regret.

Dinner concluded with the drinking of toasts, to everyone from the Pilgrims to the Pioneer Woman and the Officials of the Day. No less than 27 toasts were drunk.

In 1854, Dennison was elected Portland City Recorder, being carried into office on a general triumph of Democrats over Whigs. Portland's 458 voters cast their ballots as follows:

Democrats		Whigs
W.S. Ladd, 261	Mayor	W.P. Abrams, 197
A.P. Dennison, 250	Recorder	N. Coe, 208

At the 1855 Multnomah County Democratic Convention, Dennison was elected Chairman of the meeting, and he was also nominated by the convention to be the party's candidate for the Territorial Senate, or "Council," as it was also called. Dennison's opponent in the election was L. Limerick, a "Know-Nothing." The "Know-Nothings" were a rather vague political cluster which formed temporarily in the transitional vacuum between the dying Whig Party and the not-yet-formed Republican Party. The Senate seat, which Dennison won, represented three counties: Multnomah, Washington, and Columbia. The vote shows how scanty their population was in 1855:

A.P. Dennison		L. Limerick
59	Columbia	66
245	Washington	265
336	Multnomah	248
640	Total	579

In the Legislature of 1855-56, there were eight members of the Senate. Six of them were Democrats, and they elected Dennison President. A sample of Dennison's political style is this excerpt from his speech of acceptance:

> Gentlemen, I thank you for the honor conferred, and trust that I shall so discharge the duties incumbent on me as to meet your approbation. I shall expect your cordial co-operation in preserving order, so essential to healthy and profitable legislation.

This session of the Legislature did not convene, as heretofore, at Oregon City, but at Corvallis, and one of its first items of business was to select a permanent capital. In the debate, Dennison favored Salem, which was the choice of the leaders of the dominant Democratic Party, and he opposed the selection of Portland, whose voters had elected him. Editor Dryer, of the *Oregonian*, denounced Dennison in these words:

> We notice that one A.P. Dennison, who imagines himself to be a very great man since he was accidentally elected to that body of "Solons" called law-makers, recently made a speech against re-locating the state capital at Portland. When he said the people of this city and county were opposed to having the seat of government moved to Portland, he uttered a lie. The fact is, Dennison sold himself to vote against this question...that he may get a few crumbs which fall from the Democratic Party table. We are not surprised that Dennison would do this, knowing him as we do.

Editor Dryer's assertion that Portlanders wanted the capital at Portland was confirmed by a vote taken several years later. In the election of June 1864, asked for their preferred location for the State capital, residents of Multnomah County voted as follows: for Portland, 1317; for Salem, 21; for Eugene, 2.

While the *Oregonian* vilified Dennison, the principal spokesman for the Democrat Party, editor Bush of the *Statesman*, defended Dennison's support of Salem as capital — hardly surprising since that was where the *Statesman* and Bush were located. Bush took the occasion to pay this compliment:

> Mr. Dennison's general course in the Council, the promptness and correctness with which he discharges the duties of presiding officer, have won for him a deserved popularity in that body.

Dennison's loyal support had not gone unnoticed by the Democrat governor and other party leaders, and it did not long remain unrewarded. In March 1856, a band of belligerent Indians attacked the settlement at "Cascades" (now Cascade Locks). Some volunteer militia were sent up the Columbia River from Portland, and Governor Curry appointed two "Southern Democrat" friends, Benjamin Stark and A.P. Dennison, to be his Aides-de-Camp, with the rank of "Colonel." On March 27th, Colonel Dennison, with 20 volunteers, went up to the Cascades aboard the steamboat *Fashion*. En route, he sent the following message back by a passing riverboat to Colonel Stark, who remained in the rear, so to speak, at Portland:

> Mr. Slater just passed us in a canoe, and says all the houses are burned at the Cascades and that the Indians are from 600 to 800 strong. Our people are fighting at the Block-house, and those on board the *Belle* [a riverboat which had gone up earlier in the day to assist the people at the Cascades] are fighting, but can furnish no relief to those in the Block-house. Two of the men who went up on the *Belle* are killed. We shall take our position and try to defend ourselves and send the *Fashion* back immediately for supplies and ammunition.

Stark forwarded Colonel Dennison's gallant and graphic message to Governor Curry by way of a new telegraphic wire which had just been strung from Portland to Lafayette. From there, the news was taken to Salem by horseback. (Today, it would see odd to terminate a major communication line at Lafayette, a small town with little more population than it had in the 1850s. But at that time, few villages were larger than Lafayette, which was the market center for the farming population of the Yamhill Valley.)

The next day, the company of "Multnomah County Volunteers" to which Colonel Dennison was attached as Aide-de-camp had advanced part way from the Cascades waterfront to the Block-house, when two river steamboats, the *Mary* and the *Wasco*, arrived from The Dalles. They brought 250 regular army troops. The soldiers re-captured the Block-house and restored order. On March 30th, Stark was able to send this message to the Governor:

> Col. Dennison and party have returned from the Cascades, having rendered important assistance in rescuing the people there and re-establishing communications between Portland and the Cascades. Twelve of our people [residents at Cascades] have been killed, and two missing. The volunteers of Multnomah County have just returned on the steamer *Jennie Clark*, and have been discharged from further duty.

Editor Dryer, in the *Oregonian*, vigorously attacked Stark, Dennison, and Governor Curry, stating that if the volunteers had been taken to the Cascades more quickly and given supplies and arms, they could have repulsed the Indians without any help from the regular army. Dryer denounced the two Colonels in these words:

> Some 600 volunteers have been treated like dogs...have been living upon horse meat...while the officials [Dennison and Stark] have been swaggering around this city talking philosophically about war.

On the other hand, Editor Bush, in the *Statesman*, loyally came to the defense of the two Democrat Colonels:

> The *Oregonian* is sawing away at Mssrs. Stark and Dennison, Governor's Aides, for refusing arms to the Cascade volunteers. We know nothing of the facts in the case, but feel assured that their conduct will not admit of just censure.

From this distance in time, it is almost impossible to arrive at a fair appraisal of those charges and countercharges. Regardless of how one interprets the "Cascade Massacre," it did have the practical result, as far as Dennison was concerned, of bestowing upon him the rank of "Colonel." The title seems to have rested comfortably upon him; he retained it thereafter. But his four days of military service had necessitated his absence from Portland at a time when he was also campaigning as a candidate for mayor of Portland. Either for that reason, or perhaps because of the caustic remarks by Editor Dryer, Colonel Dennison lost the April 1856 election, polling only 81 votes, compared to 156 for James O'Neill.

It was not long, however, before Colonel Dennison had better news. That October, he was notified by the Democratic administration in Washington, D.C. that he was being named Indian Agent for the Warm Springs Reservation. This appointment was a juicy political plum worth $1500 a year. That was the same salary Oregon's governor received in the 1850s. The appointment came about through the patronage accorded Oregon's Senator Lane, who was thus able to reward Colonel Dennison for his loyalty to the Democratic Party leaders in Oregon, especially those at Salem.

While waiting to assume the office of Indian Agent, Colonel Dennison was busy looking after his various interests in Portland. By 1856, his "Dennison Building" had been converted into the "Metropolis Hotel." But the Colonel retained an office there, which was entered by a door under a portico at the right side of the hotel.

The Dennison Building and Metropolis Hotel, 1856

In 1857, when Colonel Dennison moved upriver to begin his duties as Indian Agent, he did not live at the Warm Springs Reservation, but at The Dalles, a more comfortable setting. Another advantage of having his office at the County Seat was that he could participate in local politics. During 1858, he was chairman of the Wasco County Democratic Convention. At the reservation itself, 50 miles to the south, were some administrative personnel under a resident physician, Dr. Thomas Fitch.

The *Statesman* gave Agent Dennison some publicity by sending a reporter from Salem to write about the reservation. Colonel Dennison accompanied the visitor on a tour of the facility, and in November 1858, an article appeared in the *Statesman* which included these observations:

> There are about 1200 Indians on the Warm Springs Reservation, which is in charge of Agent Dennison. The appearance of everything about the reservation speaks well for the Agent.

From Warm Springs, Colonel Dennison and his guest returned to The Dalles. From that city, the reporter added this aside: "The gambling saloons here are in full blast today, Sunday. The Lord evidently has no day east of the Cascades."

In 1859, the peaceful routine was disrupted when the Snakes, a tribe of bellicose Indians not among those living at Warm Springs, raided the reservation, stealing horses and cattle. That August, Agent Dennison received this appalling message from Dr. Fitch: "For God's sake send some help as soon as possible. We are surrounded with Snakes." Colonel Dennison promptly organized a small party and proceeded to the reservation. From there, he wrote to the Superintendent of Indian Affairs at Portland:

> I arrived here on 22nd August and was much gratified to learn that none of the buildings had been destroyed. I soon succeeded in placing the blockhouse in a position to be successfully defended. At a rough calculation, without descending to minution, I should estimate the loss... at from $7000 to $8000.

Agent Dennison's reluctance to "descend to minution" was consistent with his temperament. He was a man who preferred the broad brush, who was bored by details and impatient with financial records. His indifference to bookkeeping "minution" was to get him into difficulties a few years later.

To stabilize conditions at the reservation, a small military force was sent there. Two months later, in October, Agent

Dennison felt compelled to write this note to his supervisor at Portland:

> I have learned that the detachment of soldiers is to be called in. I hope you will use your influence with General Harney to prevent this. For the last two weeks, the Snakes have visited the Reservation almost every night. If the soldiers leave, the Indians will leave the Reservation, and, further, it will be impossible to keep any employees at the Reservation, and I believe they are good and brave men as can be found in the country, and they say that unless the soldiers remain, they will ask for their discharge.

As a result of his request, 20 mounted soldiers were assigned to the reservation for the winter.

Despite Agent Dennison's preoccupations at The Dalles, he continued to nurture his real estate investments in Portland. The assessor, reporting the principal holdings in the town in October 1859, noted that A.P. Dennison's property was worth $9,500 at market value, a quite respectable sum in terms of 1859 prices. In the same list, the property of Stephen Coffin, one of the townsite's owners, was valued at $20,000, while that of P.A. Marquam, who became one of the city's major landowners, was valued at $10,000.

At the end of October 1859, with order restored at the reservation and with his properties in Portland having attained a satisfying value, Agent Dennison announced his intention to take a leave of absence. He wished to visit his relatives in Maine and to attend the Democratic National Convention, to be held in May 1860 at Charleston, South Carolina. The *Statesman* of November 8, 1859 printed this item:

> George Abbott, Indian Agent, has been ordered to take the place of Agent Dennison, who purposes to visit the Atlantic States.

In January 1860, Colonel Dennison began the trip back to Boston, from which he had sailed just eleven years before. He must have felt a pardonable sense of achievement. He had left Massachusetts as an obscure employee in a carpet factory. Now 35 years old, he was returning as a Man of Property, with a military title and a well-paying government job. But 1860 was to be a year of crisis, not only for the nation, as the shadow of secession and Civil War fell across the land, but also for Colonel Dennison, who had tied his political future to that of the Southern Democrats.

The trip from Portland to Boston — steamship to San Francisco, thence by another steamship to Panama, across the isthmus, and then up the East Coast by steamship — took about five weeks. While in Maine that spring, he met a widow, Mrs. Lydia M. Sewall, whom he married at Bath, Maine on June 14, 1860. But before that, there was a brief interruption in the courtship. In May, Colonel Dennison had important business in Charleston. There, he met Oregon's other delegates to the Democratic National Convention. They were:

Lansing Stout, a Representative in Congress from Oregon;

John K. Lamerick, General of the Oregon Militia and later an officer in the Confederate army;

Isaac Stevens, Washington Territory's delegate to Congress;

Justus Steinberger, a Wells, Fargo Co. agent at Portland;

R.B. Metcalf, an Indian Agent at Siletz, Oregon who, like Dennison, owed that job to the patronage of Oregon's Senator, Joseph Lane.

At Charleston, the Democrats faced a difficult dilemma. If they could agree upon a compromise candidate, which they had been able to do in 1852 (Pierce) and 1856 (Buchanan), they could probably retain control of the Presidency, with all its power and patronage. But compromise between the northern and southern Democrats on the issue of slavery was becoming more difficult. If they could not find a compromise, the best that could happen would be electoral defeat and temporary joblessness; the worst: Civil War.

The Charleston convention had not been long in session before it was clear that compromise was impossible. The platform submitted by the northern wing was unacceptable to the southern delegates, who walked out of the convention. The six delegates voting for Oregon did not walk out. But they stated that if the rule requiring a two-thirds majority for selection of the Presidential candidate was dropped, thereby making possible the nomination of the northern Democrat, Stephen Douglas, they, too, would withdraw. The Oregon delegates then sent a note to Senator Lane at Washington, D.C., asking for instructions. Lane told them to withdraw with the seceding southern delegates and stand with them.

In this chaotic situation, the convention was adjourned, to meet again at Baltimore in July. It was during this interlude, between conventions, that Colonel Dennison went back to Maine and married Lydia.

At the first meeting of the convention at Baltimore, the Oregon delegation announced that they were withdrawing. They then went over to the rival convention of the Southern Democrats also being held in Baltimore at the same time, and voted with the states that shortly thereafter became the Confederacy, nominating Kentucky's John Breckinridge for President. Joining him on the ticket as candidate for Vice-President was none other than Oregon's Senator Joseph Lane. The Democrats at the "northern" convention nominated Stephen Douglas.

There was a stormy reaction in Oregon. Editor Dryer, of the Republican *Oregonian*, was, of course, delighted, as the split at Baltimore practically guaranteed Lincoln's election. Editor Bush, of the *Statesman*, a Douglas man, did an abrupt about-face in his attitude towards Dennison. Bush said that neither Metcalf nor Dennison had been chosen by the Democrats in Oregon to be delegates to the convention, "but they went to the convention anyway." Bush identified Metcalf as "formerly Indian Agent at Siletz but now a citizen of Texas." The editor called the Breckinridge delegates "a mere assemblage of odds and ends," adding:

> The Democratic Convention was engineered by the relatives and personal retainers of General Lane. They were all devoted to Lane's personal interests. Thus, Democrats of Oregon, are your wishes thwarted.

Bush went on to say "four-fifths of Oregon Democrats prefer Douglas." Bush did not get high marks for objectivity. In the election, November 1860, the results in Oregon were:

Democrats, 9210, comprised of 5074 votes for Breckinridge and 4136 votes for Douglas;

Republicans (Lincoln), 5334.

Thus the votes of Dennison and his colleagues at Baltimore did, in fact, represent the view of the majority of Oregon's Democrats. However, because of the Democrats' split, Oregon's electoral votes went to Lincoln.

Dennison, with his bride, returned to Oregon in September 1860, to resume his duties as Indian Agent at The Dalles. From then on, Dennison was fair game for Bush. A month after Dennison had returned, Editor Bush wrote:

> Lane's Indian agent at The Dalles went out to stand for him at Baltimore. Joe Lane has tied him to his coat-tails, and now Dennison ventures to "instruct" unpurchased and unpurchasable men. He'll be for Lincoln as soon as he hears of Lincoln's election. The first that will be heard of Dennison after November will be that he is figuring in a Republican meeting at The Dalles. He had better explain how sundry thousands can be "saved up" from a salary of $1500.

Bush's denunciations probably should be accepted only at some discount. Editor Dryer, of the *Oregonian*, had continually challenged Bush's probity. And even the milder-mannered H.L. Pittock, Dryer's successor, called Bush "a most accomplished vilifier" whose writings were full of "invective."

Dennison's next political appointment came in September 1861. At that time, when most of the soldiers in the Northwest had been withdrawn for action in the Civil War, the Army commandant asked Oregon's Governor to create a company of volunteers, to supplement the military forces. It was feared that some Indian bands might take advantage of the reduction in army personnel to raid established reservations or outlying settlements. John Whiteaker, a Democrat of "Southern" leanings who was Governor of Oregon from 1859 to 1862, appointed Colonel Dennison, a friend of his, to recruit 88 volunteer cavalrymen. Dennison, in turn, appointed Deputies to recruit at Portland, Salem, Corvallis, and Eugene. Editor Bush, in the *Statesman*, had this to say about the man whose every action, a few years earlier, he had defended: "The appointment of Dennison may prove unfortunate for the State treasury." Bush also wrote that, since it was suspected that Whiteaker, Dennison, and Dennison's deputies were all "Secessionists" and supporters of the Confederacy, no one was enlisting. The *Mountaineer*, a newspaper published at The Dalles, said Bush's accusations were unjust and suggested that Dennison vindicate himself. Bush retorted:

> We presume he will undertake [to vindicate himself] but it is of no use. He was a secession Indian Agent under President Buchanan for two years, got rich, and will now be a Union man for the next four years if he can get richer by so doing.

Two weeks later, Bush was able to write, with glee:

> Dennison's Enlistment Discontinued — An order has been made by the Army Department... suspending the enrollment of the Cavalry Company at The Dalles of which A.P. Dennison has been recruiting officer. How much will he bleed the State treasury for the one month he has done nothing?

The answer to that somewhat rhetorical question came the following year. Governor Whiteaker, in his final message to the State Legislature, in September 1862, submitted Colonel

Dennison's request for $1985 for "expenses incurred in recruiting." The Governor added: "The recruiting officer recommends provision for its early payment, in which I fully concur. The call was made in good faith, and those who furnished supplies, transportation, &c. doubtless did it in good faith and are justly entitled to their pay." The request was referred to the Senate Committee on Military Affairs, which reported back later that month, "No action taken, from the fact that the committee have not sufficient data to prove the correctness or justice of the demand." It was inconvenient for Colonel Dennison that he found bookkeeping details so tiresome. The request was "laid on the table" and forgotten by the Legislature but not by Dennison, who later made a trip to Washington, D.C. to try to collect. The amount involved — we would have to multiply it by about fifteen to express it in present-day dollars — was worth a little effort.

If Agent Dennison at The Dalles was having to bear some cruel barbs from former friends, life also had its more pleasant side. In December 1861, a son was born to Ami and Lydia, their only child.

About this time, Republican Indian Agents were replacing Democratic ones, as the new Lincoln administration began ousting appointees of the preceding Democratic regimes and awarding its own patronage. Early in 1862, the Dennisons left The Dalles and moved to Portland for a brief period. Here, the Colonel consolidated his affairs. In April 1862, the name of his Metropolis Hotel was changed to "Dennison House," the hotel concession being operated by Messrs. Kinney and Quin, as shown in this advertisement from newspapers of 1862:

DENNISON HOUSE
Formerly Metropolis Hotel
Cor. of Front and Stark Streets

THIS HOTEL is now open for the reception of guests, and will be conducted in all its departments as a First Class Hotel.

Kinney & Quin

Advertisements for Dennison House also noted: "Warm and Cold Lunch Served up in the Bar Room."

In September 1862, Colonel Dennison was nominated for State Representative from Multnomah County. But Democrats, especially those who sided with the Southerners, were temporarily under a cloud, and Dennison was not elected. Toward the end of 1862, he and his wife and son boarded a ship for New England. They lived at Bath, Maine for about three years. During that period, the Colonel made a trip to Washington, D.C. for the purpose, according to a biographer, of "prosecuting his claims against the Government from the Indian War" — presumably the $1985 which the Oregon Legislature had refused to pay. The final disposition of that suit remains uncertain; research has not disclosed that it was ever paid.

During this period in Maine, Mrs. Dennison died. In 1866, leaving his son with relatives in New England, Colonel Dennison returned to Portland. Perhaps, in the more structured and conventional New England, he missed the greater scope and possibilities out on the frontier. Back in Portland, he engaged in such enterprises as selling supplies to the Army Quarternasters Dept. In 1867, we find him living as a boarder at Arrigoni's Hotel. This was his old Metropolis Hotel and Dennison House, S.N. Arrigoni having purchased the property in 1864. From 1868 to 1870, he lived in an apartment on Third Street, between Main and Jefferson streets. In 1868, he was elected to the School Board, of which he was a director for nearly three years.

In 1870, two noteworthy events took place in the Colonel's career. In that year, a Democrat regained control of the Governorship, for the first time since the beginning of the Civil War. This was a happy development which opened up promising possibilities in patronage. Governor Grover took office on September 14, 1870 and on September 15th he named Colonel Dennison to be Adjutant-General of the Oregon Militia (forerunner of the National Guard). It was not an office that involved much in the way of pay, but it had worthwhile fringe benefits.

Also in 1870, Colonel Dennison joined a prosperous local merchant, H.F. Bloch (sometimes spelled Block) in a partnership, engaging in importing, exporting, and merchandising. In business directories of the day, "Bloch & Dennison" are described as "Speculators and Brokers," with offices on Front Street, near Stark Street. The partnership lasted about two years, after which Dennison appears in the directories independently, first as a broker and later as a "speculator."

About this time, Dennison again ran into difficulties because of that indifference towards bookkeeping details. In 1871, a public meeting was called to protest alleged irregularities in the bookkeeping of the School Board, of which Dennison had become chairman. It was charged that Dennison had "mismanaged" the funds. Three men were appointed, as a committee of auditors, to examine his books. The auditors found that the books, as kept under Dennison's regime, were "incomplete and informal." They were unable to account for expenditures by Dennison of $1684. Also, there was a mysterious warrant for $550 for purchase of "incidentals." Colonel Dennison countered by accusing the committee of "malice." Nevertheless, he did feel moved, probably because of the hostile tone of the press, to resign before the completion of his term. Now, a century later, it is unsafe to pronounce on the merits of the case, but it did tarnish the Colonel's image, about which any politician, however debonair, must be concerned.

It was also in 1871 that Colonel Dennison engaged in the little real estate transaction which resulted in his name becoming attached forever, as first owner, to a tract of 160 acres on the west slope of Mt. Sylvania. The acreage, which today includes the campus of Portland Community College, had been "school land" and was sold by the State of Oregon to Dennison in March 1871 for $240, or $1.50 per acre. In October 1872, Dennison sold the 160 acres to Robert Irving for $350, a remarkably short profit for a man who liked to think big.

In 1874, Colonel Dennison disposed of all his Portland interests and withdrew to San Francisco. Did he feel a growing coolness and constraint in Portland of late? In any case, he seems to have decided that the volatile atmosphere of the "Barbary Coast" would offer a more congenial environment for the expression of his enterprising nature.

In San Francisco, with an amazing ability to find a niche in the public bureaucracy — the mark of the born politician — he became Superintendent of the "House of Correction." However, he held the job for only one year. But in 1880, he was tapped for a very nice assignment. He became "private secretary" to General William S. Rosecrans, a Democrat who had just been elected to Congress. This was a signal honor for our Colonel. General Rosecrans was a man of stature. A graduate of West Point, he had been a Brigadier-General in the Civil War, and twice had been commended by Congress for winning important battles. His selection of Colonel Dennison for "private secretary" was a great tribute to the Colonel's skills.

The next two years, living in Washington, D.C. at the hub of national politics, must have been glorious ones for the Colonel, though prospects were somewhat dimmed by the fact that the Republicans (Presidents Garfield and Arthur) still held the White House and the Executive bureaucracy. The Colonel was in his mid-50s, and at the peak of his political flair.

In 1882, Colonel Dennison returned to San Francisco. For the next three years, he engaged in what he described to a biographer as "various enterprises." But in November 1884, the clouds lifted. For the first time since the ante-bellum days of President Buchanan, a Democrat (Cleveland) was elected President. Cleveland took office in March 1885, and shortly thereafter, General Rosecrans became "Register" of the Treasury, an obscure though worthwhile position. Then, as the chain reaction echoed down the ranks, Colonel Dennison was awarded a position in the San Francisco branch of the U.S. Mint!

The Mint seems a peculiarly suitable place for this soldier-of-fortune. Now in his 60s, with a comfortable office and salary, not too many duties, and a few underlings to concern themselves with the petty business of financial records, the Colonel was free to think in the broad and imaginative terms of "various enterprises."

The Colonel appears to have been of that happy disposition which regards retrospection as morbid. But, if he did look back over his somewhat checkered career, did he regret his disdain for the details of double-entry bookkeeping? We do not know. In any case, he did not return to Portland, nor did he leave any monuments or descendants here.

Despite the fact that the Colonel had reached the point of being snugly ensconced in the Mint, one feels a curious sense of incompleteness about his career. He did not seem quite to have reached the heights forecast by his obvious talents as a politician. He might, indeed, have gone far in politics — if only the Civil War had turned out differently.

Devee

John Devee and his wife Maria settled on a claim of 320 acres in February 1855. John was born in New York state in 1826 and married Maria in 1850 in Michigan. They arrived in Oregon in 1853. The tract they selected is bounded today by these S.W. streets: on the north, Alice; on the east, 25th; on the south, Dickinson-35th-Lucille; and on the west, 45th. In February 1859, they filed a "proof" of their ownership (that they had lived upon and cultivated their claim as required), and that same month they began to sell off parcels of their land. By March 1860, they had disposed of all 320 acres, as follows:

> 40 acres to Finice Caruthers, for $160;
> 14 acres to Thomas Tice, for $75;
> 226 acres to P.A. Marquam, for $1500;
> 40 acres to Boyd Quivey, for $350.

During the year, the price per acre had increased from $4 to $8.75.

The couple moved shortly thereafter to California, where Maria died. John seems to have kept in touch with friends in

Oregon, since, in 1866, he returned briefly to be married, as this newspaper announcement noted:

> Married — At the residence of William Shawley, in Yamhill County, by Elder S.C. Adams: Mr. John Devee, of San Joaquin County, Calif., to Miss Elizabeth C. Shawley, of Yamhill Co., Ore.

Reports of any successes Mr. Devee may have had in the San Joaquin valley never found their way into Oregon archives. But, in passing through Portland, he had left his name upon the land.

Dickinson

Josiah S. Dickinson was born in upstate New York in 1815 and came out to California in 1852. After a few months in the turbulence of the gold boom, he decided to move north to the more peaceful environment of Oregon. In 1853, he married

Josiah S. Dickinson

Martha Ann King, who had come to Oregon the previous year from Indiana. She was 20 years old when she married Josiah, who was 38. The couple settled on a 316-acre DLC on Mt. Sylvania. It is bounded today by S.W. 19th, 35th, Stephenson Street, and the County Line.

Besides being a farmer, Mr. Dickinson was an amateur of local politics. In 1854, he was nominated to be the Democratic Party's candidate for the Territorial Legislature, to represent Washington County, but lost the election by a narrow margin to G. W. Grier, the Whig candidate. In 1858, Mr. Dickinson was a member of the Board of Commissioners in charge of the Territorial Penitentiary, having been appointed by the Democrat Governor, Curry.

Mr. Dickinson was not, however, devoting all his time to farming and politics. He and Martha were busy raising ten children — one boy, followed by nine girls. At that time, there was no school near their farm. Josiah and Martha taught their children "the rudiments of the three Rs," as one daughter later expressed it. The son lived on the old family farm for more than 80 years. Parts of the Dickinson claim were sold off in the 1870s, but most of the original DLC remained intact into the 1930s. Mr. Dickinson died in 1899, aged 83. His wife died the previous year, aged 65.

Dillon

Isaac Dillon's career is an example of the important role played by Methodist missionaries in early Oregon religious and educational life. He was born in Ohio, into a home "where the Bible was read daily," a practice less remarkable then than today. A biographer observed, "That training so influenced Isaac that he never wandered into the byways of wickedness."

He completed four years of college and was ordained in 1844 at the early age of 21, "because of his Christian character, gifts, graces, and usefulness." For eight years, he was a circuit-riding Methodist minister in rural Ohio. In 1852, he was transferred to the "Oregon and California Mission Conference."

Preaching on the frontier posed a special problem: the diverse backgrounds to which a sermon had to appeal. As he faced his congregation, a minister might see at one end of a pew a graduate from Yale University and at the other end of the pew a worthy and valued citizen who could neither read nor write his name.

In 1853, at the annual ministers' "Conference" at Salem, Rev. Dillon was designated to be a teacher at Willamette University, the Methodists' pioneer school. There, he met Marie Carissa Plamondon, one of the teachers. They were married that year; she was 29 and he was 30.

In 1859, Rev. Dillon became principal of the church's "Umpqua Academy," at Wilbur, Oregon. The community had been named for one of the patriarchs among early Methodist ministers, "Father" Wilbur. At the school, Mrs. Dillon taught French. There were about 50 students, and most of them later became prominent Oregonians, contributing in many ways to the state's growth. Perhaps their later successes were partly due to the strict code of conduct to which they were required to subscribe in order to enter, or remain in, the Academy. The long list of rules included these things that would not be tolerated:

> "Irreverent remarks about the Christian Religion, Profane or vulgar language, Any degree of tippling anywhere. . ."

Among later assignments, Rev. Dillon, described as "a man of power and influence," was editor of the Methodists' periodical, *Pacific Christian Advocate*, published at Portland.

In 1870, Rev. Dillon became the first individual to own a 160-acre tract bounded today by North Portland Boulevard, Lombard Street, and Interstate and Delaware avenues. It was "school land," sold by the State of Oregon to Isaac Dillon for $400. A year later, he sold 150 acres to Van DeLashmutt for $3100, showing that the Reverend was not totally indifferent to the affairs of this world, where, indeed, it takes money to do God's work.

In the years around 1880, Rev. Dillon was a frequent participant in Methodist "camp meetings" at Ocean Park, in southwestern Washington. Among the prominent Methodist laymen attending meetings with him was J.K. Gill, the Portland bookstore owner.

In 1882, Rev. Dillon was transferred to the church's Puget Sound Conference, where he later became pastor of the First Methodist Church of Seattle. By 1902, he was in semi-retirement, a beloved elder clergyman "of gentle mind and thorough scholarship." He was still preaching, and, one Friday in June 1902, he set out to row across an arm of Puget Sound among the San Juan Islands, from Port Stanley, where he was staying, to Newhall, where he was to preach the following Sunday. It was a distance of seven miles by water, but though he was 79 years old, the journey seems not to have been regarded as unusual for the heroic pioneer. Rev Dillon was seen, alone in his rowboat, late Friday evening, but never afterward.

The next morning, his drifting, oar-less boat was found, but there was no trace of Rev. Dillon. His body was never recovered, and there was an element of mystery about the event. Since the oars were not in the boat, it was surmised that he had let one of them slip out of its oarlock, and, seeking to retrieve it with the other oar, had fallen overboard. A more fitting, and more daring, explanation crossed the minds of some: perhaps the Rev. Dillon, a devout and holy man, had, like the prophet Elijah before him, been translated bodily into Heaven.

Doane

Milton Doane and his wife came across the plains in 1846, settling at Portland that fall. With them came their first four children. They later had five more, beginning with Milton, Jr., who was born May 1847 in the Doane's cabin on Alder Street, in what is now the center of Portland's business district.

Milton, Senior, was born in Kentucky in 1807 and married Elizabeth in Indiana in 1831. Neither Milton nor Elizabeth could read or write. But they were ambitious for their children, and enrolled four of them in Portland's first school, which opened in the fall of 1847 in a house at the foot of Taylor Street. That school had about a dozen pupils of all ages meeting in one room. It was taught by a physician, Dr. Ralph Wilcox. It lasted one term, and was succeeded, in February 1848, by a school held in a log cabin, again a single class for all ages, taught by Miss Julia Carter. The Doane children continued in Miss Carter's school for a time.

Mr. Doane operated a flatboat, transporting goods on the Willamette River. In December 1847, the Doanes settled on a claim of 627 acres on the west bank of the river. The DLC extends from the riverfront to Forest Park and from N.W. Doane Avenue northward beyond the Burlington Northern railroad bridge. A point on the riverbank there is still identified on navigation maps as Doane Point. The property is now covered with oil storage tanks and heavy industry.

Because the Doane residence was about six miles downstream from the village of Portland, the children had to make a real effort to get to school. Perhaps they occasionally got a ride on their father's flatboat.

Milton Doane died in September 1857. His estate included: land valued at $1200; 1 yoke of oxen; 7 head of steers; 2 bulls; 3 cows; and a one-half interest in a flatboat, the other half being owned by his son-in-law, J.W. Tate.

The title to the Doane DLC was then divided among the widow and children, but one son, Josiah, seems to have bought up the others' interests, for about $60 each, and consolidated them into a single ownership. Josiah died in 1872, and, since he and his wife had no children, the full title went to his wife Henrietta. The following year, widow Henrietta married William Wandell, and that same year, she and her husband sold all their interest in the Doane claim to Alexander Gemmell for $800. Ten years later, Gemmell sold the 627 acres to P.J. Mann for $20,000. And in 1890, Mann sold most of the Doane DLC for $100,000.

These were large numbers, but they meant little to the surviving Doanes. By then, the Doane offspring were scattered, and related to the "Doane DLC" only in name.

Donner

Names become attached to pieces of geography in various ways. John Donner's name will be used forever in real estate transactions involving a 300-acre tract of hillside above the Medical School, because he was its first owner. His brother, George Donner, who was the leader of the party involved in the well-known calamity on the way to California in the winter of 1846-47, left the name "Donner" on a mountain pass and a lake near the spot where he met his sad end.

Our John was born in 1790 in North Carolina and came to Oregon in 1850. A field survey of the Donner Donation Land Claim, made in 1855, noted that it was covered with "broken and rough timber — fir, hemlock, and cedar." Today, it is covered with houses, some of which have magnificent views. The Donner DLC extends from S.W. Broadway Drive to Hamilton Street, and from S.W. 9th Avenue to about Fairmount Boulevard and Sherwood Place.

In 1857, Donner sold his claim to P.A. Marquam for $2500. Donner remained in Portland, living to be 89. His wife, Sarah, had died in 1852, aged 52. In his will, Donner left his possessions to two daughters living in Portland "and two other daughters residing, as I suppose, in States east of the Rocky Mountains," a touching phrase that shows how difficult communications and family unity were a century ago.

Duvall

Nicholas Duvall settled on a 160-acre Donation Land Claim which today includes the west half of Broadmoor Golf Course. The tract extends from N.E. 33rd to 37th and from Portland Boulevard to the Airport. Duvall came to Oregon about 1852, and was single at that time.

In 1859, he sold his 160 acres, "together with all buildings and crops standing thereon," to one Jesse Soverans for $800. Duvall signed the deed with "X," his mark.

The only other relic of Duvall contained in public records is in the *Oregonian* of January 1, 1881, where his name appears, under the heading "The Departed," in a list of those who died in Multnomah County during 1880. Duvall was 83.

Nicholas Duvall was probably related to the C.M. Duvall, one of Portland's early photographers, mentioned subsequently in connection with another pioneer landowner, William Hall. The Hall DLC adjoined the Duvall DLC.

East

Hardman E.W. East was born in Georgia in 1802 and came to Oregon as a middle-aged bachelor in 1852. The following year, he married Eliza Ann. In November 1855, the couple settled on a 301-acre claim under the Donation Land Act, just one month before that law expired. By then, the more desirable west-side locations around the village of Portland had already been taken. The tract they found was in mountainous terrain north of Cornell Road, and today includes the Bird Sanctuary and part of Macleay Park.

During the years 1864 to 1873, the Easts sold off their land, the largest parcel being 231 acres purchased by James Scott in 1869 for $500. Mr. East signed his name to these deeds, but his good wife had to be content with making "X," her mark.

Since "H.E.W. East" appears in no subsequent historical records, there is a presumption that, about 1873 — he would have been 71 years old — Mr. East left Oregon, and possibly this world.

Emerson

The name "George Emerson" is attached to a 160-acre tract of what, in the 1870s, was forest but today is the pleasant residential neighborhood extending from N.E. 24th to 33rd and Prescott to Killingsworth Street. Mr. Emerson bought the land from the U.S. Government under the Homestead Act, paying $1.25 per acre, or $200 for the quarter-section. In 1874, he sold 40 acres to William Dryden for $650. At that time, Mr. Emerson was a widower.

In 1880, he sold his remaining 120 acres to A.H. Buckman for $3000. That is all we know for certain about this pioneer landowner; his name does not appear in any other Portland records. However, he may have been the "George Harvey Emerson" who came up from California about 1870 to operate a sawmill in Douglas County, who visited Grays Harbor in the years around 1875, and began operating a sawmill at Hoquiam, Washington in 1881. This George Emerson was born in New Hampshire in 1840, was a solder in the Civil War, and came, with his wife, to California in the late 1860s.

It is possible that these were incidents in the career of one and the same George Emerson. If not, we risk offending their vanities by confounding the two, though we have no basis for judging which of the two might be more annoyed.

Finstamaker

Lying in a pool of blood with his throat cut, John Finstamaker (or Findsermacker — his name was spelled various ways because he did not know how to write) was found in his bachelor's farmhouse one day in the spring of 1887 by a neighbor, William Monies. John was still alive, so Monies got him into a buggy and whipped off to try to find a doctor before the victim bled to death. He had to drive to several offices before finding a doctor in. "At last," as Monies said in his account of the incident, he found a Dr. Coles, who "operated on the cut neck, charging $50."

This was the second time John had tried to commit suicide. The first time, Dr. John Sellwood had repaired the damage for $25. But the third time was the charm. John died by his own hand May 17, 1887, and, hopefully, found the peace he was seeking. He was 63 years old. What disappointments, what self-recrimination, regrets or remorse may have tortured poor old John, God alone knows.

Records do not show when, or from whence, John came to Oregon. Late in the 1850s, he acquired two tracts of land, both under the Homestead Act, at a cost of $1.25 per acre. One was a 67-acre parcel bounded today by N. Portland Boulevard, Lombard Street, Interstate Avenue, and Missouri Avenue. He sold it in 1862 to John Holts for $100, only slightly more than he paid for it. The other Finstamaker claim was a 40-acre tract in Parkrose. He sold it in 1865 for $40, less than the $50 he paid for it.

Though he made little profit from the two tracts which forever perpetuate his name as original owner, John invested wisely in other real estate. He seems to have been a hard worker and a good business man. His estate, at probate, was valued at $9,500, including $7,000 worth of real estate. Other assets were: cash in the bank, $1,626; several hundred dollars worth of personal notes due him from eight individuals to whom he had loaned money; his share of a potato crop; "berry caddies"; one black horse; and a one-horse wagon.

John had no wife or children, nor were any relatives found in Oregon or elsewhere. After various charges against the estate, including $235 for the undertaker, his assets went to that most impersonal of beneficiaries, the "State." His grave is in Lone Fir Cemetery, marked by a weathered shaft of marble with one simple decoration, a bundle of wheat — reference to the Biblical assurance that "He will gather His wheat unto Himself."

Fitch

As the owner of one of early Portland's many saloons, Thomas Fitch fell a victim to two weaknesses. One was his extravagance in granting credit to patrons. The other was a fondness for his own wares. Whether anxiety about the unpaid bills led to his drinking or whether intemperance induced his reckless liberality, we can only surmise. But the result was that in April 1872 he was adjudged insane, and committed to the Asylum. That institution was then located in Portland, on Hawthorne Boulevard. (Its proprietor was Dr. Hawthorne, for whom the street is named.)

Two months later, Fitch was released into the care of a guardian, James H. Frush. Fitch's estate, as taken over by Frush, included the following: wares of the saloon, $401; one horse, $35; one mule, $50; one "express wagon," $175; and "Accounts Due" from 25 customers of the Saloon, $288. What luck Frush had in collecting the "Accounts Due" is not recorded.

Seventeen years before his collapse and confinement, Fitch had already assured immortality for his name by becoming the first owner of some Portland real estate. He was born in Ohio and arrived here in October 1852. Being single, he qualified for only 160 acres under the Donation Land law. He found a claim of that size and settled on it in 1855. His DLC is bounded today by these southeast streets: 57th, 67th, Harold, and Duke. In 1863, when he was 30 years old, Fitch sold his 160 acres to Patrick Finegan for $280.

(Surprisingly, there was another Thomas Fitch in Oregon at this time, the doctor at the Warm Springs Indian Reservation to whom reference was made in the earlier account of the career of A.P. Dennison. There seems to have been no connection between that Dr. Fitch and our bartender.)

Our Tom Fitch was 39 years old when he was released from the Asylum to his guardian. He lived for another ten years. How his time was occupied we can hardly imagine. In January 1882, a newspaper gave two lines to note that Thomas Fitch, "an East Portland pioneer," had died.

Force

George Washington Force was born in New Jersey in 1819 and lived there until 1844, when he moved with his parents to Illinois. In 1845, when he was 26 years old, he joined a wagon train for Oregon. He later recalled that he had been inspired by editor Horace Greeley's advice, "Go west, young man!"

In 1848, he married Susan Wolf, who had come to Oregon the preceding year. The couple settled on a Donation Land Claim of 625 acres, extending from Columbia Slough to the Columbia River and including, today, the Expo Center and East Delta Park.

Mr. Force was Judge of Elections in 1852 for the precinct voting at the house of John Switzler, another pioneer landowner on Columbia Slough. That location attracted settlers because the river-bottom land was rich and because the Slough provided the water transportation which was so important in early days.

The Forces had eight children. Mrs. Force died in March 1898, aged 68, and Mr. Force followed her six months later, aged 79. They were buried in the pioneer cemetery on Columbia Boulevard, where many tombstones bear the names of such Columbia Slough pioneer families as Force and Switzler.

Mr. Force was a farmer, and a successful one. At his death his estate was valued at $17,461, including "cash in the bank, $12,600." For that young man, at least, Greeley's advice worked out well.

Foster

John Foster was born in England and emigrated first to Canada, where, in 1836 at the age of 38, he married Hannah Elizabeth. They moved to "the States" and in 1847 came across the plains to Oregon.

There were several men named "John Foster" in the Portland area in the 1850s. Our pioneer landowner was not the John Foster who was postmaster of "Clackamas" post office from 1852 to 1854, nor the John R. Foster who was a merchant in the village of Portland, nor the John Foster who came from San Francisco to Portland in 1855 at the age of six as an orphan. Our subject and his son, John Foster, Jr., lived out their lives on the family farm in north Portland. His other children moved to the State of Washington.

Our John Foster's name is attached as first owner to two separate claims. One is the John Foster Donation Land Claim, 287 acres between N. Peninsular and N. Washburne avenues and extending from Lombard Street to Columbia Slough. The other tract, which Mr. Foster bought under the Homestead Act for $1.25 per acre, comprises 69 acres adjoining his DLC.

John Foster sold the 69-acre "Homestead" tract in 1877 to J.C. Windle for $2400. In 1882, he sold his Donation Land Claim. This transaction involved not only his own 287-acre DLC but also 143 acres he had bought, for $600, from the adjoining Alexander Brown DLC. Mr. Foster sold the entire parcel, now comprising 430 acres, to Louis A. Banks for $25,000. Then, the following year, comforted possibly by the gratification of having done well in real estate, he died, aged 85.

Gates

Thomas Waterman Gates was born in New York state in 1821. In 1847, he came by covered wagon to Oregon. Also in that wagon train was a girl named Cynthia, whom he met and admired, and they were married *en route* to Oregon. They settled on their 640-acre Donation Land Claim in 1852. Their DLC, which surrounds today's Lents Park, is bounded by these S.E. streets: Powell, Woodstock, 82nd, and 97th-Francis-102nd.

During the years 1856 to 1871, Tom and Cynthia sold off their land, at prices ranging from $1.50 to $10 per acre. Mr. Gates died February 12, 1878, aged 57, at the home of his brother, Alonzo Gates, in East Portland.

Gatton

It was an understandable desire to find a more congenial climate than that of the Midwest which motivated William Gatton and his young wife to migrate to Oregon in 1852. William was then 21 years old. He had been born in Ohio, later moving to Iowa, where he married Nancy Hendrickson in 1850.

The couple settled on a 320-acre Donation Land Claim bordering the Willamette River just north of present-day "Terminal No. 4." At first, "home" was a one-room log cabin. The land was heavily forested, and for several years young Gatton made a business of cutting and selling wood. He was also a flatboatman on the river and, later, engaged in dairying. "By hard work and close economy," as a friend recalled, he added land to his original claim, until his tract covered more than a square mile.

Mr. Gatton played an important part in the early development of St. Johns. He was one of the first members of the community's School Board, and helped build the first Methodist Church in St. Johns. The Gattons had eleven children, five of whom died while still young. One son was drowned in the river.

In 1923, a celebration was held on Mr. Gatton's 92nd birthday. He was still living, with two sons, on his original claim. By then he had 29 great grandchildren. All of them were present at the party. A newspaper photograph showed Mr. Gatton, looking resolute and energetic, with a full white beard and small oval steel-rimmed glasses. Among the relatives at the celebration was his brother, Samuel Gatton, also hale and hearty at the age of 90, and a resident of Woodland, Wash.

Mr. Gatton died in 1924, aged 93. He was buried in the Gatton cemetery located on his property. Mr. Gatton began using that plot as a cemetery in 1871 when his wife Nancy died. The location he selected for that purpose is at the eastern extremity of the Gatton DLC, well above the danger of flooding. A visit to the cemetery today shows that six Gattons are buried there, as well as members of two other families. The little cemetery comprises about one-quarter acre.

Mr. Gatton, late in his lifetime, sold two parcels of his land for the construction of Terminal No. 4 and a lumber mill. The remainder he rented out for farming uses. By then, taxes had increased so much that they were barely covered by the small income from farm rents. After his death, the Dock Commission purchased another 50 acres, at $1000 per acre, to expand Terminal No. 4.

Individuals who had tried to buy some of his acreage criticized the tenacity with which Mr Gatton held onto his land. But his friend and attorney, J.N. Pearly, commenting on that pioneer landowner's life, rose to his defense, saying, "Through the years, Mr. Gatton helped as a pioneer to build up our community. He has done his part."

Gerow

Had Jonathan Titus Gerow married Ellen Gardner a year earlier, one might have thought he was motivated partly by a desire to double the amount of free land he could claim under the Donation Land Act. There are grounds for believing that some marriages were undertaken with that in mind. But Jonathan was still single in January 1855 when he took up his DLC, so he could claim only 160 acres. Next year, he married Ellen. The supposition that they were inspired by the purer considerations of romance is not made less likely by the fact that they proceeded to have 13 children.

The year 1856 was also significant for Jonathan because of his participation in two Indian "wars." The "war" at "Cascades" (now Cascade Locks), in March 1856, was described in the earlier biography of another pioneer landowner, A.P. Dennison. One company of volunteers had set out from Portland on the riverboat *Fashion* to go to the aid of settlers at Cascades. Another company of volunteers from Portland was organized by Captain Stephen Coffin (later "General" of the Oregon militia and also one of our pioneer landowners). Jonathan Gerow was a private in Coffin's company, which numbered 80 men. They started to march from Portland to Cascades, but before they got there, regular army troops from The Dalles subdued the Indians. So Private Gerow and his fellow volunteers turned around and marched back to Portland, where they were mustered out. During their three days of service, they had not fired a shot.

Later that spring, Gerow again volunteered "to guard the settlers of Sandy and Powell's Valley, and drive the Indians back," as he expressed it in a letter written afterward. He added, "I think there was 25 men in all in our company." This service lasted 30 days, but again no shots were fired in anger. Perhaps the rough and informal aspect of 25 pioneer Portlanders was sufficient in itself to awe the Indians.

Jonathan, now 29 years old, spent the rest of 1856 clearing his 160 acres for farming, and settling in with Ellen. His tract is bounded today by N.E. Union Avenue, N. Interstate Avenue, and Prescott and Killingsworth streets. In 1856, it was heavily timbered and "Nathan," as he was sometimes called, cut wood, hauled it to the riverbank, and sold it to steamboats. In the years around 1860, he himself owned a small riverboat, the *Ellsworth*, with which he contracted to carry freight between Portland and

St. Johns. The river was still a far more convenient artery of transportation than the unpaved country roads.

In 1868, Mr. Gerow sold his farm to D.W. Williams and moved to Clark County, Washington. Williams subsequently sold the 160 acres to Matthew Patton, whose name is memorialized by the Patton Home, a retirement institution located on the original Gerow DLC. By 1894, Mr. Gerow had moved to Pacific County, Washington. In that year, he submitted a request for a pension on the basis of his service in "the Indians wars." In his letter of application, he wrote, "I am 67 or 68 years old, my health is very poor, my legs is given out, so I am home all the time." It is satisfactory to note that his pension was granted and that he lived to enjoy it for 13 years. He died at Chinook, a fishing village across the Columbia River from Astoria, and far, indeed, from the Pennsylvania farm where he had been born 79 years before.

Gilfry

"Eden of the World" was the phrase Henry H. Gilfry used to describe the Oregon of his boyhood when he delivered the Annual Address at the 1905 meeting of the Oregon Pioneer Association. If, already in 1905, he was using that phrase in the past tense, today he might feel that Eden had, indeed, harbored a serpent, sometimes called "Progress."

The pioneers had invited their guest speaker back to Oregon from Washington, D.C., where he was in the midst of a long career as Clerk of the U.S. Senate. Henry Gilfry had first come to Oregon in 1852, at the age of eight, when he and his parents crossed the plains from Illinois, settling near Eugene. Henry attended Willamette University. It was a time when attending college was not yet a "right" but a rare privilege, to be taken with appropriate gravity. The *Oregon Statesman* in 1864 found it newsworthy that Henry Gilfry had been elected Secretary of the university's Hesperian Literary Society. Two

Henry H. Gilfry

years later, at the age of 22, he graduated from Willamette and entered law school. In 1868, he was elected to the State Legislature from Lane County. He was a Democrat.

In 1870, the Democrats recaptured the Statehouse, for the first time since the Civil War, and the newly elected governor, LaFayette Grover, chose Mr. Gilfry to be his private secretary. Their association continued throughout the Governor's term, 1870-1877. During this period, Mr. Gilfry, though only about 30 years-old, was elected Grand Master of his fraternal society, the Odd Fellows. He was also honored by being selected to represent Oregon at the Philadelphia Centennial Exposition of 1876, which celebrated the 100th anniversary of the Declaration of Independence. There, he gave a speech on the history, growth, and resources of Oregon.

It was in 1870 and 1871, when he was the Governor's private secretary, that Mr. Gilfry bought two pieces of Portland real estate which perpetuate his name as original owner. These tracts were "school land" sold to Mr. Gilfry by the State. One was an 80-acre parcel bounded today by these N.E. streets: 72nd, 82nd, Siskiyou, and Fremont. The other also comprised 80 acres, bounded by 72nd, 82nd, Halsey, and Tillamook. Three state officials signed the deeds conveying these tracts to Mr. Gilfry: his employer, Governor Grover; Stephen Chadwick, Secretary of State; and Louis Fleischner, State Treasurer. Mr. Gilfry paid the State $400 for each of the 80-acre tracts. Shortly after he had brought the tracts, Mr. Gilfry sold his acres to Stephen Chadwick, Louis Fleischner, and to Fannie Fleischner, a relative of Louis. Mr. Gilfry's Democratic cronies seem to have done him a favor; he paid $800 for his 160 acres and sold them for $2000. But Chadwick and Fleischner seem to have made little or no profit in their later sales of those acres.

After seven years as Governor, LaFayette Grover was elected U.S. Senator. Mr. Gilfry, still as his private secretary, went with him to Washington, D.C. The relationship continued through Senator Grover's term, 1877-1883. In Washington, Mr. Gilfry met and married Margaret Stouffer, the ceremony taking place in 1878 when he was 35 years old.

The fascination of the nation's political hub was such that, when Senator Grover was replaced by a Republican (Joseph Dolph) in 1883 and returned to Oregon, Mr. Gilfry remained in Washington. He became a clerk in the Senate, where he continued to work for the rest of his life. There are several "clerk" positions in the Senate and Mr. Gilfry at different times filled three of them: reading clerk, minute and journal clerk, and parliamentary clerk. He became an authority on parliamentary procedure, and wrote a book on the subject. The clerks were appointed by the political party having a majority in the Senate. At the beginning of each session, if there was a change in majority, the previous clerks were usually let go. It was a tribute to Mr. Gilfry's ability that he was retained steadily as a clerk for 42 years, through periods of Republican as well as Democratic majorities. He continued to work in the Senate until his death in 1925, aged 81. A photo taken in his later years shows him bald, with a walrus moustache, wearing a high starched collar, a black ribbon tie, and a gravely serious expression. An editor who knew him wrote these words: "He was an able and an excellent man of high character. As a companion and conversationalist, he was equalled by few."

Friends in Oregon regretted that Mr. Gilfry, who had begun a promising career here as a young man, chose to remain in Washington. Evidently, he found it more satisfying to be a small cog in a large and important setting than to play a large role out in the provinces, however Eden-like. Perhaps the only occupational hazard of working where he did was the necessity of listening attentively to decades of pompous oratory. In 1905, when he delivered his speech to the Oregon Pioneers, his style already suffered from the effects of his Senatorial habitat. He closed that speech with a peroration urging us to hand Oregon history and traditions "down to those who travel in our footsteps along the great highway of time."

Gilham

Forty covered wagons, drawn by slowly plodding oxen, left Missouri in the spring of 1852 for Oregon. The families making the trip could muster 70 men who had guns. Before moving out, the wagon train was "organized" by the election of a captain, Newton D. Gilham. One of the men who came to Oregon in this group wrote, "Captain Gilham's authority was almost absolute, but right well did he perform his exacting duties."

Mr. Gilham was born in Illinois in 1811 and, when he was 34, married Marecy, aged 28. With them in their wagon, as they crossed the plains, was a two-year-old son, Newton L. Gilham. They selected a 322-acre Donation Land Claim. It is an irregularly shaped tract bounded by these streets: S.E. Stark; N.E. Tillamook; 60th-Halsey-62nd; and 67th-Halsey-72nd. There, the family grew to seven children. Mr. Gilham was a farmer and a Methodist.

Marecy died in 1882 and the next year Mr. Gilham, aged 72, made his will. He wrote it himself, with a shaky hand and

Newton D. Gilham

some highly personalized spelling. It provided that a son, Charles, was to have "all livestock, waggons, plows, harness, all hous holed and kitcy furiture, in fact evry thing in the house or petaig to the house." The household furniture included an organ.

Of his original land claim, Mr. Gilham had sold 80 acres in 1864 for $500. At his death in 1887, the remainder was divided among his children. A friend who had known Mr. Gilham since the 1852 covered wagon trip paid him this tribute: "His name recalls the memory of a faithful, useful life."

Gradon

A 213-acre tract of land, part of which is now in the "Mall 205" shopping center, was covered with heavy timber in 1855 when Israel and Isabella Gradon settled on it as their Donation Land Claim. Israel was born in Ohio in 1821. When he was 29, he married a widow, Mrs. Isabella Chopin Creich, and the couple came to Oregon in 1852. They retained the claim only long enough to establish their title to it. In 1859, they sold 210 acres for $3000, retaining only the three acres on which their house stood. The boundaries of the "Gradon DLC" are 80th, 102nd, Stark and Salmon streets.

Mr. Gradon, who died at "Powell's Valley" in 1891, aged 70, was a wagon-maker by trade. He was active in the Odd-Fellows Lodge, and in 1860 was its Grand Warden. He was also interested in politics and was elected Justice of the Peace. As such, he performed many marriages in the late 1860s.

Another surviving record of Mr. Gradon, and one which gives an intimation of his political preferences, is his name, along with 27 others, signed in 1862 to an affidavit opposing the seating of Benjamin Stark in the U.S. Senate. Mr. Stark, another pioneer landowner whose career will be described in later pages, was a sympathizer with the Southern Confederacy. Stark did represent Oregon in the Senate during 1861-62, despite Mr. Gradon's protest.

Gray
　　　　Robert
　　　　George

Two brothers, Robert and George Gray, both of whom were among early Oregon's amateur tobacco growers, have their names preserved on pioneer land claims in east Portland. The Grays came across the plains to Oregon in 1853. They were originally from Ohio. The family group making the trip included Robert Gray, Jr., aged 41, and his wife, Sarah Ann, aged 26; his brother, George B. Gray, aged 32 and single; their father, Robert Gray, senior; and other family members not recorded by name.

Robert Gray, senior, was a saddlemaker. He settled in Polk County. He was probably accompanied by his wife and other children. He died at Corvallis in 1857, from typhoid.

Robert Gray, Jr., and his wife Sarah Ann lived on their Portland DLC until about 1866. It was during this period that he became famous as a tobacco-grower. A newspaper in Portland, the *Times*, printed this item in November 1863:

> Robert Gray has furnished us with a sample of tobacco of his own raising. It is of the "Orinoco" variety, and in appearance is as good an article as was ever produced in any country. Parties who profess to be good judges of the raw material pronounce it as good as was ever raised on Missouri or Virginia soil.

In 1866, the *Statesman* reported that, at the State Fair at Salem, Robert Gray had an exhibit of leaf tobacco "said by connoisseurs to be of a good quality."

About 1866, the Robert Grays moved from Portland to Polk County, where other members of the family had established themselves. Robert sold his Portland land claim, parts of it going to Erastus Gray and Lyman Gray, probably his sons. His 160-acre DLC is bounded today by S.E. 72nd, 85th, Powell, and Division-80th-Lincoln streets.

Robert's wife, Sarah Ann, died near Corvallis in January 1868, and Robert died at Corvallis in 1892, aged 79. There is a "Robert Gray School" in southwest Portland, but it is not named for our pioneer landowner but for Captain Robert Gray, who in 1792 discovered the Columbia River, which he named for his ship.

George Gray, after living alone on his DLC for about ten years, married a widow, Mrs. Sarah Jean Gordon, in 1865, when he was 44 years old. The previous year he had been elected Justice of the Peace and, as such, had been performing a great many marriages, which perhaps put him in a mood to take the step himself. George also grew tobacco and a newspaper item noted that he was making cigars. George and Sarah Jean sold most of their land to J.H. Mitchell in 1870 for $500. The George Gray DLC is bounded by 67th, 72nd, S.E. Stark and N.E. Halsey streets.

By a surprising coincidence, considering how small the Territory's population was, there were three distinct individuals called George Gray in Oregon in the 1850s. One of them even came across the plains in the same year as our George, but settled near Eugene. The third one, George Berry Gray, lived at Salem. Also, there was in Oregon in the 1850s a Robert D. Gray, a pioneer Baptist minister in Lane County. Genealogical data indicate that this could not have been our DLC Robert Gray, which is fortunate, since the vision of a cigar-chomping Baptist evangelist would be too astonishing.

Greenleaf

Robert Stevens Greenleaf was a professional surveyor who, in the course of his work, discovered a little tract of ten acres which, though close to the city, still remained in the public domain as late as 1892. In that year, he acquired title to it under the Homestead Act for $1.25 per acre. The next year, he sold the ten acres to Seneca Smith for $2000. That land today is in Tryon Creek State Park.

Mr. Greenleaf was born in St. Louis in 1848, and was related to the poet John Greenleaf Whittier. During the closing months of the Civil War, he served as a drummer boy, though he was only 17 years old. Later, he studied engineering at St. Louis. He came to Oregon in 1884 and, as a surveyor, laid out many subdivisions, including Rose City Park, Laurelhurst, Westmoreland, Eastmoreland, Euclid Heights, and Greenhills. In 1891, he was appointed County Surveyor, to fill an unexpired term, and in 1892, he was elected to that office. It was while he was County Surveyor that he acquired the 10-acre tract perpetuating his name as original owner.

During the Spanish-American War, he was a captain in the Oregon Militia, passing the war months stationed at Vancouver, Washington. After the war, Captain Greenleaf returned to surveying, which he practiced until the day of his death, in 1915, at the age of 67. A newspaper editor wrote of him as "a man of unassailable honesty, satisfied only with absolute accuracy. A

'Greenleaf' map was accepted in any court as incontrovertible evidence. All over the downtown area, in the sidewalks and curbs, are small brass screws placed there, while surveying, by this accurate engineer."

Groom

Orson Alonzo Groom (the name sometimes appears as Grooms) was born in New Jersey and arrived in Oregon in March 1852, a single man 36 years old. He settled at Oregon City where, seven months later, he married a widow, Mrs. Artemisia Sweeza. The marriage was performed by the city's mayor. As man and wife, the couple were entitled under the Donation Land Act to 320 acres free. The claim they chose is bounded today by S.W. 45th, 55th, Stephenson Street, and Taylors Ferry Road.

As soon as they had completed the residence requirement, the Grooms sold their claim. Half of it was sold to John Kilgore for $500. Artemisia signed with "X," her mark. A year later, they sold the other half to David Groom, probably Orson's brother, for $1600. This time, Artemisia wrote her name, showing that she had used the intervening year constructively.

The Grooms moved to the town of Dayton, in Yamhill County, and there, in 1858, Orson died of consumption. A newspaper noted, "He left a wife and four small children to mourn his loss. He obtained a hope in Christ before God called him to rest."

Guild

The first "tavern" or "public house" in the vicinity of Portland was the cabin Peter Guild built in 1849 on his 598-acre Donation Land Claim. The DLC today includes the "Guilds

Lake" district in the city's northwest industrial area and the Port of Portland's "Terminal No. 2." Guild's Tavern became a favorite rendezvous of immigrants and sailors. The cabin, an eight-cornered edifice of logs, was located on the west bank of the river near a different kind of bar — the Swan Island Bar, a sand and gravel obstacle in the channel that often detained sailing ships when the river was low or winds were contrary. The captains of such ships would anchor near the bar and then spend a night or two at Guild's pub, awaiting a favorable wind. The tavern, pioneers recalled, was "a scene of dancing and general merrymaking, interspersed with well-spun yarns of old sea dogs."

Though he may have derived entertainment as well as profit from it, operating a pub had not been Mr. Guild's original intention. He had planned to be a stockman. He came to Oregon in 1847 with his wife, five children, and 50 head of cattle. Mr. Guild was born in Rhode Island, had married Elizabeth Richardson in Illinois in 1839, and was 54 when he decided to bring his family across the plains.

When the Guilds reached The Dalles, late in the fall of 1847, they decided to leave the cattle there rather than try to drive them around Mt. Hood during the winter, and the family came on to Portland to select a land claim. They spent the winter at Linnton, which, according to a visitor who saw it at that time, "contains only a few log houses; its few inhabitants are very poor." One of the Guilds' poverty-stricken companions at Linnton that winter was James Johns, later the pioneer landowner of St. Johns.

In the spring of 1848, Peter Guild selected his claim. It had nearly a mile of riverfront, a lake, and bottomland that would provide fine pasture for his cattle. Leaving his family at Linnton Mr. Guild went up to The Dalles, but, though he looked high and low, he could find no trace of his animals. Upon inquiry, he was appalled to find that they had, all 50 head, been eaten. It had been a hard winter at The Dalles; supplies had been short and the population was augmented by a regiment of volunteer militia mobilized to suppress the Cayuse Indians following their massacre of the Whitman missionaries. What arrangement

Mr. Guild had made for the custody of his cattle is not recorded, but it appears to have been less than satisfactory. He filed a claim against the U.S. government for reparations, but was unable to collect.

Mr. Guild returned to his claim, under the necessity to change his plans, and built his octagon-shaped log house. It was two miles downstream from the village of Portland, which then was just a cluster of cabins at the foot of Washington Street. Mr. Guild's log house, where he offered food, drink, and lodging, gradually turned into a haven for becalmed sailors, immigrants, and pedestrians *en route* to or from the California gold fields. A reason for its popularity was probably that, as an old pioneer later recalled, "Peter Guild dispensed good cheer with a lavish hand." In the 1850s and 1860s, Guild's Tavern and Guild's Lake, located on his DLC, were well-known recreational resorts. Mr. Guild added to his log building until, by the time of his death in 1870, it was an imposing structure.

Meanwhile, the number of Guild children had increased to nine. They were aged 35 to 12 when the father died. Half of the DLC went to the widow. The other half, according to Peter Guild's will, went to the children, "to be so partitioned that each has a building spot on high ground and each having as nearly as possible the same amount of high ground and pasture."

Of her part of the claim, Mrs. Guild gave 36 acres to a son. Then, in 1881, she received $10,000 from Nicholas Versteg for 35 acres as a site for a sawmill. She sold her remaining 220 acres to P.L. Willis for $40,000. Mrs. Guild signed the deeds with her mark, "X." But it was a valuable X.

Guntley

Anton Guntley was first owner of an 80-acre tract in southwest Portland bounded today by 12th, 25th, Dickinson, and Palatine streets. He acquired it in 1861, using a "Military Bounty" land warrant. The warrant was originally issued to

Thomson Ward, who had been a captain in the Kentucky militia in the War of 1812. Ward, many years after that, sold the warrant to Guntley, probably for about $80. Guntley held the land for 10 years, then in 1871 sold it to B.C. Cardwell for $650. Title remained in the Cardwell estate until his widow sold the 80 acres in 1906 for $3600.

Aside from these transactions, the records contain no reference whatsoever to Anton Guntley. Except for his signature on the deed to Cardwell, he might have been quite mythical. Certainly, if he ever lived in Portland, he led a very quiet life.

Hall

The biography of pioneer landowner William Hall is somewhat uncertain, not due to any dearth of references to "William Hall" in the archives of early Oregon, but because there were several individuals with that same name. We do know that our William Hall was born in Ohio in 1822 and settled on a 320-acre Donation Land Claim in 1851, at which time he was still a single man. Those facts are recorded on his application for the land claim. His DLC is bounded today by N.E. 37th, 42nd, and Holman Street, and extends northward across Columbia Slough to and including part of Broadmoor Golf Course. Records also show that in 1865 he acquired an adjoining 80-acre tract under the Homestead Act, paying $1.25 per acre for that land. The 320 acres in his DLC were, of course, free.

It is also evident that William Hall had come to Oregon before December 1850. A single man arriving after that time could have claimed only 160 acres under the Donation Land Act.

According to an article written in 1885, there was living in Beaverton at that time a William Hall, who had been born in Ohio in 1822, and we assume that this was our William. He had married a woman whose first name was Christiana and they had six children. Newspaper files show that a William Hall, born in

1822, died at Hillsboro in 1895, and that Mrs. William Hall died at Hillsboro in 1897. Her obituary gives the additional information that she was born in North Carolina in 1826 and came to Oregon in 1853. The article adds. "For a number of years, she and her husband lived near Beaverton."

Another bit of evidence helping to identify our William Hall is an item which appeared in July 1853 in the *Oregon Weekly Times*, a pioneer newspaper published in Portland, under the heading "Marriages":

> July 13th, at the residence of David Powell, by E.S. Quimby, Esq., Mr. William Hall and Mrs. Christiana DeVall.

So far, we can be fairly confident that we are on the trail of the right William Hall, since real estate records confirm that his wife's name was, in fact, Christiana. Deeds signed by William and Christiana Hall show these sales of land from his Donation Land Claim:

> 1856, 104 acres, for $416;
> 1861, 22 acres, for $500;
> 1866, 194 acres, for $1500.

Another reference which was probably to our pioneer landowner shows that, at the first Multnomah County Agricultural Society Fair, held in October 1860, William Hall was an exhibitor and won an award.

In the Portland City Directory of 1873 are listed "Hall & DuVall, Photographers," and the partners, identified as William Hall and C.M. DuVall, were living at the same address, in East Portland. Since our William had married the widow, Mrs. Christiana DeVall, the same combination of almost identical names gives a strong presumption that William had become one of Portland's early photographers, in partnership with his wife or a step-son. In the 1875 City Directory, C.M. DuVall is still shown as a photographer, but William Hall has become a carpenter. The name DuVall does not appear in subsequent directories, but William Hall is shown as a "Clerk" in the

Portland directory of 1876. If this is our DLC William, he would then have been 54 years old. And, if our deductions are correct, he moved sometime during the following few years to Beaverton, and later to Hillsboro.

An earlier historical record may shed additional light on our pioneer landowner's first years in Oregon. The Minute Book of the West Union Baptist Church for 1847, when that congregation was just a small group of people meeting in a private home between Beaverton and Hillsboro, contains this entry:

> On Sabbath, July 11th, Elder Snelling preached to a Respectable audience after which the Church congregation repaired to Darie Creek, where the ordinance of Baptism was administered to Sister Brazilla Constable and Brother William F. Hall.

If, as is not improbable, this was our William, he would have been 25 years old at the time. Evidently, William was a promising convert; a few months later, he was appointed to a building committee "to effect the erection of a meeting house at Hillsboro."

The passage of the Donation Land Act in September 1850 seems to have drawn William from Hillsboro to the vicinity of Portland, with a view to establishing a claim which, as the village became a city, would appreciate rapidly in value. The move led, if we read the records correctly, to a chain of destiny: marriage, farming, photography, carpentry, and, at the end, a return to the neighborhood where, many years before, on a summer Sunday, he had been immersed in the then clear waters of Dairy Creek.

Clark Hay's Wagon Factory, 1865

Hay

Widely Known Pioneer Passes Away in 90th Year

Established First Wagon Factory Here And was a Citizen of Sterling Worth and Character

Such was the heading in the *Oregonian* in 1906 at the death of Clark Hay, familiarly known as "Father" Hay. In his latter years, the gentler honorific "Father" had replaced the sterner title "Captain," by which he had been known when he was leader of a train of 70 covered wagons in 1853 and also when he was an officer of the Oregon militia in the Indian wars of 1855-56. His obituary closed on this eulogistic note: "No man possessed a more amiable disposition, or was more honorable in his business dealings."

Mr. Hay's long and richly varied career began in Ohio, where he was born in 1817. There, he learned the trade of "carriage blacksmith." When he was 30, he married, and in 1853, he and his wife Clara Belle and three infant daughters came to Oregon. They travelled by steamboat from Ohio to Missouri, where they joined a wagon train. A note in a diary kept by a member of Captain Hay's train reminds us of the three constant concerns of covered-wagon pioneers — water, grass for the animals, and firewood:

> Aug. 11, 1853: Drove from John Day's River to the Columbia River. Got there at 8 o'clock p.m. Good grass on the side of the mountain. Camped in the bottom. Wood very scarce.

The Hays first settled at Skipanon, a little community at the mouth of the Columbia River. They lived there about a year. Then, for all his amiability of disposition, Clark and Clara Belle decided to be divorced. It was a step that was not only more unusual but also more difficult than it is today. And it required an act of the Legislature when Clara Belle wanted to marry another man two years later. Records of the House of Representatives show that, in 1856, a bill was passed to change the name of Clara Hay to Clara Hay Pease.

About 1854, Clark Hay moved to Portland and entered business as a wagon and carriage blacksmith. His shop was on Front Avenue at Madison Street. The business grew until Mr. Hay was employing about 20 men.

When he moved to Portland, Mr. Hay had not yet availed himself of the free land to which he was entitled under the Donation Land Act, though his divorce, by transmuting him to single status, had cut in half the number of acres for which he was eligible. In 1855, he claimed 160 acres, bounded today by these N.E. streets: 50th, 57th, Halsey, and Brazee.

In 1865, when he was 48, Mr. Hay remarried. His second wife was Josephine Burch, by whom he had one son. The couple lived in East Portland, probably on the "Hay DLC," and Mr. Hay was a daily commuter on the Stark Street Ferry. In 1870, the Hays sold 47 acres to Hiram Tuttle for $1200. In 1879, Mr. Hay sold the remainder of his claim for $6500. By that time Josephine had evidently died, since only Clark Hay's name appears on the deed of sale.

Mr. Hay continued to manage his wagon factory until 1883. Then, at the age of 66, he embarked on an entirely new venture. He had long believed that people could "associate themselves together and carry mutual benefit insurance at a very low cost, within the scope of the smallest wage-earner's purse." In 1883, he incorporated the "Washington Co-operative Life Insurance Company," also known as the "Order of Washington." He was its treasurer and manager. The business flourished and by 1906, when the founder had become "Honored Past Supreme President," it was a large and profitable enterprise, "proving in a most vivid way the soundness of Mr. Hay's idea."

In his later years, "Father" Hay was an active participant in the annual "Camps" of the Indian War Veterans. For example, at the Portland Camp Meeting of 1894, when 33 veterans were present, he was appointed to a "relief committee" to organize aid for needy veterans.

Mr. Hay was, according to biographers, "a lifelong and ardent supporter of the Republican Party" and "a consistent believer in the principles of temperance." When he was a child, he gave his mother "his pledge to abstain from alcoholic beverages, to which he faithfully adhered."

Gay Hayden and his wife Mary Jane

Hayden

Hayden Island, on the Oregon side of the Columbia River north of Portland, perpetuates the name of Gay Hayden, who occupied it as his Donation Land Claim. He was born in New York state in 1819 and later moved to Wisconsin, where he married Mary Jane in 1846. Crossing the plains, the family reached Oregon in October 1850. The timing was good; they arrived just two months before the December 1st deadline after which they could have claimed only 320 acres instead of 640. The island on which the Haydens settled had a nominal area of 644 acres. However, during floods in those early days when there were no dams on the Columbia River to help regulate its flow, the island's dimensions could shrink alarmingly. Perhaps it was this variability which caused the Haydens to sell the island in 1869 to William and John Switzler for about $2000.

The Haydens also owned 25 acres which are now part of the Portland Airport. They acquired that tract in 1863 under the Homestead Act, paying $1.25 per acre, or a total of $31.25. They sold the 25 acres in 1869 for $32.

The Haydens later lived in Vancouver, Washington, and Mr. Hayden was mayor of that city for several years. He died there in 1902, aged 83.

When Mr. Hayden built his first cabin, about 1851, he incorporated in it some brick tile which he had purchased from the Hudson's Bay Company store at Vancouver. After his death, his widow donated some pieces of this tile to the Oregon Historical Society. Mr. Hayden was, it appears, a man of sensitivity, who wanted his log cabin to have a touch of gentility.

Hendrickson

Swan Island (those aren't swans you see thereabouts; they're well-fed seagulls) really was an island when Lemuel Hendrickson, in November 1851, claimed it as his Donation Land grant. Lemuel was from Ohio and had arrived in Oregon in November 1848. The landfill linking the island with the mainland was built many years later.

From his island, Lemuel made frequent trips across the river to the DLC of Milton Doane, who had a daughter named Sarah Ann. The result was that Lemuel and Sarah Ann were married in August 1853. He was 27 years old and she was 17. The wedding took place at his cabin on Swan Island, with everyone arriving by boat. Lemuel's brother William, an "elder" of the Church of the Brethren, performed the ceremony.

Lemuel's island DLC had a nominal area, according to Land Office records, of 266 acres, but that would have varied widely with the seasonal level of the river.

There are no indications as to how the Hendricksons spent their time, but we do know that Lemuel died in October 1887, aged 60, and Sarah Ann in 1901, aged 64.

Hildburgh

A tract of 160 acres in northeast Portland was sold in December 1870 by the State of Oregon to David H. Hildburgh for $800. This had been "school land," and the deed was signed by the three members of the Land Board: Governor Grover, Secretary of State Chadwick, and State Treasurer Fleischner. The boundaries of the Hildburgh tract are 62nd, 72nd, Fremont, and Prescott streets.

In 1882, Hildburgh sold 80 acres to Jacob Haas for $1200, and in 1888 he sold his remaining 80 acres to Fannie Fleischner for $600. In these deeds, there is no mention of a wife, so we may assume that Hildburgh was a single man. At the bottom of the last deed, this note was pencilled: "David Hildburgh died 1905 at Mount Sinai Hospital in New York City." Except for these glimpses, an impenetrable cloud obscures the origins, vocation, and character of the man whose name survives as the first individual to own this real estate.

Hill, Isaac

References to an Isaac Hill who crossed the plains to Oregon in 1852 and became a prominent citizen of the Rogue Valley are so numerous in the annals of Oregon that they eclipse the few records left by another Isaac Hill, who led an obscure but no less worthy life in Portland. Our Isaac and his wife Mary were both from West Virginia, where he was born in 1836. The couple came to Oregon in 1862 and Mr. Hill became a farmer in what is now northeast Portland. He died in 1917, aged 81, survived by Mary and five children. "He took a active part in most of the religious and charitable movements of the day and was an active member of Centenary Methodist Church," according to a newspaper obituary writer.

The 165-acre tract bearing his name, which he acquired under the Homestead Act at $1.25 per acre, is bounded today by these N.E. streets: 37th, 47th, Killingsworth, and Prescott.

During the years 1882 to 1888, the Hills sold most of their claim for about $40 an acre. Subsequently, each of those acres was divided into eight residential lots.

Hill, Lorenzo

Title to a 40-acre tract along the west side of N.E. 82nd Avenue between Prescott and Killingsworth streets goes back to Lorenzo D. Hill. He acquired it in February 1874 as a "homestead" at $1.25 per acre, or $50 for his claim. After holding it for only ten months, he sold the tract for $150 to Laban Hill. Lorenzo was a single man and Laban may have been his brother. Lorenzo may also have been related to Isaac Hill, another pioneer landowner, but we found no evidence of such relationship.

Those two deeds, showing his name as buyer and seller, are the only surviving relics of Lorenzo Hill. One looks in vain through the files of our 19th-century newspapers for any reference to him. Since in those days, even as now, the surest path to publicity was involvement in some crime or catastrophe, there is the pleasing reflection that, if Lorenzo's life was unrenowned, at least it was lawful.

Holland

About the time of the Great Potato Famine, there lived in western Ireland two young men whose paths were later to cross in Oregon — Patrick Daly and Patrick Holland. Whether they knew each other in the Old Country is not revealed by the records, but they may well have been friends. Daly left Ireland in the 1850s and, after several years which were probably not without adventure, finally came to rest about 1865 in Portland.

In that year, he took up a claim under the Homestead Act on the 160 acres bounded today by N.E. 15th, 24th, Prescott, and Killingsworth streets. Daly paid $200 for the land. In 1869, just before he would have completed the residence requirement necessary to have the title issued in his name, he died. He left neither wife nor will, and the court appointed one Thomas Ryan, who had been a friend of Daly, as administrator. Ryan found that Daly's only relatives were a father and mother on the Old Sod of Ireland and a brother who had last been heard from living "somewhere in Boston." Though Daly had not, at the time of his death, acquired final title to his land, he did have, by claim and occupancy, a right in it. Ryan auctioned off that right, and it was purchased by Patrick Holland for $250. Holland completed the residence requirement, and title to the tract was issued in his name.

Patrick Holland had come to America in 1859, had enlisted in the Ohio infantry, and served in the Civil War. After that, he re-enlisted and fought against Indians in California and Arizona. He came to Portland in 1867 and we may suppose that, in the small community of that day, he and Daly were friends during the two years before Daly's death.

Holland, not long after his arrival in Portland, had married a woman named Margaret, and in July 1871, Patrick and Margaret Holland sold their 160 acres to John Dunning for $2000. At that time, Patrick was unable to read or write; he signed the deed with "X," his mark. Margaret, however, could write her name.

For about 30 years, Holland engaged in dairying. But the handsome profit he had made on his real estate transaction must often have suggested to him that there could be an easier way to make a living than milking cows. About the turn of the century, by which time his wife had died and he was in his 60s, Holland retired from dairying and became a real estate dealer. He had, meanwhile and perhaps with Margaret's help, learned to read and write. For the next 20 years, he dealt in real estate, in a small and quiet way, living alone in the Lenox Hotel. He died in 1919, and, after a funeral service at St. Mary's Cathedral, his body was buried beneath the new sod of Lone Fir Cemetery. He had only one fraternal affiliation: membership in the Grand Army of the Republic.

Holmes

For Byron Zebriski Holmes, the path towards worldly success had already been paved by his pioneer father, Thomas J. Holmes. The elder Holmes, a shoemaker by trade, had migrated from England to New Jersey, where he married and had six children. His wife died before she was 30, and in 1849, Thomas left his children in the care of relatives and sailed for the California gold fields. After a few months there, he came to Portland, where he set up a shoemaker's shop. He invested his earnings in real estate and soon became one of the town's wealthy men. By 1855 he had remarried, and in that year some of his children came out to join him in Portland, travelling via steamship and the Isthmus of Panama. One of these young voyagers was Byron, aged eight.

The pioneer Holmes house stood in the center of the block bounded by N.W. 2nd, 3rd, Davis, and Everett streets. Byron received what a biographer called "a liberal education in the public schools of this city." But in 1867, when he was 20, he was left an orphan, though not a poor one. His father had just engaged in a vigorous campaign to be elected Mayor, but, two days after his successful effort, he dropped dead.

In 1871, Byron, aged 24, married Miss Huldah Francis, of a well-established Portland family. The marriage took place at Victoria, B.C., where her father, Allen Francis, was temporarily serving as U.S. Consul. By 1873, B.Z. Holmes was listed in the Portland City Directory as a "speculator." Some of his speculation was in real estate.

Byron also inherited from his father an interest in politics. Though he was "a lifelong Democrat," he was a candidate for

Byron Z. Holmes

public office only once, in 1876, when, at the age of 29, he was elected to one term in the State Legislature.

Byron Holmes' name is attached as original owner to 160 acres bounded today by N.E. 72nd, 82nd, Fremont, and Prescott streets. The tract was "school land" sold to him by the State of Oregon in December 1870. The sale was made by the same Democratic triumvirate (Governor Grover, Secretary of State Chadwick, and State Treasurer Fleischner) who sold land to three other pioneer landowners discussed in preceding pages. Could it be only a coincidence that Holmes, Cann, Dennison, and Gilfry were all active in the Democratic Party? About a month after Holmes had bought the quarter-section for $800, he sold a half-interest in it to S.F. Chadwick, the Secretary of State, for $600. On January 11, 1882, Chadwick sold his half-interest to H.B. Oatman for "one dollar" — lawyer's language for saying that it was a gift. Two days later, Holmes transferred the half-interest he still held to Oatman, also for $1. And on that same day, Oatman, now in possession of both half-interests, sold full title in the 160 acres to William Denholm for $4400. Four months later, Denholm sold it for $8000, a substantial sum in

1882, though not in terms of today's value for the equivalent of about 160 city blocks.

The 1870s were the magnificent years of the Volunteer Fire Department, and Byron Holmes was one of its active members. There were several companies of volunteers in Portland, and the city provided each with a pump mounted on wheels, and also its own headquarters. Each company's building was much like a clubroom, and membership was select and exclusive. Many of the town's leading citizens were members, and when a vacancy occurred, it could only by filled by someone acceptable to all members. The volunteer companies were something like today's college fraternities, lodges, or athletic clubs. Membership was a sign that one had "arrived" socially, whatever one's occupation or condition. Membership was also proof that one was considered a jolly and clubable fellow.

On public occasions, the volunteer companies would parade, with pomp and pride. And if a fire should occur, the volunteers were expected to hasten to their headquarters, drag their engine to the fire, and work the manual pump with all possible energy. On the day after the fire, the universal topic among sporting types and in the saloons would be: Which company got to the fire first, or squirted its stream farthest. By about 1880, however, steam pumpers were replacing those operated by manpower, and equipment became so heavy that it had to be pulled by horses. That, plus the more elaborate machinery, required full-time attendance, and professional firemen replaced the glorious amateurs.

Mr. Holmes was also interested in industry. He was associated with Willamette Iron & Steel Co. during its early days. But in 1903, when only 56 years old and in the midst of a successful career, he died of typhoid. He had no children, and his entire estate, valued at $93,000, went to his widow. Real estate comprised nearly all of his assets.

A friend wrote of Byron Holmes: "Nothing could give him greater pain than to see anyone abuse a dumb animal" — a concern that could have caused him daily anguish at a time when nearly everything that moved on wheels was pulled by horses.

Mr. Holmes was, the friend continued, "one of the most unassuming and retiring of men, yet possessed of a keen sense of wit and humor. I have never known him to lose his temper nor speak an ill-word of anyone."

Holtgrieve

Working his way across the plains as a hired driver of an ox team, Henry Holtgrieve reached Portland in October 1850. He was 22 years old. But that was not the first long migration he had made. Eight years earlier he had come from Hanover, Germany with his parents, who settled on a farm in Missouri.

In Oregon, Henry worked as a hired hand on farms that were just being cleared along Columbia Slough. Then, in 1852, he found a small tract that had not yet been possessed and took up a Donation Land Claim of 80 acres. It lies between N.E. 82nd Avenue and Airport Way and is now part of Portland Airport. His claim was heavily timbered. He built a cabin and industriously cleared the land. Part of his motivation came from romantic thoughts of a girl he had met on his trip across the plains, Miss Elizabeth Shepherd. She was travelling with her parents, and settled with them at The Dalles. Henry and Elizabeth kept in touch, while he lived alone in his cabin and began cultivating his farm, and in 1855 they were married.

Mr. Holtgrieve used a sail-powered flatboat on the Columbia River to bring produce to Portland and get supplies. He added to his farm by buying acreage from neighboring landowners and also from the State of Oregon, which sold him an adjoining tract that had been "school land." That latter purchase ($609 for 40 acres) took place in July 1869 during the Republican administration which ended in September 1870. At that time, the Statehouse was taken over by the Democratic officials whose land sales were mentioned in the preceding article about Byron Holmes and who seemed prone to sell land to Democrats. It would be interesting to know if Mr. Holtgrieve was a Republican,

Henry Holtgrieve

but that question has defied our inquiries. Mr. Holtgrieve held onto his land and at his death in 1906 still owned his 275-acre farm on the rich Columbia River bottom land. He also owned land in Clackamas, Clark, and Yamhill counties.

Mr. Holtgrieve was one of the original members of the Multnomah County Agricultural Society, organized in 1859. Annual membership at first was $3 but the next year, "owing to the indifference of the people of Portland," the fee was cut to $1. Overcoming such discouraging "indifference," the Society held the first County Fair in 1860. Among the 40 exhibitors was Henry Holtgrieve, who won three prizes.

Besides his lifelong career as a farmer, Mr. Holtgrieve was active in the Masonic Lodge. He also was one of the early members of the Oregon Historical Society.

A year after Mr. and Mrs. Holtgrieve celebrated their Golden Wedding Anniversary, he died, aged 77. At his death, he was, as a newspaper writer expressed it, "surrounded by his wife and all his children [eight in number], who had been waiting for the end for several days." The obituary stated, "It became apparent to the pioneer and his family a few days ago that death was near," and, with philosophic coolheadedness, "Mr. Holtgrieve made arrangements accordingly." His body was buried far from his Fatherland, but in the new land he had tilled so well.

Howe

Evander Howe came from Vermont to Oregon in the 1860s and established a claim under the Homestead Act to 160 acres in north Portland. The tract is bounded today by Interstate Avenue, Kerby Avenue, Killingsworth Street, and Portland Boulevard. He paid $200 for his land. In 1870, he sold 80 acres for $400. He was not married, and when he died, in 1882, his remaining 80 acres, then valued at $6000, went to a brother, Estey Howe, of Battleboro, Vermont. No record tells what sort of man Evander Howe was, nor how he occupied his time in Oregon.

Humphrey

"One of our strong, positive, hardy men of the early days, whose grip of hand was like a vise [wince!], whose activity and endurance of frame were remarkable even among early Oregonians, and whose force of will was equalled only by his clearness of mental outlook!" Thus was Homon Munson Humphrey described in 1888, the year after his death, by a fellow pioneer.

To recount the highlights of Mr. Humphrey's life-story is to trace the westward movement of the American frontier. His father, descendant of an old Eastern family, was an early Congregational Church Deacon who, after serving in the War of 1812, became a pioneer in western New York state, then a distant and wild part of the Union. There, way out west in Wyoming County, New York, Homon was born, one of a family of seventeen children.

Homon M. Humphrey and family, 1860

When Homon was 20, he married Lydia Snow and the young couple set out westward, to take up new land in the remote wilderness of Iowa Territory. The younger Humphrey, like his father, became a Deacon in the Congregational Church and "a Christian of strong convictions."

In 1852, Deacon Humphrey felt called to come to Oregon, to help establish the Christian way of life on this last frontier. Harvey W. Scott, the *Oregonian's* editor, writing in 1890 about Mr. Humphrey, said, "He incorporated in his character the inflexible virtues of his ancestry and the added facility and adaptability of mind gained from Western life." The Deacon seems to have been a strongly-motivated, somewhat obdurate individual, and it is not surprising that he was chosen to be "Captain" of the wagon train in which he travelled. Perhaps, as he met his fellow wagoneers, he had shaken their hands in his vise-like grip. A peculiarity of his leadership was that he did not allow anyone to travel on Sunday. This Sabbath inactivity, as the wagons stood inert and no work was done, must have puzzled the watching Indians.

Mr. Humphrey, with his wife and five children, reached Portland in August 1852 and began looking for a promising place to settle. He asked one of the "old-timers" at Portland — the village itself was only six years old — how far up the Willamette River sea-going vessels could sail.

"Not above Ross Island," was the reply.

Mr. Humphrey concluded that Portland was destined to be the metropolis of the region, and he took up a Donation Land Claim of about 320 acres in the hills west of town, where Hewett Boulevard runs today. His property included the hilltop just south of Sylvan, which was known as "Humphrey's Mountain." There, by October 1852, Mr. Humphrey had built a cabin and was busy with the chores of pioneer life — splitting shingles and fence rails, gardening, and raising livestock. He had brought 27 head of cattle with him across the plains.

For the Humphrey family, which now included six children, the daily routine also included Bible reading. And each Sunday, the family would come down the mountain to attend services at the Congregational Church, then located at Second and Jefferson streets. During the following years, Deacon Humphrey supported the Congregational Church with many gifts.

In January 1859, Mr. Humphrey's wife, Lydia, died at the age of 42. Shortly thereafter, Mr. Humphrey made a trip back to his native Wyoming County, New York, where, on June 23, 1859, he married Miss Eliza Carson. A few weeks later, in August, the *Oregon Statesman* carried this announcement: "H.M. Humphrey and wife arrived at Portland from San Francisco on the steamship *Northerner*." Since the trip between Portland and New York by steamship and the Isthmus of Panama took about six weeks, one way, it is clear that the Deacon was a man of decision.

Mr. Humphrey was probably anxious to get back to Portland to tend to his financial affairs. By putting into real estate any money he could save, he had expanded his property to include about 1500 acres of "Portland Heights." However, most of his holdings were mortgaged. The result was that in 1861, when a financial panic occurred at the outbreak of the Civil War, his ownership was wiped out, except for 100 acres and his cabin. But he was a sufficiently skillful husbandman to make a living from that reduced area.

The marriage of Homon and Eliza proved to be an unhappy one. Perhaps the brief courtship back in New York in the spring of 1859 had not allowed time for Miss Carson to learn fully what being a frontier housewife involved. Tending six step-children in a mountain cabin, while her husband's property dwindled as mortgages were foreclosed, cannot have been an easy life. In any case, the marriage ended in divorce. A few years later, in 1865, Mr. Humphrey married Mrs. Lemira Mercer, a widow. He was then 46 and she 41. In 1869, Homon Humphrey and one of his sons, Theophilus, went to Yakima to raise cows and operate a dairy. They later moved back to Portland.

Deacon Humphrey made one other trip back to the Eastern states. In 1880, he was a delegate from the Congregational Association of Oregon to the Church's national convention. That was only the fifth time, in the more than 30 years since the beginning of the Congregational Church in Oregon, that a delegate from this state had attended the annual meeting. As a church report stated in 1881:

> The distance from other States is so great that but few delegates have ever been received from Congregational Associations in other States and but few of our members have visited the Associations of other States.

The careers of the six children of Homon and Lydia illustrate Portland's increasing variety and urbanization as it changed, in the span of just one generation, from a farming village to a city. Wolcott, the eldest, was first a farmer and later a printer, learning his trade on the *Pacific Christian Advocate*, a Methodist periodical published at Portland. The other son, Theophilus, became one of the city's best-known physicians during the last part of the nineteenth century. One daughter, Eliza, married a printer on the *Oregonian*, Henry Denlinger, when she was 21 years old. Then, in her 30s, she attended Philadelphia

Medical School, graduating as a doctor in 1882. But the next year she died, aged only 37. Orpha, another daughter, was married when she was 16 years old to I.H. Gove, who began his career as a carpenter, became a builder and contractor, and then a grocer. The youngest daughter, Lydia, married Daniel McClain Gault in January 1878.

Homon Humphrey died in 1887, aged 67, leaving an estate valued at $12,000. His will granted one acre to the Home Missionary Society and another to the American Missionary Association. The rest of his property was divided among his widow, Lemira, and his five surviving children. In addition to those material possessions, he had accumulated among his fellow Portlanders a large treasure of goodwill.

The body of Homon Humphrey was buried in "Jones Cemetery," located near Sylvan and named for another pioneer landowner, Nathan Jones, who was a neighbor of the Humphreys. Nearby are the graves of his wives Lydia and Lemira. A plaque bears this testimonial to Homon's faith:

> There is no Death;
> What seems so is transition.
> This life of Mortal breath
> Is but a suburb of the Life Elysian
> Whose portal we call Death.

Irving

During the 1840s, the brig *Tuscany* plied, as regularly as sails would permit, between New York City and England, and William Irving was her mate. Though only in his 20s, he had already seen most of the famous and romantic seaports of the world, having left his native Scotland to go to sea while only a lad. With him on the *Tuscany* were two other young men who, like Irving, helped in later years to develop navigation on the Willamette and Columbia rivers. They were Richard Hoyt, captain of the *Tuscany*, and Richard Williams, her steward.

In 1849, Irving, as captain and part owner of the brig *Success*, sailed with a load of gold-hunters around Cape Horn

Captain William Irving

to San Francisco and then entered the coastal trade between California and Oregon. On one of his trips to Portland, he brought, lashed onto the deck of the *Success*, a little steamboat, the *Eagle*, which he put into operation on the Willamette River. It was on the Portland-to-Oregon City run by late 1851, in competition with the steamboats *Lot Whitcomb* and *Black Hawk*. Richard Williams, the young friend from the *Tuscany*, had also come to the West Coast on the *Success*, and he was installed as the *Eagle's* captain and crew. The *Eagle* earned a good income for Irving and Williams during the 1850s. Passenger fare between Portland and Oregon City was $5, until competition forced it down.

On his visits at Portland, Captain Irvin came to know Miss Elizabeth Jane Dickson, whom he married in September 1851, when he was 36 years old. Now committed to a more domestic way of life, the captain gave up the sea and settled on a 644-acre Donation Land Claim embracing the present-day "Irvington" district. The claim had originally been taken up by one David Sheldon, who, after occupying it for six months, sold his rights in it to Captain Irving, in whose name the original title was issued. Sheldon had cleared two acres; the rest of the land was covered with heavy forest. The "Irving DLC" is bounded today by these N.E. streets: Halsey, Fremont, 24th, and the riverfront-Hancock-7th.

Captain Irving continued to invest in and operate river steamboats, but in 1860 he sold his shipping interests here and moved to New Westminster, British Columbia, where he pioneered steamboating on the Fraser River. He sold 103 acres from his DLC in 1870 to P.J. Martin for $15,000. Captain Irving died in 1872 and shortly thereafter his son, John, laid out about 200 acres as the "Irvington" addition to East Portland. Then, in 1882, John Irving, identified as "an unmarried man residing in British Columbia," sold the remaining 288 acres of the Irving DLC to a syndicate headed by D.P. Thompson, mayor of Portland, for $62,100.

Though Captain Irving had lived in Portland for only ten years, he left, as namesakes, a Donation Land Claim, a neighborhood, a tennis club, a park, and a street.

Johns

"Old Jimmy Johns" he was called by some, and he was described as "a hermit and recluse." Others called him "Saint" Johns. And saintly it was of him to bequeath his extensive real estate holdings for the establishment of public schools in St. Johns, the community which grew up on his Donation Land Claim.

James Johns was born in Ohio in 1809, according to the application he filed for his DLC. In the spring of 1841, he crossed the plains to California, and lived in the Sacramento Valley until May 1843. He then came to Oregon with a party of Hudson's Bay Company employees. He first settled on Tualatin Plains, but in 1844 he moved to Linnton, an almost uninhabited townsite which had just been laid out. There he bought a town lot and helped build a warehouse which was expected to make

The home of James Johns, on the riverbank at his townsite.

Linnton a great seaport. The venture did not prosper. In 1846 a visitor described Linnton in these words: "Its few inhabitants are very poor, and severely persecuted by musquitos [sic] day and night."

In 1847, Mr. Johns, perhaps seeking higher ground with fewer insects, took up a claim on the bluff across the river, where St. Johns is today. By 1850, he had laid out some lots and was operating, in a quiet way, a country store. By 1851, there were about a dozen families living in the vicinity. In 1852, he began a ferry service, using a rowboat, across the Willamette River between his claim and Linnton, from which a trail took off for the Tualatin Valley. The plat for the town of St. Johns was filed in 1865. In 1915, St. Johns was annexed to Portland. The "Johns DLC" is bounded today by N. John Avenue, N. St. Johns Avenue, N. Central Street, and the riverfront.

Mr. Johns died in May 1886, aged 77. The *Oregonian* reported that "James Johns, the founder of St. Johns" had been found dead in his bed by some neighbors, adding "he left considerable property." This included much of his original 320-acre DLC, by then divided into valuable town lots. Mr. Johns had never married, and his only relatives were in Indiana: a brother and his children, and the children of a deceased sister.

In his will, Mr. Johns instructed his executors to lease all his real estate for 15 years. After 15 years (during which, as he had correctly anticipated, property values increased greatly) the real estate was to be sold. The will created a trust fund, and the money coming into it was to be used to build public schools in St. Johns and to pay teachers, who were to be "competent" — a wise proviso.

Six months after Mr. Johns' death, the brother in Indiana, named Ira, died, aged 80. The remaining Indiana relatives (nieces and nephews of James Johns) felt somewhat neglected by the terms of the will, and brought suit contesting it, alleging that Uncle Jimmy was of unsound mind. The decision, twice appealed, went against the contestants, but the legal maneuvers cost the Johns estate $10,000 in attorneys' fees.

Besides his real estate, James Johns' generous will also ordered that his personal property was to be sold, the proceeds also going into the trust fund for schools. In addition to household furniture, his possessions included a Bible, a dictionary and a 10-volume encyclopedia — a not unimpressive library at a time when so many early settlers could neither read nor write.

During the two decades after Old Jimmy Johns' death, the citizens of St. Johns frequently charged the executors of the estate with failing to carry out the spirit and intent of his will. The executors originally named by Mr. Johns had died or had refused to accept the appointment, and others had been named by the court. Whatever the merit of those charges, some substantial benefits to public education in St. Johns did flow from the will of this public-spirited benefactor.

In accounts written after Mr. Johns' lifetime, his name is sometimes spelled without the "s." Perhaps this inconsistency came about because some of his Indiana relatives involved in the lengthy litigation in Oregon courts spelled the family name "John." Also, several unsuccessful attempts were made over the years by residents of the community to change its name to

St. John — perhaps in honor of the Biblical prophet — and those efforts added to the confusion. However, it seems clear that the proper spelling is "Johns." That is the way it appears on the deed to his DLC and in his newspaper obituary. Even more conclusive evidence is an advertisement which he himself placed in the *Oregonian* in 1852, announcing his new ferry service, which is plainly signed "James Johns."

Some uncertainty about James Johns' name and career may have arisen from the fact that there were in Oregon during his lifetime two other men of similar name. One was Jacob John, who came to Oregon in 1854 and lived at Portland with his 13 children; he later moved to Woodland, Washington. The other was James McClelland Johns, who came to Oregon in 1858 and lived near Salem. These men were not related to our saint-like pioneer landowner.

Old Jimmy Johns was buried in the pioneer Columbian Cemetery, and for 23 years his grave was ornamented by no special monument other than a small plain headstone. Then, in 1909, the directors of the school district which included the St. Johns area placed a large concrete slab on the grave. On its rounded top are the benefactor's vital statistics. The designers fell into the error of spelling his last name without the "s," but the three-word epitaph justly summarizes at least the final act of his adventurous life:

FRIEND OF EDUCATION

Johnson

There were at least a dozen men in Oregon in the 1850s named William Johnson. One of them was the original owner of 640 acres in the Lents district.

This William Johnson was born in Maryland in 1801, later migrating to Ohio, where he married Elizabeth in 1824. There, several children were born. The whole family came to Oregon in 1846 by covered wagon. They first settled in Oregon City. One day in 1849, while on a cross-country walk, Mr. Johnson came over the hill we now call Mt. Scott. He liked the look of the valley just to the north with the small stream winding through it, and resolved to settle there. His Donation Land Claim is bounded today by these S.E. streets: 92nd, 112th, Duke (as extended), and Clatsop. In the 1850s, he built a sawmill on his property on the bank of Johnson Creek, named for him.

During the years 1859 to 1879, Mr. and Mrs. Johnson sold several parcels of their land to one of their sons, Jacob Johnson, who became a farmer. Elizabeth signed the deeds with "X," her mark. By 1888, both parents were dead. In that year, their children sold some of the remaining acreage to Columbus Whitlock for $42 per acre.

There still is today a sawmill at the same site where Mr. Johnson built his mill more than a century ago, though the modern one is not powered by a water wheel.

Jones

At the western edge of Portland where Sylvan is today, there was, in the "Gay '90s," a little hilltop community known as "Ziontown." Whatever reputation the "90s" may have deserved elsewhere, Ziontown presented, at least in outward appearances, very little gaiety. Its few houses, humble and shabby, clustered around a saloon operated by the Lepper brothers. Nearby, in a squalid cabin, lived the threadbare owner of the townsite, Nathan B. Jones, an eccentric bachelor. It was the belief of the idlers who played cards in "Lepper's Saloon" that Old Man Jones' poverty was only apparent, that he dwelt amidst dust and dirt out of sheer perversity, and that he was, in fact, "filthy rich." Rumor, which turned out to be unreliable, placed his fortune at $200,000 in gold coins, said to be secreted in his cabin.

Nathan B. Jones

In January 1894, the gossip-mongers were particularly talkative because Mr. Jones had just sold some property for $1071. Four days after that real estate transaction, about nine o'clock on a dark, wintry night, a man carrying a heavy stick entered Mr. Jones' cabin and savagely beat the old man in an unsuccessful attempt to force him to reveal the location of his treasure.

Earlier that day, Mr. Jones and two friends had been down to Portland. When they returned late in the afternoon, they found waiting for Mr. Jones inside his cabin an unemployed bricklayer, 22 years old, named Charles D---. According to newspaper accounts, D--- had been "hanging around" Lepper's Saloon and Mr. Jones' cabin for about two weeks, during which time he had got on speaking terms with the old man. It was intimated in a newspaper story that, on this particular afternoon, D--- had entered the cabin to try to find the hidden money, but had been unable to do so before being interrupted by the return of the owner and his friends.

During a conversation among the men in the cabin, D--- remarked that the fireplace needed repairing, and said he would do the job for $2. D--- made the offer, it was implied, merely as a trick to enable him to poke about for the treasure. But Mr. Jones replied, "The fireplace suits me fine." D--- then left, but returned early in the evening. After a short conversation, Mr. Jones gave him some small change with which to "treat the boys" at the saloon to beers. D--- went back to the saloon and it was about two hours later that Mr. Jones was assaulted. The next morning a neighbor came to visit Mr. Jones and discovered him, severely wounded, on his bed, "weltering in his own blood," as a journalist of the day expressed it. The neighbor asked what had happened, and, according to newspaper accounts, the following dialogue took place:

> "That fellow did me up last night," said Mr. Jones.
> "Who?" asked the neighbor
> "Charley D---," was the reply.

The assailant took a $5 gold piece — in those days gold coins circulated freely — and two watches. But he had not been able to find the "secret hiding places" presumed to contain thousands of dollars. Mr. Jones, under the care of two friendly neighbors, grew steadily worse, despite frequent doses of medicinal whiskey. Lepper's Saloon later submitted a bill against the estate for $4 "for whiskey during deceased's last illness." A week after the assault, Mr. Jones died, aged 74. With his death, newspapermen had the pleasure of running the headline:

IT IS MURDER

and the charge against D---, lodged in the county jail for assault and robbery, was elevated to a capital crime.

Today, a reader of old newspaper files is led to a clear conviction that D--- was guilty. And those newspaper stories, written before the trial began, must have had a similar impact on citizens of the day, for it proved to be difficult to find jurymen who had not already come to that conclusion. The evidence assembled by the newspapers included these items:

1. Mr. Jones, in the presence of several witnesses, identified D--- as his assailant, and named him as such in an affidavit he signed;

2. On the afternoon of the crime, D--- "was known to have little or no money" but, about an hour after the time of the assault, "he passed a $5 gold piece over the bar of Lepper's Saloon for a drink, received his change, and left." There seemed to be little doubt that this was the same $5 gold piece that had been taken from Mr. Jones.

When the trial commenced, the *Oregonian* described D--- in these words:

> The stupidity which had formerly characterized his movements had, at the time of his arraignment, given way to a cunning look; a sardonic smile played on his features.

The trial was a popular diversion for the community. "From near and far came the morbidly curious crowd that thronged the criminal courtroom . . ." And, as at any sporting contest, there was much excitement and partisanship. A newspaper gave this account of events on the day the verdict was announced:

> When the jury entered, their countenance did not exhibit the proverbial gravity of a jury about to impose capital punishment, and a glance served to show that the verdict was acquittal. As the words "Not guilty" fell from the lips of the clerk, there was a deafening uproar. Hats were thrown in the air, handkerchiefs waved, and lungs exercised. D--- left the courtroom followed by a crowd which persisted in congratulating him.

Having been indoctrinated by the pre-trial evidence gathered by those energetic journalists, the researcher of old newspaper files is startled by the verdict, "Not guilty." But D---

had had a trio of astute defense attorneys, Edward ("Ed") and Elbert ("Bert") Mendenhall, brothers, and E.B. Watson. They had managed to get their client out of a tight corner by introducing three witnesses who raised some doubts in the minds of the jurymen:

1. An habitué of Lepper's Saloon who was prepared to testify, under oath, that D--- had been playing cards in the saloon about the time the crime occurred;

2. D---'s mother, who swore she had given her son the $5 gold piece; and

3. A man who said he had heard Mr. Jones name a person other than D--- as his assailant, intimating that Mr. Jones was confused. The jurymen seem to have attached considerable weight to this inconsistency, though several witnesses swore that Mr. Jones had plainly named D---. One such witness, recalling a conversation, quoted Mr. Jones' quaint and archaic style of speech:

> I asked Mr. Jones "Are you sure it was D---?" and he replied, "I am that."

The "State" also introduced a "Mr. Bush, of Ziontown," who said that Jones flatly told him that D--- came into the cabin, demanded the $1000 from the land transaction, and when Jones refused to comply, struck him with a club.

There were hints in the press at dark rumors that D---, apparently not a very clever young man, had really been a pawn in the service of other and more sinister individuals who remained, and must forever remain, nameless. The whole truth, from this distance in time, is as elusive as Mr. Jones' treasure. When the old man's friends located what they believed to be his "secret hiding places," they found, according to their statement to the court, exactly $17.85.

Mr. Jones, for years before his pitiful death, had been a well-known "character" and the subject of several newspaper stories. One, written in 1888, began: "Who has driven out Canyon Road and not wondered what sort of individual inhabits the old vine-clad cottage on the hill?" The cabin was almost hidden from view by apple trees and rose bushes growing in wild profusion. "The old cabin is rapidly crumbling into decay but the place is typical of its owner. Jones is an eccentric ard cranky old bachelor, to be sure."

In his obituary, he was described as "a hermit who loved the society of his dogs and cats more than the conventional shows and shams of society. His bent form was a familiar figure to those who had occasion to travel over the Canyon Road. Almost any day, he could be seen, attired in a suit of black clothes, slouch hat, and coarse flannel shirt. He was never without his crook-handled cane, while his faithful dogs trailed after him and brought up the rear of the procession." Among his dogs were Rover, Big Boy, Little Boy, and many others.

Despite his idiosyncrasies, Mr. Jones had a keen eye for business. Of his original 320-acre Donation Land Claim, he had, by 1894, sold off 223 acres, mostly in small parcels of an acre or two. In the years around 1890, he was selling half-acre lots for about $125. Just four days before the assault which caused his death, he had sold 3½ acres. He was much involved in lending money to men who had pledged real estate as surety, and at the time of his death he held several mortgages. The "Jones DLC" extends from West Burnside Road to a line about one-quarter of a mile south of Canyon Road, and from about S.W. 56th to the County Line (65th).

Mr. Jones had laid out some of his acreage in blocks and streets and hoped it would become the nucleus of an important town. He wanted it to be called "Zion," after the Biblical city, and the small community there, consisting of a saloon, a post office, and a few ramshackle dwellings, was informally known as "Zion," "Zionville," "Ziontown," or "Mount Zion," even though the official name of the post office was "Sylvan."

In an interview a few years before his death, Mr. Jones revealed a pleasing spark of humor in talking about his townsite: "I think the seat of government [the State capital] ought to come here on this hill. An expenditure of seven or eight million dollars would help this place wonderfully."

Mr. Jones' choice of the name "Zion" reflected his religious convictions. He once said, "I never belonged to any church, but I believe the Bible and all it contains. I believe its predictions are true." He also had an interest in politics, particularly in promoting political harmony. In the saloon, which he leased to the Lepper brothers, was this sign:

REPUBLICANS AND DEMOCRATS: UNION BEER

He said he hoped to unite the two parties by feeding them on union beer!

Nathan Jones was born in New Hampshire in 1819 and spent his early manhood in Illinois. When he was 28, he and a friend, Dennis Hardie, travelled to "St. Joe," Missouri and then crossed the plains together, reaching Oregon in December 1847. They were part of the "advance guard of civilization." After roaming around the Willamette Valley for about a year, they settled at Portland. During 1849 Mr. Jones lived on Front Street, where he bought two lots for $100 each from D.H. Lownsdale. In March 1850, when he was 31 years old, he staked out his claim at Sylvan, later acquiring title to it under the Donation Land Act. If he had married, he could have claimed twice a much free land. Apparently he didn't think it was worth it. Or perhaps even the hardy and stoical pioneer women found him too "cranky."

From 1850 to 1894, Mr. Jones lived on his claim, and he boasted that, during those 44 years, he had not spent a dozen nights away from his cabin. For the first two years, his only companions in that hilltop forest were cougars and owls. Occasionally an Indian would visit him. Then, in the fall of 1852, H.M. Humphrey, another pioneer landowner, established a claim adjoining the Jones DLC and built a cabin about a mile southeast from that of the recluse. Also in 1852, Mr. Jones' father, William Jones, then aged 74, came out to Oregon from Illinois to live with him. Two years later, in April 1854, the father died, and Nathan buried the body on top of a knoll in the southeast corner of his property. In 1872, by which time there were numerous settlers in the vicinity and Canyon Road was busy with wagon traffic, Mr. Jones decided "to protect the grave of my deceased father" by dedicating two acres around it as a cemetery. The two acres were deeded to Multnomah County "for a public cemetery and burying ground free to all persons."

Beside the grave of his father, Mr. Jones installed, somewhat ahead of time, a rather handsome tombstone for himself. He said he put it up himself because his heirs "certainly would not do it." On the tombstone is the emblem of the Masonic Lodge, and also this little couplet:

> David charged Solomon, he being his son,
> To finish the work which he had begun.

Just what "work" Mr. Jones had in mind is not clear, unless he visualized his rudimentary townsite as potentially rivalling the splendor of Solomon's temple. Mr. Jones had been a member of the Masonic Order when he was living in Illinois, but his name does not appear among the early members of Portland's first Masonic Lodge, founded in 1850. Somehow it is difficult to imagine the old hermit as a member of any fraternal order. He seems to have been a misanthrope rather than a "joiner." But perhaps he had been more gregarious in his twenties.

Today, the cemetery, known as the "Jones" or "Sylvan" Cemetery, contains about 200 graves, though many of them are unidentified by name. Several members of the neighboring Humphrey family are buried there.

Mr. Jones left no will and his estate, as it came to probate, was rather tangled. Many claims and charges against the estate were submitted and authorized, some puzzling to justify. His remaining 97 acres were valued at $36,000. He had $1496 deposited in a bank. The remainder of his property, besides miscellaneous household furniture, consisted of the following: one horse, harness, and an old buggy having a total value of $22; five chickens and one rooster.

The heirs were a sister and ten nieces and nephews in Illinois. Some of them came out to Oregon to look after the estate. They offered a reward of $100 for information leading to the conviction of Mr. Jones' murderer. When informed of the offer, the District Attorney is quoted as saying that the amount was "sufficient for the purpose" — a curious remark considering the outcome of D---'s trial, and the fact that no indictment was brought against anyone else. Perhaps the District Attorney, lulled into complacency by the newspapers' convincing statements against D---, had taken his conviction for granted.

When the body of Mr. Jones was laid in the "Jones Cemetery" beside that of his father, the inhabitants of the "Zion" community as well as the old settlers in the surrounding countryside all attended the funeral, giving him in death the respect and attention they seem to have omitted when he was alive and cantankerous.

Kelly

Clinton
Albert
Thomas
Plympton
Hampton
Archon

It was in the Cumberland Valley of eastern Kentucky that there lived, in the early part of the nineteenth century, a strong-willed widow named Nancy Kelly, mother of twelve. All of the six Kellys whose names are attached to original Portland land claims were her sons or grandsons.

The cradle-land of this Kelly clan — the mountainous region where Kentucky, Virginia, and Tennessee come together — is notorious as the home of the Martins and the Coys and reckless mountain boys distilling illicit corn whiskey by moonlight. Popular folklore suggests that all adult males

Rev. Clinton Kelly

Plympton Kelly (seated), his wife Elizabeth and some of their children.

thereabouts are moonshiners. Like most stereotypes, this is a gross generalization, and one which certainly does not apply to our Kellys. Every one of the pioneer landowners led westward by Clinton Kelly was a teetotalling enemy of alcohol.

Their convictions were due to Mother Nancy, whom a biographer described as "a woman of noble character," uncompromisingly opposed to the use of "ardent spirits," and "faithful and true to her religion." She transmitted these admirable qualities to her sons, whom she "consecrated to the ministry of the Methodist Church."

Nancy (nee Kennedy) married Samuel Kelly in 1807. Clinton was born in 1808 and there followed a stair-step-like procession of eleven other children until, after the birth of Thomas in 1829, Samuel died. Clinton became the nominal *pater familias*. He had already demonstrated the self-discipline and motivation which were to characterize his entire life. His boyhood was spent on the family farm, and he had almost no schooling. Kentucky was still pioneer country, though it had become a state in 1792, and there were few schools. Nor did frontier farm families have much time to attend any schools there may have been. But Clinton taught himself, acquiring by reading and study on his own "a good education for those times." He did it so well that he was hired as a school teacher, though many of his pupils were older than he was.

In 1827, aged 19, he was ordained a Methodist minister. That same year he married Mary Baston. Clinton and Mary had five sons (Plympton, Hampton, Archon, Calmet, and Bengal). Since frontier ministers received no regular stipend, Clinton supported himself and his growing family by rafting logs on the Cumberland River. But in 1837 Mary died. In 1838, Clinton, now aged 30 and with five young boys, married Jane Burns. Jane died in 1840 in childbirth. In 1842 he married Moriah Crain, with whom he had nine more children, for a total of 14, thus outdoing his father by two.

Clinton, his wife Moriah, his children, and several of his brothers and their families all left Kentucky in the fall of 1847 — a great caravan of Kellys headed for Oregon. Their exodus was caused by two social forces at work in the country in the 1840s. One was the turmoil resulting from the slavery question. On that issue, the States were divided politically along the Mason-Dixon Line, and other institutions began to follow that division. For example, the Methodist Church split in two: "Southern Methodists" and, in the North, the "Methodist Church." Kentucky was a border state, and Rev. Clinton Kelly took up his hierarchic relations with the Southern Church. But (as a contemporary of his wrote), Clinton Kelly, "seeing, though then far off, the terrible strife that would result from slavery, longed to get away from its influences."

At the same time there was a complementary magnetic force — the attraction of free, fertile land, with a mild climate, in a far-away and peaceful place called Oregon. Until 1846, the political future of "The Oregon Country" was in limbo, but in that year, a treaty with Great Britain gave Oregon to the U.S. The very next year, our Kellys headed west, even though no "Free Land" law had yet been enacted. But it was widely and correctly assumed that Congress would soon pass such a Bill. That legislation was temporarily delayed by complicated compromises between the "Slave" and "Free" forces in the Capitol. In 1850, the Oregon Donation Land Act finally passed. By then, thousands of pioneers, including the Kellys, had already staked out their claims in Oregon.

Clinton and his company of Kellys spent the winter of 1847-48 in Missouri, and reached Oregon City in October 1848. The trip must have been a glorious adventure for the many young people in the wagon train.

Six of these Kellys (four of whom were Methodist ministers) took up claims and developed farms within the area that has since become Portland. Their names, relationship, and the approximate boundaries of their claims are:

Rev. Clinton Kelly (1808-1875), 640 acres, S.E. Division to Holgate, 26th to 42nd.

Rev. Albert C. Kelly (1814-1873), brother of Clinton, 640 acres, S.W. Hamilton to Vermont, 25th to 45th. "Albert Kelly Park" is located near the center of this DLC. The names of both

Albert and his wife Nira are usually used to identify this DLC because Albert, who filed the initial application, died before the title was issued, so the DLC was assigned officially to his widow.

Thomas Kelly (1829-1903), brother of Clinton, 320 acres, N.E. 29th to 36th, Halsey to Fremont. This includes the Dolph Park neighborhood and Grant High School.

Rev. Plympton Kelly (1828-1906), son of Clinton, 322 acres, S.E. Lincoln to Powell, 85th to 101st. This includes the hill known as "Kelly Butte."

Hampton Kelly (1830-1898), son of Clinton, 323 acres, S.E. Division to Holgate, 42nd to 52nd.

Rev. Archon Kelly (1832-1890), son of Clinton, 317 acres, an irregular parcel bounded on the west by S.E. 38th, on the north by Reedway-42nd-Raymond, on the east by 52nd, and on the south by Henry Street.

The newspapers of the 1850s to 1880s contain many small references to the doings of this Kelly clan: ministers appointed to churches, marriages performed, land donated to churches, land bought and sold, etc. Clinton was one of the incorporators of the First Methodist Church in Portland. He was also a Trustee of the Portland Academy, a Methodist institution which was one of the community's first schools. He built a large two-story log house on a hill in his claim, near what is now S.E. 28th Avenue and Clinton Street. One biographer described the location as "the most sightly knoll on the east side of the river." From there, he constructed, through the primeval forest, the first road from that vicinity to the bank of the Willamette River, from whence, by rowboat, one could reach the village of Portland on the opposite shore.

Clinton preached regularly in the Methodist Church at Milwaukie in the 1850s, walking there every Sunday along a woodsy trail. It was about four miles from his log cabin to the church. A contemporary of Clinton wrote of him: "By great industry and frugality, he surrounded himself and family with an abundance of this world's goods. Though so well situated in life, he ceased not to teach men of Jesus and the higher life they might live by squaring their lives by His laws."

Clinton derived some income by selling parts of his claim. The *Oregonian* in 1872 printed an item, appearing below, about a subdivision he made. To understand the newspaper's petulant tone, one needs to recall the rivalry among developing townsites. East Portland had been incorporated in 1870 and had expanded its territory by annexing adjacent farmland. The newspaper scribe in the village of Portland, as he looked across the river at the relatively bucolic and even smaller village of East Portland, was somewhat contemptuous.

> ANOTHER ADDITION
> TO EAST PORTLAND
> East Portland has indulged in another spread. This time, Rev. Clinton Kelly is the man who contributes to expand the borders of our ambitious rival municipality. He has laid off a tract of land adjoining Stephens' Addition to the east, and has called it Kelly's Addition. He offers blocks or lots on terms of part payment down and the balance in easy installments.

Clinton devoted much effort to what was then known as "the temperance cause." His obituary, in the *Oregonian* in 1875, noted that he "had seen much of the ravages of the drinking custom during his lifetime, and worked to abate its dreadful power. He spared neither time nor money . . . and though earnestly he fought, he made no enemies, for all felt that love for his fellow man urged him to this work."

Clinton was described as ". . .a prominent figure in the streets of Portland, well known because of his strange, coarse garb." — a reference to the homespun cloth from which his clothes were made.

The other five original landowner Kellys were also producing newspaper items for future historians to discover in the archives:

Brother Albert, also a preacher, had, before the trek to Oregon, married Nira in 1837. He farmed his Portland claim and was proprietor of an early "Portland Hotel" at Second and Taylor streets. The records show that he was "a Methodist and a

Republican." In the 1850s, he sold half of his claim for $2000 to Finice Caruthers, another pioneer landowner. Albert sold five acres to the Methodist Church for the token amount of $1. With brother Clinton, Albert was one of the incorporators of Portland's First Methodist Church. In 1863, he was appointed a minister in Yamhill County.

Thomas, Clinton's youngest brother, farmed his Portland claim for 22 years. In 1853, he married Christina Sunderland, daughter of another pioneer Portland landowner. Thomas joined "Wilson's Company" of volunteers during some difficulties with the Yakima Indians. It was a short tour of duty: he enlisted in October 1855 an was discharged in February 1856. His nephew, Plympton, was in the same Company. Uncle Thomas was a year younger than nephew Plympton, an anomaly which can occur with families of 12 and 14 children. Such genealogical aberrations can confuse the unwary archivist. Fortunately, Samuel and Clinton Kelly had an inexplicable but happy inclination to choose unusual first names for their offspring (Archon, Bengal, Gilmore, Hercules, Penumbra, Plympton, Richmond, etc.). This is a great help to the researcher in tracking each specific individual. In 1871, Thomas moved to Yakima and spent the rest of his life there, farming and raising cattle.

Plympton, Clinton's eldest son, was 6 feet 1 inch tall, with black hair and blue eyes, according to his military record from the "Yakima Indian War" of 1855-56. During 1858-59, he operated the steamboat *Multnomah*, used to transport people and cattle among the various villages on the Willamette River. In 1864, he married Elizabeth Clark. He was an ordained minister and though he did not fill a pulpit regularly, he preached many sermons in Methodist churches in the Portland area. He was a Republican and a member of an organization called "Sons of Temperance." In his later years, he lived in Portland's "Lents District."

Hampton married Margaret Fitch in 1853, the ceremony taking place at his father's big log cabin. In 1862, he placed an advertisement in the *Oregon Statesman* reporting that he had found a stray horse. Hampton had asthma and, in 1881, he moved to Eastern Oregon to find a more congenial climate. He died in Wasco County in 1898. His estate was valued at $15,700. He had made a will, signing it with "X," his mark. His newspaper obituary contained this intriguing observation: "He was a singular man of eccentric habits, but was well beloved by all who knew him." Unfortunately, the writer gave no clue as to the nature of his eccentricities, a frustrating omission.

Archon married Susan Roork in 1855. In 1863, Archon Z. Kelly and wife Susan sold 377 acres to Clinton Kelly for $2500. This included all of his original land claim plus 60 acres he had bought from Edward Long, another original landowner, for $387. Susan signed the deed with "X," her mark. Our attempts to discover Archon's middle name, beginning with "Z," have been unsuccessful, which is a pity because, considering the bizarre names in the family, it may have been quite extraordinary. During the years 1858-1862, Archon was a Methodist minister at The Dalles, Butteville, Rock Creek, and Clear Creek.

Another of Clinton's sons might be mentioned here, even though he was not an original DLC land owner, because a public building has been named for him. This was Penumbra Kelly, born in Kentucky in 1845 and one of the children Clinton had with wife Moriah. Penumbra became a state legislator, Multnomah County Sheriff, County Commissioner, and U.S. Marshal for Oregon. The "Penumbra Kelly Police Center" at 47th and East Burnside is named for him. Penumbra died in 1928.

In June 1875, at the age of 67, Clinton "passed from earth to his reward," as the *Oregonian* obituary writer expressed it, adding ". . . he has diligently served his God, and after a long life of usefulness, full of sufferings and privations, he has gone to reign with Him." The obituary writer, in the flamboyant and gossipy style of nineteenth century journalism, wallowed in the medical details:

> His last sickness was accompanied with most excruciating pain. For nearly a score of years, he had been afflicted with a severe type of dyspepsia. . . It was found his heart

was diseased, the valves having become thickened from rheumatism... The two diseases combined caused a smothering sensation, and for the last three months, he has almost constantly been in an upright posture. The disease completely baffled the best efforts of his physicians. His strong physical system refused to yield, and the fight was long and terrible; but amidst it all, his mind was calm and serene, and with pleasure he looked for the coming of his Master. His life was an example of integrity, and his memory will long remain fragrant in the hearts of scores and hundreds who have known and loved him.

Another biographer summed up Clinton Kelly's life with an encomium anyone would be proud to receive: He was a man of "unwavering integrity."

Well done, Mother Nancy!

Kennedy

The Kennedys are a numerous clan in Ireland, and Michael is a popular first name in the "Old Sod." Even so, it's surprising that, among the small number of early-day Portlanders, there were at least three men named Michael Kennedy, all of whom had been born in Ireland. The one in whom we are most interested (the Portland Donation Land Claim settler) is, unfortunately, the one about whom we know the least. There was Michael W. Kennedy, who subsequently became a homesteader near Bandon. A newspaper item in 1892 reported of him: "On Saturday, Mr. Michael Kennedy, of Ten-Mile Creek, breathed his last. He had ridden his horse up to town and home in a hurry a week earlier, and contracted a cold, which developed into pneumonia." And there was Michael J. Kennedy, born in Ireland in 1841, a long-time employee of the Portland Water Bureau.

As to *our* Michael, who used no middle initial, the archival residua are meagre. From the certificate filed for his Donation

Land Claim, we learn that Michael was born in Ireland in 1827. He emigrated because, no doubt, of the Great Potato Famine. A large part of the Irish peasantry had become dependent for existence on potatoes, and a potato blight in 1845-46 caused a terrible famine. From 1845 to 1850, the population in Ireland declined from about nine million to about seven million. More than one million emigrants were registered, and many more left without being recorded officially. Most of them went to North America, but many, including our Michael, went to Australia. We don't know the exact year he left Ireland, but "about 1848" would be a good guess. We do know that he was in Sydney in 1850, where he married Ellen Connors (sometimes spelled O'Conner).

At the time of their marriage, Michael was about 23 and Ellen about 15. Ellen was also born in Ireland, and perhaps they had known each other "back home." Or possibly they met aboard ship on the voyage out to Australia. They would have had ample time to get acquainted. The trip, by sailing vessel, would have taken about 140 days, allowing for a short call at Capetown for the ship to "re-victual." However they met, we know of no reason to doubt that it was a happy and cordial marriage. Certainly, it was productive, as we shall see.

Michael and Ellen were an adventurous and daring young couple. Shortly after their marriage, they decided to make another great voyage — from Sydney to Oregon. It may well be that they were motivated to move to Oregon by reports in the Australian newspapers about the "Free Land in Oregon" bill passed by the U.S. Congress in 1850. In any case, when they arrived in Oregon in July 1851, Michael applied for U.S. Citizenship and sought out a donation land claim. A man could settle on a claim and begin the required four consecutive years of cultivation if he had applied for citizenship, but the eventual title to the land grant could be given only to a U.S. citizen.

The Kennedys chose an L-shaped claim totaling 320 acres, in what is now southwest Portland. It contains present-day Gabriel Park. They settled on it in July 1852. The claim's boundaries are marked today by S.W. Vermont Street on the north,

Dolph Court on the south, 45th on the west, and 19th, Nevada Court, and 40th on the east.

U.S. citizenship was awarded to Michael on May 4, 1857. Four citizens signed the affidavit testifying that he had done what he was supposed to do, in terms of residence and cultivation. His sponsors were Albert Kelly, John A. Slavin, and David Nelson, who were DLC settlers with claims close to Michael's, and Francis Niebur, a friend of the Kennedy family.

On December 31, 1859, Michael and Ellen Kennedy sold their 320-acre claim to "Finis" (usually spelled "Finice") Caruthers, for $2000. During the seven years they lived on their claim, two noteworthy things happened to the Kennedys. One was that Michael learned to read and write, or at least to write his name. When he had signed his application for the Donation Land Claim in 1852, he signed with "X," his mark. But for the sale to Caruthers in 1859, both he and Ellen signed their names. "Illiterate" is an adjective which, today, is quite a put-down. But a century ago, it was much less pejorative. Quite competent people often had not had time nor opportunity to learn to read and write.

The other significant event — actually a series of blessed events — was that their household had grown to seven, by the births of five children.

By early 1860, Michael had taken his growing family to Forest Grove. There, he invested the $2000 from the sale of his claim in a house. He also became what the census taker called a "saloonkeeper." Here, again, we have a word which might, today, be a bit demeaning. But we would like to think that Michael sought to reproduce in Forest Grove his recollection of pubs in England and Ireland, which are quite respectable social institutions and where the publican (the proprietor of the pub) is a not unworthy person. And the Kennedys seem to have flourished in Forest Grove — five more children were born to them through 1870.

The Kennedys were devout Roman Catholics and, as shown by church records, saw to it that each of their children was promptly baptized. One of the sponsors who frequently attended at the baptisms was the same Francis Niebur who was present at Michael's citizenship ceremony.

Michael died in 1878. He, his wife, and several of their children are buried in a predominantly Catholic cemetery near Cedar Mill. Or rather, it is the *flesh* that is moldering in the ground. Their souls, we assume, are in Heaven with their Creator. And there we leave them — parting, as seems fitting, with an old Irish blessing:

UNTIL WE MEET AGAIN
MAY GOD HOLD YOU IN THE PALM OF HIS HAND.

Kern

There is confusion in the archives because two Donation Land Claim settlers in the Portland area had almost identical names: William Kern and William Kerns. Our "facts" for these biographies often come from the files of early newspapers, and pioneer newspapermen did not always get the "s" on the right name. But the affidavits the two men filed for their claims make it clear that they were, indeed, two distinct individuals, unrelated, and with different origins. We will consider Mr. Kern first, and then Mr. Kerns.

William Kern was born in Pennsylvania in 1813. In 1834, he married Mary Ann Shull. The couple moved to Illinois, where the children began to appear. These included Emma, born in 1835; John William, 1838; Camelia, 1842; and Thomas, 1848.

In 1851, the family came across the plains to Oregon, arriving in December. Mr. Kern cut some trees, cleared the land, and became a farmer on what is now Portland's "East Side." In February 1854, they settled on their Donation Land Claim, 320 acres bounded by these present-day streets in southeast Portland: 72nd, Powell Boulevard, 82nd, and Harold.

In 1855, Mr. Kern made a tentative venture into politics, as a candidate for County Commissioner. There were 8 candidates altogether (3 Democrats, 3 Know-Nothings, and 2 Whigs), with 2 to be elected. Mr. Kern was a Whig. It is sad to have to report that our Mr. Kern came in 8th, receiving only 15 votes, compared to 319 and 317 for the two (both Democrats) who were elected.

But Mr. Kern persevered. In 1862, he ran again and was elected Multnomah County Commissioner. By that time, there had been (as a result of the Civil War) a reformation of political parties, and Mr. Kern was a candidate of the "Union Party." Here are the results of that election, as reported in the *Oregon Statesman* of June 16, 1862: Kern, 584; Burrell, 580; Charleton, 190; Nottage, 189; Quimby, 4.

Meanwhile, two more children were born to William and Mary Ann (or "Maggie," as she was called): Eldon Augustus, in 1858, and Lilly W., in 1859. The 1860 Census shows that son John, by then 22 years old, was a carpenter, and that Mr. Kern was a farmer whose property was valued at $2000, a respectable sum in those days.

In April 1861, Mr. Kern's son John married Miss Sarah M. Kelly, daughter of another DLC settler, Rev. Clinton Kelly. The marriage took place at the home of the bride's father, and the Rev. Kelly performed the service. John went on from carpentry to steamboating, and became a riverboat pilot and captain. He also engaged in real estate development. In 1890, he built a magnificent Victorian mansion, with towers, gables, and 15 rooms (later enlarged to 32 rooms). It was located at what is now S.E. 30th and Powell Boulevard. The house was often called, incorrectly, "the Clinton Kelly Mansion." But Clinton Kelly died in 1875, 15 years before the house was built. It *was* built on land that was part of the original Clinton Kelly DLC, and an earlier house of Clinton Kelly may have stood at that spot. And, of course, the wife of Captain John Kern was Clinton Kelly's daughter. The house was a landmark for many years until it was torn down in 1950. Today, a hamburger restaurant occupies the site.

But all that is a slight diversion from the *curriculum vitae* of William Kern. In May 1862, William and his wife Maggie sold two acres from their claim to School District No. 12, for the token amount of $1, which was a generous gesture. Sometime before 1870, Maggie died. At her death, one-half of the 320-acre DLC was inherited by the Kern children. In 1875, Mr. Kern sold his remaining half of the claim (160 acres) to his son Eldon for $400. Mr. Kern senior died at Portland October 13, 1895, 82 years and many adventures and joys after his birth in faraway Pennsylvania.

Kerns

"The poor man never realized what hurt him," wrote a witness of the death of William Kerns, who was killed August 1, 1878 by a cave-in at a mine. The writer gave these further details in a letter which was printed in the *Oregonian* August 8, 1878:

> Kerns & Co. were sluicing out a slide on their claim when another heavy cave-in came on, covering three of the men up to their necks and killing Mr. Kerns instantly. . . .Go to Mr. Reddick and you and he break it as gently as you can to his wife and children.

The letter was addressed to Mr. J.S. Williams, of East Portland, a friend of the family. Mr. Kerns' mine was a gold prospect at Spanish Gulch, in Grant County, Oregon.

Mr. Kerns was 68 years old at the time of his death. He was born in Ohio in 1810. In 1848, he married Lois (sometimes spelled Louisa). They came to Oregon in 1852, arriving in September. In January 1853, they settled on their Donation Land Claim, which encompassed 320 acres. Its boundaries were at these present-day streets: 82nd, N.E. Glisan, 102nd, S.E. Stark.

The couple had several children, including (as of the Federal Census of 1870) Wilbur, Mary, Anna, Heddie, and Elmer.

William and Lois gradually sold off their DLC claim. In March 1859, they sold 160 acres to John S. Newell for $200. In November 1859, they sold 120 acres to Julia Lewis for $2800. Then, in 1872, they sold their remaining 40 acres for a token $1, which means that it was a gift, probably to a school or church.

King

Eulogies written about our pioneers are sometimes entertaining studies in hyperbole. But those about Amos Nahum King, while highly complimentary, do not seem unreasonable. In 1899, when Mr. King was 77 years old, he was praised as "one of the most substantial and upright men of Oregon, who largely assisted in building it up to what it now is." And the record does show that Mr. King was an outstanding citizen. But first, before looking into those details, we observe that he was named not for one but for *two* Old Testament prophets — Amos and Nahum, who spoke much about tribulation and the wrath of God, but who also foresaw eventual bliss and happy endings. Thus spake the prophets, and so it was with our Amos.

Amos was born in Ohio in 1822 and grew up on his father's farm. His parents were Nahum and Serepta King. His first enterprise, as a young man, was operating a ferryboat. But the floods came and wiped out his ferryboat and all his worldly goods. He then studied the tanning trade. But those were lean years in Ohio and the Kings did not prosper. About that time, travellers began to bring back tales of a distant valley out West, where there was free land, fertile soil, a mild climate, where there were few and not unfriendly inhabitants, no poisonous serpents, beautiful vistas of snow-clad mountains — a land of milk and honey, so to speak, and all Free! It was called Oregon, and it sounded like the promised land. Perhaps it was. So Amos's father said, "Amos, let us go out of the land of Ohio and into the land of Oregon." And so it came to pass that in 1845 Amos, his father, his 3 brothers, his 5 sisters, together with their oxen and other animals and all their possessions, travelled in wagons across the seemingly endless plain called Nebraska and over the wearisome mountains aptly called Rocky.

After many tribulations. the King caravan came to a great river. On the bank of that river was a village called The Dalles, and the river was called Columbia. The hills thereabouts were covered with tall trees. The Kings cut down some of those trees and used their oxen to drag the logs to the river, where they built an enormous raft. On this raft, the Kings drifted down the great river, with all their possessions except their oxen, which they left to proceed on hoof in the company of the animals of some other immigrants.

On this voyage, Amos's experience as a ferryboat operator was a blessing. But soon they began to hear a mighty roar and then they saw ahead of them a great falls, or cataract, called "The Cascades," over which it would have been disastrous to attempt to float their raft. So they abandoned their raft, and carried all their possessions around the falls, below which they bought, from travellers and residents, several small boats in which they drifted and rowed on down the river. Mr. King later recalled that "the passage was a thrilling one, full of hair-breadth escapes."

After many difficulties, the King flotilla arrived at an even smaller village, called Linnton. From there, a road (really just a semi-improved trail) led over the West Hills to the green pastures and still waters of the Tualatin Valley. And they looked at the valley and saw that it was good, and they rejoiced, for the tribulations were over and it was, indeed, the Promised Land.

It was November 1845 when the Kings came to rest at a settlement called Forest Grove. In 1846, Amos married Miss Melinda Fuller, who had also come to Oregon from Ohio. A biographer described her as "an estimable lady," and she bore him (as nineteenth-century phraseology would have it) six children. In 1849, Amos and Melinda moved to the village called Portland. Amos had decided, as had several other men, that the Portland townsite was destined to become the metropolis of the Oregon Country, and that it would be the most advantageous place to establish a land claim.

There was living near the Portland townsite at that time a tanner named Daniel H. Lownsdale. Mr. Lownsdale had a "squatter's rights" claim on a tract of land just west of the original Portland townsite. His claim encompassed more than 500 acres. His tannery was located where Multnomah Stadium stands today. A creek, which had come to be known as "Tanner's Creek," flowed through his property, providing water that was useful in the tanning operation. Mr. Lownsdale had, as his claim, the right of first occupancy, but he did not plan to make that property his Donation Land Claim. Amos King saw that this property had a great real estate potential, besides having the tannery, so he bought the rights to it from Mr. Lownsdale for "a nominal sum." We have not been able to determine the exact sum, but it was trivial compared with the land's future value. Amos and Melinda settled on it, as their Donation Land Claim, in May 1849. Their claim included 535 acres. Within 3 or 4 decades, it was covered with the mansions of Portland's affluent entrepreneurs.

Why, one might ask, would Mr. Lownsdale, who was an astute businessman, sell such a claim? The answer is quite simple. He had his eye on an even more valuable tract for his Donation Land Claim — the very townsite of Portland itself! And since a settler was entitled to only one DLC, he sold his other property to Amos. Mr. Lownsdale and his DLC are discussed in later pages. The complex dealings in the ownership of the Portland townsite are described in our previous book *Early Portland: Stump-Town Triumphant*, pp. 40, 43, and 64-67.

Amos worked at the tanning business from 1849 to 1860, "with very flattering results," according to a biographer. By 1860, his property interests had become so absorbing, with the growth and westward expansion of the city, that he sold his tannery and devoted all his time to real estate.

The Amos King DLC is bounded approximately by these streets: on the north, Lovejoy and that line extended westward; on the south, Jefferson from 18th to about 21st and then due west through Washington Park; on the west, where 33rd Avenue would be if it were put through. On the east, the boundary is more complex. Originally, it ran northward from Jefferson along 18th to Burnside and then diagonally across streets and blocks from Trinity Place to 22nd and Lovejoy. But that boundary became the subject of a land dispute. The controversial line separated the King claim from the claim of Captain John H. Couch, another DLC settler. The original line had been determined by a survey which Captain Couch had ordered to be done in 1845 by Thomas Brown, the principal surveyor in the Portland area at the time. But in 1860, Mr. King had the line re-surveyed, by D.P. Thompson, the deputy U.S. surveyor. This later survey pushed the line eastward, into Captain Couch's territory. But Captain Couch had had his survey recorded and had occupied his claim continuously since August 1848. So there was a confrontation between two of Portland's wealthiest and most influential clans. The battle between the Couchs and the Kings was finally settled by a compromise which moved the line eastward about 300 feet, running from about 18th and Burnside to about 20th and Lovejoy. The compromise transferred 25 acres from the Couchs to the Kings.

In the 1850s, the King claim was undeveloped. An old-time resident, who was a child in Portland from 1855 to 1860, recalled that "Amos King's tannery hillside was a great place for blackberries — the most delicious in the area. The whole hillside was covered with wild blackberries."

In 1856, Mr. King built a "mansion" at the corner of 20th and Washington streets. It was the family home for the rest of his life.

Mr. King "was highly in favor of Portland having a City Park," and, in 1871, he sold 40 acres from his property to the City, to make what is now called Washington Park. The price paid by the City was $800 an acre, for a total of $32,000, a substantial sum in 1871. One biographer calls $800 "only a fraction of the actual value of the property." A different writer calls it "a handsome price." It's difficult, and perhaps unfair, to attempt to judge Mr. King's generosity. We do know that in 1859, the Multnomah County Assessor listed the King property at a true cash or market value of $12,000, or an average of about $240 an acre.

Then, in 1860, at the time of the dispute with Captain Couch, the land involved there was valued at $300 per acre. But property values were appreciating rapidly, and in 1871 Amos and Melinda King sold five acres to Mary Burnside for $1000 per acre. So the $800 Amos charged the City in 1871 was probably a fair price, especially if one considers the pleasures enjoyed over the years by the users of the park. The King DLC today is covered by high-rise apartment buildings, the "Uptown Shopping Center," and some of Portland's most elegant homes.

Mrs. Melinda King died in 1887. Amos later married Fanny G. Roberts, described as "a woman of rare culture and refinement, with the added charm of a natural affectionate disposition."

By 1899, two of Amos's children had died, but there were living near him his daughter Nartilla (Mrs. E.J. Jeffery), his daughter Lucy Ann (Mrs. A. Lumsden), and a son, Edward A. King. Nartilla was "Treasurer of the King Real Estate Association," and Edward was its President, managing the family's property interests while Amos enjoyed some leisure. Another son, N.A. King, was a wealthy rancher in Lake County, Oregon. Some details about the subdivisions and streets named for Mr. King and his family are given in our previous book, *Portland Names and Neighborhoods*, pp. 69, 70, 96, and 161.

Mr. King was one of the original stockholders in the Multnomah Street Railway Company, Portland's first horse-drawn streetcars. They were later electrified, and, as a contemporary wrote, "the cars glide swiftly through his property," a reference to King's Heights and King's Addition.

In 1899, a writer could say of Amos King: "He lives in a beautiful mansion, surrounded by all that wealth can contribute in comfort and ease." In the City Directories of the 1870s, Mr. King's occupation had been listed as "Speculator." In the 1900 issue, his occupation is "Capitalist." Verily, it had been the Promised Land.

Mr. King died in 1901, aged 79. The funeral service was conducted by Rev. Edgar P. Hill, pastor of the First Presbyterian Church.

The end was a peaceful one. Mr. King had hardly ever been ill throughout his whole life, but in November 1901, he "came down with" pneumonia, and died three days later. "Everything that medical science could suggest was done to relieve the venerable patient" but "it became apparent that the end was near. . . . Surrounded by his family, the respected citizen passed quietly away, after bidding them all 'Good-by.'"

Kittridge

George Kittridge was born in Vermont in 1808. In 1835, he was in New York state, where he married Mariah. Later, the family came across the plains to Oregon, arriving probably in the fall of 1848. In March 1850, they settled on their Donation Land Claim. It contained 640 acres, located in what is now northwest Portland, and extending from the riverfront about a mile up the hillside into present-day Forest Park. Kittridge Street, named for this pioneer, is within his DLC, which today is covered with "tank farms" (storage tanks for petroleum products) and other industrial operations. For many years, part of the property was inundated, during seasons when the Willamette River was at high stages, by a shallow seepage called Kittridge Lake. That area has now been filled in.

Mr. Kittridge farmed his claim. He also was a partner in a general merchandise business with Colonel William King, who had come to Oregon from upstate New York in the fall of 1848.

In May 1855, George and Mariah sold half of their claim to William Meek for $1100. They both signed the deed, but, curiously, their signatures were "George Kitrege" and "Mariah L. Kitrege." The name is spelled Kittridge in the Land Office records dealing with their DLC. Some newspaper items of their day spelled it Kittredge. Perhaps George and Mariah were themselves unsure of the spelling.

In June 1855, Mr. Kittridge was a candidate for County Commissioner. This was the same election in which William

Kern, another DLC settler discussed a few pages earlier, was a candidate. Mr. Kittridge came in sixth in a field of eight candidates, running as a "Whig-Know Nothing." His peculiar political denomination needs, perhaps, to be explained. The Whigs were a well-established political party during the years 1836 to 1856. There was also in the 1850s a political faction whose members called themselves the "American Party." They were opposed to influences they regarded as "alien" or "foreign," and also to immigrants. But they were reluctant to show their hostility openly, not wishing to seem intolerant, so when asked about their attitudes towards such "un-American" groups, their standard reply was "I know nothing about that." Hence the name "Know-Nothings." This political movement joined forces with the Whigs, but even together they did not win locally or nationally, and both parties disintegrated before 1860.

George Kittridge seems to have used the $1100 he received for half his claim to buy a hotel. The 1860 census of Portland shows him as a "hotel keeper." According to that census, his hotel was valued at $6000, which suggests that the rapid growth of the town during those years had given him a nice appreciation on his investment. At the time of that census, his hotel had 27 residents, and George was 51 years old.

After 1860, his name vanishes from the archives. Did he leave Oregon? Was he simply leading a blameless, low-profile life, producing no news items, no waves? We do not know. No further references indubitably about him are in the records we searched. But we did find one newspaper report which may be about our George. If so, it would go far to explain the silence. The item appeared in the *Oregon Statesman* December 14, 1863:

> MAN KILLED — QUARTZ DISCOVERED
>
> A man named Kittridge was shot and instantly killed at Placerville, Idaho Territory, on the 13th Nov. The killing grew out of a dispute about a mining claim. A rich quartz ledge has been discovered about 2 miles from Bannock, on Bear Run.

Mariah Kittridge died in Alpine County, California, in May 1868. Her will left her property, consisting of "the Kittridge farm on the bank of the Willamette River," to her daughter Henrietta. The executor was instructed to sell the farm and invest the proceeds "for Henrietta's best interest." The size of the farm was not stated, but presumably it comprised the 320 acres remaining in the Kittridge DLC after the 1855 sale of 320 acres to William Meek. The value of the property bequeathed to Henrietta was estimated at $3000. Mariah's will made no mention, no reference whatever, to George, which suggests that he may, indeed, have been the loser in that fatal altercation at Bear Run.

Kyle

Some odd-shaped remnants of the Public Domain were sometimes left between or around the claims of settlers who had selected the most advantageous locations for their 640, 320, or 160-acre grants. One of these was a strip of land about six hundred feet wide and about one mile long, between the Carter and Stewart DLCs, in the hills west of the Portland townsite. Samuel M. Kyle and his wife Fanny settled on that 73-acre tract in September 1855. Pioneers Carter and Stewart had staked out their much larger claims in 1851, and how Mr. Kyle became aware of the unclaimed strip between their properties we do not know. Nor do we know much about the Kyles, other than that Samuel was born in Pennsylvania in 1825 and married Fanny in Ohio in 1847 and that they arrived in Oregon in October 1852.

Lawrence

The life story of Charles Lawrence, as related to the theme of this book, is typical of thousands of immigrants. As a young single man, he left a crowded eastern city (in his case, Boston) to seek greater opportunities on the western frontier. He arrived in Oregon in February 1853. In 1854, at Portland, he married Ruth (who had been born in Illinois), and in December 1854 the couple settled on their Donation Land Claim. It contained 160 acres, bounded today by S.W. Dolph Court, Taylors Ferry Road, 45th and 55th. They lived on and cultivated their claim for the required four years and then, as soon as they had received final title to the land, they sold it March 3, 1859. The buyer was Finice Caruthers, another DLC pioneer settler discussed earlier. Finice paid Charles $700 for the 160 acres. On the deed, Ruth signed with "X," her mark.

Eleven years later, this Lawrence family appears in the 1870 census of Portland. Charles is shown as a "laborer" and Ruth as "keeping house." There were five children, Mary, Isaac and William being "in school" and Elmira and Abatt being four and two years old. We know of no reason to doubt that they were a happy family, with many descendants hereabouts today.

Lemmons

In the Columbia River just downstream from Government Island and opposite the Portland Airport is a strip of land, narrow and low-lying, called Lemon Island. It is named for Peter Lemon, who once claimed it. During high water, it shrinks to a few acres, though it never reaches the vanishing point. During low water, the shallows around it can grab the keel of a carelessly-skippered sailboat. We don't know if Peter ever lived on it, but we can see why he would be glad to sell whatever claim he had to it. Not so easy to understand is why anyone would buy it. Today, it is a refuge for migratory water fowl. There are on it no so-called "improvements" and it must look very much as it did 130 years ago.

But Lemon Island is not the namesake which justifies including Peter in this book about first settlers in Portland. This is merely background information.

In northeast Portland is a 160-acre tract of which Peter Lemmons was the first owner. This is the same Peter Lemon who claimed the island — his name is spelled various ways. His claim in Portland is bounded today by N.E. 33rd, 37th, Fremont, and Killingsworth streets. He acquired title to it under the Homestead Act of 1862, paying $1.25 per acre. This was more than land cost the Donation Land Claim settlers, who paid nothing, but it was still a bargain. Peter sold 60 acres in 1873 for $1000, and the remaining 100 acres in 1879 to Louis Nicolai for $1500. Mr. Lemmons was unmarried at the time of those sales. He also appears in the 1870 census of Multnomah County, as Peter Lemmins. At that time, he was also unmarried, aged 49. He was born in Illinois and his occupation was "plasterer."

The reason for the inconsistencies in spelling his name is that Peter was illiterate. He used a cross, "his mark," on legal documents. But not being able to read or write was nothing against a man on the frontier in the 1870s. You could always find some paper-shuffling fellow — probably a lawyer — whom you could hire for a few dollars to do whatever writing you needed. People like Peter were too busy, from childhood on, trying to make a living to have time to learn reading and writing. Also, in their environment, there wasn't much to read even if they had time. In any case, the fact that he could not write his name helps our story; it's really the most interesting thing we know about Peter, however you spell Lemon.

Lent

Fremont Lovett Lent was born in 1856 on a farm southeast of Portland. His parents, for whom the "Lents" district was named, were Oliver P. Lent and Martha Buckley Lent. They came to Oregon from Ohio in 1852. They had 12 children.

Fremont had a business selling wood and was also "a prosperous farmer." He was the first owner of a 40-acre tract bounded by these present-day streets: S.E. Holgate, Raymond, 67th and 72nd. He acquired title to it under the Act of Congress of 1820 "for the sale of the Public Lands," at $1.25 per acre. In 1891, Fremont, then 35 years old and unmarried, sold the east half of his claim to Henry Fleckenstein for $2000.

Long, Edward

To begin with his obituary is to tell the story of a man's life in reverse, but in this case it does give a neat resumé of the character of our subject. Here are some excerpts:

"Edward Long was as close a practitioner of the Golden Rule as can be found in this day and age... Having spent his whole life on the frontier, his education was necessarily limited, but he was nevertheless well-read... He took great interest in public schools and was for 12 years a director of schools in Multnomah County... He delighted in working for temperance and was a thorough prohibitionist...".

Edward was born in Ohio in 1817. When he was 20 years old, he went out to Iowa, which was still a frontier territory. There he farmed and raised cattle. In 1846, aged 29, he married Martha J. Wills. She was the daughter of George Wills, another Portland DLC settler discussed later. In April 1847, Edward, Martha, and the Wills family all started for Oregon. They traveled in a wagon train called "The Oskaloosa Company" — so named for the sufficient reason that their point of departure was Oskaloosa, Iowa. Six months later, the Oskaloosians reached

Edward Long

The Dalles. There they built rafts and floated down the Columbia River to the Cascades. Below the Cascades, they boarded a large rowboat belonging to Hudson's Bay Company. Such a vessel was known by the French term "bateau," showing the influence of the early French-Canadian fur trappers. They reached Fort Vancouver at the end of October 1847. An adventurous journey, we might call it, but it was commonplace for our pioneers.

Edward and Martha found a small cabin in the wilderness of unbroken forest that today is East Portland, and there they passed that first winter. Edward made some money by cutting wood for Hudson's Bay Company. In the spring of 1848, Martha's father and brother (George and Jacob Wills), in partnership with Edward Long, began operating a sawmill on Johnson Creek. The sawmill location came to be known as "Willsburg" (named for the Wills family), and was between Sellwood and Milwaukie near the mouth of Johnson Creek. From there, the sawyers could deliver their lumber to boats operating on the Willamette River. They also shipped lumber to San Francisco, where it could be sold at a large profit because of the frenzied growth resulting from the Gold Rush. Small coastal sailing ships came up the Willamette River to Milwaukie, taking the lumber directly to San Francisco.

In 1849, Edward, then 32, bought a claim right from Seth Catlin, an earlier settler. This became the Edward Long Donation Land Claim. It is bounded today by these southeast streets: Holgate, Reedway, and 42nd. On the west, it extends to the Willamette River.

In 1850, Edward sold his interest in the sawmill and thereafter devoted his time to growing fruit on his 636-acre DLC. He and Martha had four daughters: Sarah, Mary, Margaret, and Adelma. But in 1855, Martha died, leaving Edward with the four young children. In 1856, he married Avis M. Creswell, and they had three children: Henry, Edward E., and Avis E. Then his second wife died, and, in July 1863 he married a widow, Mrs. Nancy Chase.

Edward sold various parcels of his DLC. In 1856 and 1857, he sold 126 acres to Hampton Kelly and 60 acres to Archon Kelly, at prices ranging from $6 to $12 per acre! In 1871, he sold 7 acres to Edward Murphy, by which time the price had risen to $100 per acre.

Edward died February 20, 1889, aged 72. The *Oregonian* (Friday, Feb. 22, 1889) printed this death notice:

> Gone to His Reward — Mr. Edward Long, a pioneer of 1847, died at his home in East Portland Wednesday after a long and painful illness. Although suffering intensely, there was no word of complaint from the lips now silent forever. At 6 o'clock on the evening of the 20th, he began to rapidly fail, and at 9:45 his spirit took its flight to a rest beyond. Peacefully he passed away, surrounded by his family and kind friends, who had done all that loving hearts could prompt to ease his hours of sickness. He leaves a wife, son, and four daughters to mourn the loss of a kind husband and father. He was an earnest Christian and strongly upheld the principles of temperance.

Death was attributed to "dropsy." The funeral service was at the First Baptist Church of East Portland, of which he was an active member.

Though his life seemed so well disciplined in other respects, he had never made a will. Perhaps, as with most of us, he found it hard to believe it would all end so soon.

Long, George M.

Several George Longs walk through the pages of early Oregon history. One, for example, was born in Devonshire in 1820, arrived in Oregon in 1848 as a sailor on an English vessel, and "liking the country, decided to stay." Perhaps, after the stormy voyage around Cape Horn and seven months at sea, it was simply dry land for which he longed. He became one of Oregon's pioneer carpenters. Then there were at least two George Longs who were Indian War pensioners. Another George Long's wife was murdered on Applegate Creek — an intriguing story but we can't use it because that was the wrong George. *Our* George did meet a violent end, but there was nothing mysterious about it. The *Oregonian* of September 27, 1883 gave the details:

> **SERIOUS FALL**
> Yesterday, Mr. George Long, the well-known farmer of Columbia Slough and late county commissioner, met with a severe and probably fatal accident. He was engaged on the pile driver being used in the construction of the bridge across the slough when he fell therefrom, alighting upon a pile of rocks, sustaining thereby severe injuries both external and internal.

He died that evening, aged 61. When his will was probated, it was found that "a great many cows were listed individually."

George was born in Ohio in 1822, arrived in Oregon in September 1850, and settled on his 319-acre Donation Land

Claim in October 1852. It is bounded by N.E. Lombard, Killingsworth, 85th, and 99th. In November 1852, he married Elizabeth Seelye. The ceremony was performed by "Elder" George Wills, another DLC pioneer.

Over the years, George sold these parcels from his DLC: In 1858, 16 acres to Thomas Stallard for $100; in 1862, 19 acres to Adam Fisher for $150; and in 1876, 22 acres to Henry Holtgrieve for $800.

George Long may have been related to Edward Long, the DLC settler discussed previously. They both were born in Ohio, though George came to Oregon three years after Edward. George was named guardian of three of Edward's children during a distribution of property after Edward's wife died, so they must have been at least friends. However, we found no clear evidence of family relationship.

Loomis

Giving a glimpse of travel along the Oregon Trail, a pioneer wrote in his diary, October 1844: "From Mr. Loomis, we purchased a little buffalo pemmican — 10 pounds I think." This is our James Loomis. He and his wife Sarah and their children were on their way from Missouri to the Willamette Valley. The transaction took place in eastern Oregon, near the Grande Ronde River. By then, the migrants of 1844 were, doubtless very gratefully, approaching the end of their long journey. The fact that James Loomis was able to part with some of his family's food shows that he had been an efficient provider for the six-month trek.

The Loomis family reached the Willamette River in the cold, rainy month of November 1844. At that time, "Portland" was just a clearing on the riverbank, with one cabin on it — it wasn't even named as a townsite until early 1845. James settled on the claim he selected in May 1846. It contained 642 acres, and is bounded today by North Burgard Street and St. Johns

Avenue, and extends for one mile northeastward from the Willamette River.

Mr. Loomis became the proprietor of one of Portland's first hotels, as shown by this advertisement in the *Oregonian* of December 4, 1852:

> WILLAMETTE HOUSE
> The undersigned would respectfully inform his friends and the public generally, that he has recently taken charge of the above house, which is pleasantly situated on Ash street, in the City of Portland.
> J. Loomis, Proprietor

Mr. Loomis was also a merchant in St. Johns and in Portland. He died at his St. Johns residence in January 1859. The newspaper death notice gave his age as 43, but his application for his Donation Land Claim states that he was born in New York state in 1813, which would make his age, in January 1859, 45 or 46. James and Sarah had six children: Mariah, Clancy, James A., Charles, Christen, and Edward.

Love

In 1836 when Lewis Love, aged 18, was living on a farm in Illinois with his parents and his eight brothers and sisters, he married Nancy Samantha Matilda Griffith, aged 16. His total assets at the time were $3 in cash; Nancy's dowry was a bed tick. They filled the tick with leaves, went into the woods, slept outdoors, and Lewis cut wood rails "to get a start." From these humble but energetic beginnings, Lewis worked his way to become one of Oregon's first millionaires. In fact, his prominence in the community was such that, at his death, July 3, 1903, the *Oregonian* put at the top of his obituary what newspaper copy-editors used to call a "four-deck head." Here it is:

VETERAN OF OREGON

Captain Lewis Love Dies at Ripe Old Age

Leaves Many Descendants

Illness of Less than a Day Carries Off Sturdy Pioneer who Boasted Descendants Extending to the Fourth Generation

Lewis was born in Chautauqua County, New York in 1818. In 1833, the family moved to Illinois, where Lewis married Nancy. In 1849, the couple with their seven children came to Oregon. That April, their wagon train left Lawrence, Kansas, then a dusty outpost of civilization. The emigrants experienced the usual tribulations, especially in getting the wagons across rivers. Lewis devised a method of weaving vines together to make a long, strong cable, with which they pulled the wagons across on rafts. If the stream was shallow enough to ford, they put ropes on the horns of the lead oxen and pulled them across.

The Loves spent that first winter where Washougal, Washington is today, and Lewis worked at a sawmill there. He would row down the Columbia River in a skiff to the Hudson's Bay Company settlement at Fort Vancouver to buy flour and meat.

In the following spring, the family moved across the river to a little log cabin on Columbia Slough, where, in August 1850, Lewis established his Donation Land Claim. It contained 636 acres, and is bounded today by the Columbia Slough, Lombard Street, Minnesota Avenue and N.E. 8th. Another child, Lewis P., was born in Oregon. The seven born in Illinois were William, Jeremiah, Melinda Jane, Mary, Joseph, Frederick, and Green.

Lewis was enterprising, and he engaged in many and various businesses, with considerable success. As one biographer expressed it, though neither Lewis nor Nancy had much formal education, "they both possessed good judgment and sound common sense." Lewis had the imagination to see opportunities and the venturesomeness to find ways to meet those needs. He had the kind of enterprise which, in the open society of the West, was both greatly needed and richly rewarded. The records of his endeavors show that he:

1. Farmed his DLC, which he continued throughout his life. And, over the years, he added to his real estate holdings.

2. Maintained a grocery store on his farm for the benefit of immigrants and settlers. He was also a Justice of the Peace.

3. Operated from his farm a ferry service across Columbia Slough.

4. Acquired property in Clark County, where he established the Vancouver Steam Sawmill, and also a grist mill which used waterpower from Love Creek.

5. In partnership with his son-in-law, George W. Shaver, owned a general merchandise store in Portland.

6. Built several steamboats and operated some of them himself — whence his title "Captain"! The vessels were built on his property at Vancouver, using his sawmill for boat-building materials. His steamboats included four that became famous in river history: the *Iris*; the *E.D. Baker* (named for Oregon's U.S. Senator of 1861); the *Traveler*; and the *Calliope*. Captain Love gradually retired from the steamboat business during the 1880s.

7. Owned a hotel and sawmill on Front Street, until they were destroyed by the Great Fire of 1873.

8. Operated the "Jefferson Street Ferry" across the Willamette River.

9. Built and managed another hotel, The Gray Eagle, at Front and Clay streets. He sold that business in 1890.

His beloved wife died in 1892. The remaining 11 years of his life were devoted to managing his various property interests, which included many buildings on Front Street and on the East Side, as well as his farm on Columbia Slough.

His energy and enterprise carried him through life with little illness until just a few hours before his death. His obituary, in the chatty style of Victorian journalism, described the final scene in detail: "He complained of a pain in his chest...(a doctor) was called, who said the pain was caused by gas in the stomach pressing on the heart. After taking some medicine, the Captain seemed relieved and talked freely... (a few hours later) he again complained of pain... (his granddaughter) gave him some medicine, but he was seized with an attack of vomiting and in a minute was dead."

In some records, the Captain is identified as "a pioneer industrialist" and "a Unitarian." A different biographer wrote that "Captain Love was noted as a shrewd trader... he had no decided religious views, but was liberal in giving aid to the churches."

His descendants living at the time of his death numbered 66 (sixty-six!), including a great-great-grandson. Captain Love's father (Frederick Decatur Love) had nine children; the Captain himself had eight. Even at the less prolific rate of eight, if that sort of thing were to go on for many generations — and there is a formula, which we remember vaguely from Math 101, for calculating such a progression — the entire globe would soon be covered with Love — which might not be a bad idea.

Lowenberg

Julius Lowenberg's name was often spelled "Loewenberg" in newspaper items and other nineteenth century references. The difference depends on how one tries to reproduce with the English alphabet the sound of the German umlauted o, that is, ö. But it is "Lowenberg" in the records related to his land tract, so we will use that spelling. Either way, it is German for "Lion Mountain."

Julius was born in 1833 in Prussia, and was a German Jew. He was an early member of Portland's first Jewish synogogue, Temple Beth Israel. He emigrated from Germany to New York City in 1847. Two years later, lured by the Gold Rush, he came via the Isthmus of Panama to San Francisco. He was then 16 years old. In 1857, he moved to Portland.

There was a small-scale "gold rush" in the Pacific Northwest in the 1850s and 1860s, with pay-dirt being found in Idaho and eastern Oregon. Julius made his economic start in those adventures — not, however, by looking for gold but by selling supplies to the would-be miners. Merchandising was less glamorous, perhaps, but it was more dependable — the prospectors might not find any gold but they still had to buy shovels, pans, and food. A biographer wrote: "Nightfall often found him still on his way, leading the pack-mules to and from the mining camps."

From that beginning, Julius's prosperity grew greatly, as he engaged in various mercantile, manufacturing, and financial enterprises. In this respect, it is revealing to compare Julius Lowenberg with the pioneer settler we discussed just previously, Lewis Love. They were so much alike — in humble beginnings, in many and diverse enterprises, in imaginatively seeing needs and opportunities. And yet, they were so different — Lewis a relatively uneducated farm boy and Julius from a cosmopolitan European culture. An example of their different personalities was the housing which seemed to satisfy them. Both became wealthy, but while Lewis appears to have been satisfied with the farm house on Columbia Slough, Julius was pleased to build, in an elegant setting near Washington Park, a 32-room mansion. But that came later, as the culmination of his career.

After his initial venture, peddling provisions to prospectors, Julius acquired the land that forever bears his name as first individual owner. It had originally been "school land" — the Donation Land Act provided that one section, out of the 36 sections in each township, was to be alloted to the state, which could sell it to help finance public schools. Julius bought 160 acres for $800. The tract is bounded today by these northeast streets: Fremont, Brazee, 62nd, and 72nd. In January 1871, he sold 80 of his acres to Fannie Fleischner for $600. At that time, according to title records, he was still a single man. But shortly afterward, Julius went on a buying trip to San Francisco, where he met Bertha Kuhn, lately arrived from Bavaria, Germany. They were married in April 1871, Julius being 38 years old, and Bertha 23. They had four children: Ida, Zerlina, Rose, and Sidney.

By the early 1870s, Julius was a dealer in stoves and tinware. He was a partner in the firm "Goldsmith and Lowenberg," located on Front Street. The firm later engaged in metal manufacturing. And he was becoming a businessman of substance in the community. On August 2, 1878, Portland's first telephone system began operation. The list of "subscribers" was published in the *Oregonian*. There were 32 telephones in town. One of them was at the firm of "Goldsmith and Lowenberg," and another was at the residence of Julius Lowenberg, on Park Avenue.

In 1885, a municipal water service was established. Theretofore, water had been supplied by a private company. Fifteen prominent Portlanders were appointed to a "Water Board," which was to issue bonds, build a pumping plant, and lay pipes. The 15 names sound like a roster of eminent citizens: Henry W. Corbett, Frank Dekum, Henry Failing, Louis Fleischner, John Gates, A.H. Johnson, R.B. Knapp, William S. Ladd, Cicero H. Lewis, Julius Lowenberg, Simeon Reed, Thomas M. Richardson, F.C. Smith, William K. Smith, and L. Therkelsen. They were among the town's most influential burghers. Clearly, our Julius had "arrived."

In 1886, Julius became vice-president of the Merchant's National Bank, and later was its president. Also in 1886, the Northwest Fire and Marine Insurance Company was incorporated, with Julius its president. A biographer, writing in 1890, described Julius Lowenberg as "prominently identified with some of the strongest financial organizations in the Northwest."

A conventional ritual among wealthy Victorian Americans was the Grand Tour of Europe. Julius took his wife and four children to Europe during 1891-92. While there, he acquired some of the ornate furnishings for the new "chateau" he had ordered to be built. He returned from Europe in 1892 to supervise its construction. This was the aforementioned 32-room mansion, an enormous *residence* which, according to some writers, was conceived by Julius as an imitation of the German castles he had seen in his youth or on the Grand Tour. Financing such a structure must have strained the resources of even a well-connected financier, because the record shows that Julius, in 1893, used the remaining 80 acres of his land tract as collateral for a loan from the Security Savings & Trust Co. The mansion was completed in 1893, but unfortunately Julius was able to enjoy living in this sumptuous "family seat" for only six years — he died in 1899.

The obituary in the *Oregonian* of October 10, 1899 gives some insight into Julius's character:

"Mr. Lowenberg was a man of business integrity who had the respect of the community. . .in the large enterprises in which he was engaged, he was known to possess a marked ability for detail . . . giving his personal attention to many small matters. . . Personally, he was modest in expenditures, but hospitable and generous to others. . ."

His will left all his property to his wife Bertha, "in confidence that she will provide for our children."

The mansion proved to be a bit "roomy" for the widow Bertha, with her children grown, so in 1903 she sold it to Frederick Leadbetter, a paper and lumber tycoon. His wife was Caroline Pittock, daughter of Henry L. Pittock, publisher of the *Oregonian*. The Leadbetters raised their four children in that house, during which time the establishment required a staff of five servants, not counting the children's nursemaids. The mansion belonged to the Leadbetter family from 1903 to 1951. Its address was 2407 S.W. Park Place, located at the entrance to Washington Park.

In 1951, Caroline Leadbetter gave the house and its one-acre grounds to the Oregon Historical Society, with the idea that it might become the office and museum for that Society, which was then housed (as old-timers will remember) in an ill-lit alcove in the basement of the Public Auditorium. The Historical Society put in a new heating plant and made some other repairs, but by 1954 concluded that the cost of turning the residence into a fireproof and suitable museum would be "exhorbitant." No conditions had been attached by Mrs. Leadbetter to her gift, so in November 1954 the Historical Society sold the property to Commerce Investment Company for a net gain of $35,000, which the Society used to help pay for its present site on the Park Blocks.

In 1952, the mansion, described as a gray stone house with a red slate roof, was appraised at a "replacement cost" of $300,000. But a practical use for the enormous structure, considering taxes and maintenance, was hard to find. The real estate investment company decided that it would be too costly to modernize the building to make it meet the city building code requirements that would allow it to be operated as an apartment building. So in 1960, after the elegant interior fittings had been auctioned off, Julius Lowenberg's castle was "reduced to rubble." The site is now occupied by a concrete condominium.

It does seem a pity. Not a tragedy on the scale of the demolition of the old Portland Hotel — that *was* outrageous rapine — but a pity nonetheless. During the years 1951-60 while the house stood empty but demanding constant upkeep, those burdened with the problem of what to do with the Lowenberg-Leadbetter legacy seem to have done what they could to save it. But one would hope the community in general would be willing (by tax incentives or grants) to pay the cost of preserving our cultural heritage, so that the short-run "bottom line" need not be given ruling consideration. By comparison (which shows what can be done), how fortunate that some dedicated private citizens were able to save the Pittock Mansion, which narrowly escaped a similar fate.

Lownsdale

Daniel H. Lownsdale was one of the principal developers of the original Portland townsite, along with Francis Pettygrove, Stephen Coffin, and William Chapman. His activities in that regard are discussed in detail in our previous book, *Early Portland: Stump-town Triumphant*, pages 36, 43, 64, 67, and 147. Information about him is also given in our *Portland Names and Neighborhoods*, pages 16 and 68. And we have already met him in *this* book, in the article about Amos King, to whom Mr. Lownsdale sold the land that became the King DLC. As for the Lownsdale Donation Land Claim, it is a portion of the original Portland townsite. After the various dealings in ownership of that site, described fully in the references just mentioned, the portion finally owned by Mr. Lownsdale, his DLC, was an irregular shape comprising the heart of Portland's business district. It is bounded today by these streets, listed in clockwise order: S.W. Madison; the park squares between S.W. 3rd and 4th (one of which is called Lownsdale Square); S.W. Salmon; 15th; Burnside; S.W. Stark; and the riverfront up to Madison Street.

Mr. Lownsdale (the name is sometimes spelled Lounsdale) was born in Kentucky. He was married there, but that wife died in 1830. He was 42 years old when he arrived at the Portland townsite in December 1845 and began the activities and enterprises which helped make Portland "the metropolis of the Oregon country."

Mr. Lownsdale was married a second time, at Portland in July 1850, to a widow named Nancy, but she died in 1854. He died in May 1862, at the age of 59.

Luelling
Henderson
Alfred

It is difficult for us in the Pacific Northwest today to imagine what it would be like without the apples, peaches, pears, cherries, prunes, plums, and berries for which it is famous. But our luxurious fruits, in their cultivated forms, did not exist here until brought from the eastern states. The first person to bring them was Oregon's pioneer nurseryman, Henderson Luelling.

Henderson was born in North Carolina in 1809. His parents were Quakers. His father, Meshach Luelling, was a physician who combined that profession with a nursery business. From him, Henderson learned the trade. He went to Indiana and

Henderson Luelling

there, in 1830 at the age of 21, he married Elizabeth. The couple moved to Iowa ("way out west in Iowa") where, from 1837 to 1847, Henderson operated a nursery. But he had a restless and adventurous spirit, and accounts of the Lewis and Clark Expedition awakened in him a desire to see the Far West. He decided to transport to the Willamette Valley a nursery stock, foreseeing that there would be a great demand among pioneer Oregonians for the fruit and fruit trees they had known "back East."

For the journey, he constructed a "traveling nursery" — two long boxes to fit in the bed of a covered wagon. The boxes contained a foot of soil and several hundred (some recollections say as many as a thousand) grafting sprouts of various fruits, and also many shrubs. Railings were built around the cargo to prevent the cattle in their wagon train from eating the plants. The wagon with the nursery was pulled by four yoke of oxen.

With Henderson were his wife and eight children, the oldest being his son Alfred, aged 16. The youngest was born shortly before they started. They named him Oregon Columbia Luelling, in a burst of enthusiasm for their new venture.

Accompanying them was a friend, William Meek, who brought a sack of apple seed and additional fruit tree grafts.

The 2000-mile journey, which began April 17, 1847, took six months. Their wagon train was small and relatively defenseless. On one occasion, an Indian attack was averted by the "traveling nursery" — apparently the Indians regarded living trees as under the special care of the Great Spirit and therefore didn't interfere with the Luellings. The trees and plants were tended with great care, and about half of them survived. The children had some responsibilities for watering them.

From The Dalles, the nursery boxes were taken by flatboat to a point on the Oregon riverbank opposite Fort Vancouver. Here, the party remained temporarily while Henderson selected a location for his nursery. The area he chose, just north of the townsite of Milwaukie, became his Donation Land Claim — 642 acres bounded today by Knapp Street on the north, 17th on the east, Lava Drive on the south, and the Willamette River on the west. It now contains Waverly Golf Course and the southern part of the Sellwood district.

It was late November when the Luellings reached their claim, but the trees and shrubs were planted as quickly as the ground could be cleared. This was the first grafted fruit stock on the Pacific Coast.

Henderson's son Alfred later took up a DLC just north of his father's. Its boundaries, today, are S.E. Reedway, 36th, Knapp, and the river. It contained 640 acres. Alfred was born in Indiana in 1831. He settled on his claim in December 1850. William Meek took up a Donation Land Claim just to the east of Henderson and Alfred Luelling. He married Henderson's oldest daughter, Mary. William Meek and his DLC are discussed later in this book.

In 1848, Henderson Luelling and William Meek formed a partnership to engage in the nursery business. They found that they could graft their cultivated varieties of apples onto the wild crab apple trees native to western Oregon. The trees would bear the cultivated variety within two years from the time of the graft.

There are many references in early Oregon history to the Luelling & Meek apples. One noted that there would often be "beautiful large apples, grafted on the native stock, growing to fine fruit, beside little crab apples on the same tree."

According to a resident of 1850, the first box of apples offered for sale in the village of Portland drew an admiring, fruit-hungry crowd. "The apples were eagerly bought at $1 each, and Mr. Henderson Luelling made a neat little profit of $75." (Those dollar values would have to be multiplied by at least 10, to equate them to the price level of the 1980s.)

In 1850, Henderson went back east to get more varieties of trees and plants. He brought them to Oregon by ship via the Panama route, using mules to carry them across the Isthmus.

A pioneer, reminiscing about life in early Portland, wrote: "I saw single Bellflower apples sell in the winter of 1851 in a saloon for a half-dollar an apple. These apples were raised in the orchard of Luelling and Meek, near Milwaukie, they having brought their grafts across the plains in 1847. . . . Luelling and Meek did make a fortune, first in selling trees from their nursery and then in shipping apples to California."

While these were the first *grafted* apples on the West Coast, they were not the first domesticated apples. Seedling apple trees (which produce smaller and less attractive fruit) were planted at Fort Vancouver in 1825. There is a comment about those fruit trees in the diary of Narcissa Whitman, wife of the missionary Dr. Marcus Whitman. She wrote, September 18, 1836, during a visit to the Hudson's Bay Company settlement:

"What a delightful place this is [describing various fruit trees]. I must mention the origin of these grapes and apples. A gentleman, 12 years ago, while at a party in London, put the seeds of the grapes and apples which he ate into his vest pocket. Soon afterwards, he took a voyage to this country and left them here, and now they are greatly multiplied."

Henderson's brother, Seth Luelling, came from the east to Oregon in 1850 and joined the Luelling & Meek enterprise. He was also a nurseryman and eventually became even more famous than brother Henderson. The business was flourishing, and it was an important stimulus to the economy of the Milwaukie townsite. Apples, other farm products, and lumber were shipped in small coastal sailing vessels directly from the riverside at Milwaukie to California. The fruit was in great demand in San Francisco, where the gold dust led to boom-inflated prices. Oregon became known as "The Land of Big Red Apples." Henderson Luelling and his exports are discussed in greater detail in a chapter on Milwaukie in our previous book, *Early Portland: Stump-Town Triumphant*, pp. 58-63.

Testifying to Henderson's financial success is a letter written in 1853 by Charles Stevens, a resident of Milwaukie, in which he says: "There is a nursery here. . . they sell trees for from one to two dollars each. . . this man brought his trees from the states . . . and he has made a fortune at it."

While Henderson's financial affairs were going so well, other aspects of life were sad. In December 1850, his oldest daughter died. This was Mary, who had become the wife of his partner, William Meek. William was left with an infant to care for. Then, in March 1851, Henderson's wife Elizabeth died, leaving him with nine children. Then Henderson's grandchild, William Meek's infant, died. We don't know the cause of these deaths. But there were many references in early Oregon history to the damp and unhealthful environment at Milwaukie, with deaths ascribed to "ague" or malaria. In any case, these discouragements together with his restless disposition led Henderson to move again. He took part of his nursery stock and most of his children with him to Oakland, California in 1854. Among the children accompanying their father was Oregon Columbia Luelling, now seven years old, who lived thereafter in California, where his name was at least inappropriate and perhaps even a burden for a schoolboy. By 1856, Henderson had a 10-acre nursery there and was selling trees and fruit. Within five years, he had accumulated a considerable fortune. He operated his nursery business until his death, at San Jose, in 1878.

About 1859, William Meek also left the Milwaukie nursery and moved to California. Henderson's brother Seth continued the nursery business and became famous as the developer of the Bing cherry. Why Bing? Because Seth had a Chinese helper named "Bing" and Seth named the cherry for him. It was first produced in 1875.

Henderson's son Alfred remained in Oregon. He became one of the promoters of the idea of the initiative and referendum. He was also county clerk of Washington County.

Luelling or Llewellyn?

In southeast Portland there is a public school named "Llewellyn." It is said to be named for "Henderson Llewellyn, pioneer nurseryman." This is our Henderson Luelling. His father migrated to America from Wales, where the standard spelling of the name is Llewellyn. To simplify it for non-Welsh speakers, he changed it to Luelling, though why he chose that particular spelling is nowhere explained. Both Henderson and Alfred spelled their name Luelling, but in some records and newspaper items it appeared as Llewellyn. The name Llewellyn, cut in large Roman letters on the front of the school, must have been adopted by a mason or architect who knew more about the Welsh language than about this family's history. Incidentally, Llewellyn school is not located in Henderson's DLC but in that of his son Alfred. And it was Seth Luelling who eventually became the best known member of the family, in terms of Oregon nursery development. But the most dramatic feature of this pioneer story was Henderson's "traveling nursery." So perhaps we should say the school is named for the entire family.

Luther

Albert Luther was born in Rhode Island, arrived in Oregon in January 1853 when he was 37 years old, and settled on a 160-acre Donation Land Claim in November 1853. The tract is bounded today by these northeast streets: Prescott, Fremont,

102nd and 112th. In 1858, almost as soon as the required period of occupation and cultivation had passed and he had received the formal title, Albert sold all 160 acres to E.D. Shattuck for $400. Albert was not married. To follow along the chain of title, as an aside, Mr. Shattuck, in 1870, sold the tract to E.B. Dufur for $800.

But, poor Albert! In 1865, when he was 49 years old, he was judged insane. A guardian, Oliver P. Lent, was appointed by the county court, and Albert was put into the asylum. We don't know the nature of his infirmity, but, a year later, the visiting physician issued a permit for him to leave the asylum.

An inventory of his assets at that time showed that he owned 30 acres of land (no longer his DLC acres), valued at $600. He also had a wagon (value $25), one yoke of oxen ($90), 18,000 shingles ($30), farming tools ($15), one gun ($5), potatoes and hay ($13), and miscellaneous other personal property. Everything was sold, presumably to pay for his care. He retained only a silver watch, two blankets, and the clothes he stood in. Thus minimally equipped, he went. . .we know not where.

Marquam

The crowd at the opening of the Marquam Grand Opera House, February 10, 1890, was judged by the scribes of the day to have been "the most brilliant assemblage ever seen in Portland." In the *Oregonian* next morning was a list of those who had occupied the Dress Circle and other desirable seats — a roster of the local aristocracy which provided a prestigious mailing list if such promotional tools were used in those days. The entertainment on the stage was "Faust," but eyes were somewhat distracted from Monsieur Gounod's opera by the splendor of the *beau monde* in the audience, described at length in the newspaper reports. For example "Mrs. R.B. Knapp caught all eyes in a Paris gown of yellow satin and a superb necklace of diamonds. . .and in her coiffure a tiara of rare gems." (Mr. Knapp

Philip A. Marquam

doesn't appear in this book because he was not a Donation Land Claim settler, but he was one of the town's tycoons, having done very well in buggies and carriages, not to mention in having married an attractive woman who looked well in diamonds.)

As for the Opera House itself: "It is not surpassed in elegance, comfort, beauty of decoration and elaborateness of appointments by any play house on the Coast." Other acclaim: ". . . Portland's first completely fireproof theater, lighted by electricity and heated by steam."

The theater seated 1800, and on opening night every seat was occupied. Among those present was Philip Augustus Marquam, who had conceived this elegant edifice. The Opera House adjoined an eight-story office building, the Marquam Building, completed about the same time. The dual structure covered the block from SW 6th to Broadway and from Morrison to Alder. It was thought to be the crowning achievement of Mr. Marquam's life, whose attainments had already included successes as a lawyer, judge, state legislator, and real estate developer. Unfortunately, the Opera House and office building turned out to be disasters for Mr. Marquam. It is a sad story. But first, the vital statistics.

Philip Augustus Marquam was born in 1823 on a farm near Baltimore, Maryland, the eighth of eleven children. The family moved to Indiana, where Philip studied law and began to practice in 1847. But in 1849, tales of the Gold Rush lured him to California. His brother Alfred had set a precedent, having already gone west. Alfred, who was six years older than Philip, migrated to Oregon in 1845, taking up a DLC where the village of Marquam (named for him) is located today, about 10 miles southeast of Woodburn.

The young Philip, then 26 years old, arrived at a ranch near the Sacramento River in October 1849. At first, he worked at gold mining, but in April 1850 he was elected "Judge" of Yolo County, the scene of much Gold Rush activity. It was a role in which he must have witnessed and adjudged many altercations of the sort we now see in Wild-West melodramas. Thereafter, he was forever known as Judge Marquam.

Some months later, he came to Oregon to visit brother Alfred. The area pleased him, and he decided to move to Portland. He returned to California, closed out his affairs there and, on August 13, 1851, arrived back in Portland, where he lived the rest of his life. His trip to Portland was aboard a little coastal steamboat, the *Sea Gull*, commanded by Captain Tichenor. It was a tiny vessel, 226 tons, whose passages between San Francisco and Portland took about seven days.

Here, Judge Marquam practiced law. In 1853, he married Emma Kern, daughter of pioneer settler William Kern, who was discussed earlier in this book. Philip was 30 years old, and Emma 18. The marriage service was performed by Reverend Calvin Kingsley, of the Methodist church. In February 1854, the couple settled on their 160-acre Donation Land Claim. It adjoined and was just west of the Kern DLC, the property of Philip's father-in-law. The Marquam tract is bounded today by these southeast streets: Powell, Holgate, 62nd, and 72nd.

Philip and Emma lived, at least intermittently, on their DLC, because of the requirement to cultivate the land for four years. But he must have found that location inconveniently remote from the courts and offices in Portland. So he bought a block in what was to become the center of the city, the block upon which he built the aforementioned Opera House. Judge Marquam held that block undeveloped for many years, except for "a little New England cottage" he had built there, where he and Emma lived and where their first three children were born. He paid $500 for that entire block, located in the Daniel Lownsdale DLC. In 1858, the family moved to "Marquam Hill." Judge Marquam, in 1857, had purchased the 300-acre Donner DLC on that hill for $2500 (see the John Donner entry). Here, eight more children were born, for a total of eleven — the same number, by a surprising coincidence, that his parents had had.

In 1862, Judge Marquam was elected a Multnomah County Judge. He served two terms, 1862-70. He was also a state legislator, elected in 1882. He was a Republican and active in party affairs. And, over the years, he was much involved in real estate purchases and development. Marquam Street, Marquam Hill, and the Marquam Bridge are named for him. More information about his real estate activity is given in *Portland Names and Neighborhoods*, pp. 175-6.

In the small pioneer community, the early families were closely interwoven. For example, one of Judge Marquam's daughters became the wife of Penumbra Kelly (see Clinton Kelly, a DLC settler discussed earlier). Besides his own large family, the Judge also had numerous relatives descended from his brother Alfred, among whom he was known as "Uncle Gus" (short for Augustus). Brother Alfred, like Philip and their parents, also had eleven children — which makes the coincidence even more remarkable.

The culmination of his career seemed to be the Opera House and office building. But the difficulties began even before the structure was completed. Construction was much more costly than he had anticipated, about $100,000 more — equivalent to about $1 million at today's prices. Judge Marquam had to borrow a large sum in order to complete the building. Despite — or perhaps because of — its lavish luxury, the sumptuous theater couldn't be made to pay for its expenses. The community's population and resources wouldn't support frequent repetitions of the gala opening night.

There were, of course, occasional successes. A noteworthy one was the appearance on the Marquam Grand Theater's stage of Mark Twain, who gave a humorous lecture there August 9, 1895. He was on a world tour and made a side-trip to Portland from Vancouver, B.C. where he was waiting to take ship to Australia. But most of the time, Judge Marquam had on his hands what observers called "a large white elephant." The phrase was aptly chosen. "White elephant" refers to the albino animal that is born on rare occasions in elephant lands, where it is regarded as sacred — wherefore it does no work, though it has continually to be fed and watered.

Adding to the Judge's problem was his difficulty in renting the offices in the Marquam Building. Tenants would not pay the amount of rent he had expected. One reason was that a very large crack appeared in the building's Morrison Street façade, which was so alarming that tenants were afraid to go into the upper stories. Also, according to a contemporary critic, the halls were lighted only by candles and "the elevator service was execrable. A prominent lady was killed by the gross carelessness of an elevator boy." That cost Judge Marquam "several thousand dollars" — an inconvenient amount in his desperate financial condition but a pittance in comparison to what the litigious lawyers and generous juries of the 1980s might have exacted from him.

Partly due to those imperfections and also to the financial squeeze of a business recession, Judge Marquam could not repay the money he had borrowed. He was forced to mortgage the building, and when he couldn't pay the interest on that mortgage, due to the inadequate rents from the building, it was sold at auction. A Ladd corporation (connected with the family of pioneer William S. Ladd, the Ladd & Tilton Bank, etc.) was the successful bidder.

But Lawyer Marquam believed he saw a legal defect in the proceedings. He claimed that the man who had acted as agent for the Ladd corporation in its purchase of the property was also the trustee of the property under the mortgage. If so, that individual might have committed a breach of fiduciary trust, which would have made the transaction illegal.

The issue went into the courts. There was considerable feeling in the community, with pro-Marquam and pro-Ladd partisans. The final decision, by the Oregon Supreme Court, was against Judge Marquam. The *Oregonian*, in an editorial by Harvey Scott, said, "The Marquam case is ended, and Marquam has lost his property. The old man did not take care against the sharpers who were after his estate." Others said that Judge Marquam had not managed his building efficiently, that he had understated the debts upon it and overstated its rental income, and that the Marquam Block was not worth the amount due on it. But the court had spoken, and that was the end of it, though the dispute did cause "some ill feeling between the Marquams and the Ladds." Judge Marquam lost not only his city-center Block but various other real estate, including 80 acres on N.E. Sandy Boulevard.

Judge Marquam was about 75 years old at the time the mortgage on his property was foreclosed, but "he determined to rebuild his shattered fortunes. . . he did not lose courage." And he did manage to rebuild his financial affairs to some extent. But not long afterward, he received another blow — the death of his wife, who was 12 years younger than himself. Emma Kern Marquam died in May 1902, aged 67. Her obituary noted that "She was of a philanthropic nature, and many needy families were helped through her charity." Thereafter, Judge Marquam lived with one of his married daughters.

On March 31, 1906, the Marquam Grand Theater was found to be "unsafe for theatrical use" and it was closed. Repairs were made and the theater was re-opened under a new name: The Orpheum Theater.

Judge Marquam died May 8, 1912, which happened to be the 59th anniversary of his marriage to Emma. There was an "impressive public funeral service" at the Orpheum Theater (formerly his Marquam Grand Opera House). The old-time newspaperman who was sent by his City Editor to describe the event has left us some vivid prose, under the heading "Homage Paid by Hundreds of Friends":

"Draped with an American flag, and banked with flowers, the coffin occupied the center of the stage...The theater was filled...A male chorus sang 'Nearer My God to Thee'...which seemed peculiarly appropriate" (!) "He was for more than 60 years closely identified with the legal, commercial, and social life of Portland... He was for many years the largest landowner in Multnomah County... He spread his large capital thinly and in the financial depression of the 1890s, his fortune was wiped out." . . ."All that was mortal" of Judge Philip Augustus Marquam was buried at Riverview Cemetery.

It had been an eventful and, on the whole, a happy journey from the Maryland farm to Riverview Cemetery, whose acreage, as destiny would have it, was part of Judge Marquam's own Fulton Park real estate development.

Six months after the Judge's death, an event occurred which suggested that tenants' apprehensions about the safety of the Marquam Building may not have been unfounded. In November 1912 when it was being renovated, part of the building collapsed. Fortunately, the tenants had been moved out and no one was injured. New owners decided to demolish the building. Other structures were erected on the site, the Selling Building and the American Bank Building.

Maxey

There was, in the early 1850s, a soldier, a private in the Second Regiment, U.S. Dragoons, who saw a little action during an Apache Indian disturbance. His name was Charles Vincent. In those days, there was no "G.I.Bill of Rights," but, with all that empty space out West, the Federal Government deemed it fitting to reward its military men with free land. An Act of Congress in 1855 granted "bounty land to certain offices and soldiers who have been engaged in the military service of the U.S." A warrant good for 160 acres was given to Private Vincent. A convenient feature of such a warrant was that it was negotiable — if the veteran did not want any land, he could sell his warrant. Private Vincent sold his to Robert S. Maxey, who used it to acquire a tract of 152 acres in what is now north Portland. The Maxey claim is bounded today by these streets: Kilpatrick, Lombard, Minnesota, and Peninsular.

Mr. Maxey used his "soldier's warrant" to file for his claim in October 1860. Two months later, he sold all rights in his claim to William Love for $1025. But Robert Maxey had been the first claimant of that land, so his is the name to which all property titles in that tract go back in a "chain of title." Mr. Maxey seems to have taken his money and left town — we found no further references to him in the archives.

Title to this tract changed hands several times in the next few years and, as one would expect with the town's growth, at ever higher prices. William Love died in 1879 and his widow (Sarah Catherine, known as "Sery") sold the 152 acres in 1882 to Joseph Buchtel for $3192. Mr. Buchtel sold 76 of his acres to George Ainsworth for $6600. The land eventually became a subdivision in the Kenton district.

McClung

William McClung settled on his Donation Land Claim in December 1850. He was born in Maryland and was 36 years old, and unmarried, when he took up his 320-acre claim. His tract is bounded today by the Columbia Slough, N.E. 8th, N.E. 18th, and Holman Street.

In August 1856, he enlarged his domain by purchasing from William and Christiana Hall an adjoining parcel of 104 acres, for which he paid $416. This gave him a total of 424 acres, all of which he sold in March 1859 to John Switzler, another DLC settler, for $1310.

Except for these few facts, Mr. McClung's life story is lost in the impenetrable chaos of unrecorded frontier life. Probably he took his money and left town.

McEntire

Henry McEntire bought a "Military Bounty" land certificate from one Edward DeLashmutt. All we know, or need to know, about Soldier DeLashmutt is that he had been a teamster in the Quartermaster Corps during the war with Mexico. For that duty, he received a negotiable certificate good for 160 acres of government land. We don't know how much Mr. McEntire paid him for that certificate but it was probably about $1 per acre (or slightly less), which was at least some recompense for the vexatious months he spent driving mules.

Mr. McEntire exchanged the certificate in April 1866 for 160 acres in what is now northeast Portland. Shortly before that, in November 1865, he had acquired, under the Homestead Act, 49 acres, for which he had to pay $1.25 per acre. The two tracts adjoined each other, giving Mr. McEntire a total area of 209 acres. In September 1870, Henry and his wife sold their 209 acres to James Abraham for $1025. Mr. Abraham (a DLC settler discussed earlier) sold the 209 acres, in three separate transactions during the years 1871 to 1882, for a total of $7201.

The 209-acre tract, named for Henry McEntire as original owner in title records, is bounded today by these northeast streets: 19th, 33rd, Holman, and Killingsworth.

As for Mr. and Mrs. McEntire, where or how they spent what years remained to them we do not know.

McKeown

The records pertaining to James McKeown are fragmentary and inconsistent but it seems clear that he:

Was born in Ireland about 1805;

Emigrated to North Carolina, where he became a U.S. Citizen in 1833;

Arrived in Oregon in January 1852 and settled on a 160-acre Donation Land Claim in October 1854, at which time he was unmarried;

Died at Portland April 2, 1882.

There are few clues as to how he may have spent the time from 1854 to 1882. We do know that on March 8, 1855, when he was about 50 years old, he married Mary Olney. The ceremony was performed at Portland by Rev. P.G. Buchanan, a Methodist minister. The only other record is his will, made shortly before he died. He left his property (his real estate and personal belongings had a total value of $5000) to two nieces. The executor he named was William Wadhams, a "dear friend and Christian brother."

Strangely, there is in his will no mention of his wife, though Mary Olney McKeown was still living — she died at Portland in 1885. Perhaps, when Jim made his will, his mind was so preoccupied with other things (imminent death, for example) that he simply forgot about Mary. But the will wasn't contested, so probably they had been divorced. The probate record states that "deceased left no wife nor children." The body of James McKeown was buried in Lone Fir Cemetery.

The 160-acre tract that forever bears Mr. McKeown's name is bounded today by these northeast streets: Union Avenue, 14th, Prescott, and Fremont.

McLean

Hugh A. McLean acquired, under the Homestead Act of 1820, a 160-acre tract in what is now southeast Portland. He received title to the land in June 1870, paying $1.25 per acre. He later sold all 160 acres to Uriah Dannals for $450. The tract is bounded today by Harold Street on the north, Ogden Street on the south, 72nd on the east, and, on the west, by 62nd, Duke Street, and 67th.

For Donation Land Claim settlers, some facts (date and place of birth, etc.) are available in Land Office records, but for those who acquired land under a Homestead Act or by a "Military Bounty" certificate no such records were kept. All we know about Mr. McLean is that he was unmarried and that he died in January 1875 without having made a will. To settle his estate, the court appointed an administrator, who sold some wood which had been chopped by Mr. McLean for $46. The probate file also contains a receipt from a Masonic Lodge, of which Mr. McLean had been a member, for the price of his coffin. The Lodge hired one L. Kiernan to dig Mr. McLean's grave.

McMahan

Samuel W. McMahan (his name is sometimes spelled McMahon, but it is McMahan in Land Office records) was born in Indiana in 1824. In 1844, he married Martha, and in October 1850 they arrived in Oregon. They settled on their 640-acre Donation Land Claim in March 1851. It is bounded today by these southeast streets: Flavel, 75th, and 92nd, and by the County Line.

Samuel died in 1856. In 1858, the widow Martha married a Mr. Price Fuller.

Except for these scant records, the silence lies over Samuel McMahan as impenetrably as over an unmarked grave.

William Meek

Meek

We have already met William Meek, as he came across the plains with the Luellings and worked in the fruit tree nursery at Milwaukie (see DLC settler Henderson Luelling). William was born in Ohio and was 28 years old in November 1847 when he and the Luellings reached the site of their land claims, near what is now Portland's Sellwood district.

In July 1848, William married Henderson Luelling's oldest daughter, Mary. The ceremony was performed by the Baptist preacher, Rev. George Wills, another DLC settler who had a neighboring claim. That year, William was further united with the Luelling family by becoming a partner in the nursery and fruit business. Details about "The Luelling & Meek Nursery" are given in the preceding biography of Henderson Luelling. Also in 1848, William (along with many other Oregon men) went to California to join the search for gold. What luck he may have had is not recorded, but before the end of the year he was back at Milwaukie working in the nursery.

In September 1849, he and Mary filed the application for their Donation Land Claim. It is bounded today approximately by these southeast streets: 17th, 36th, Knapp, and Harrison.

Mary Luelling Meek died in December 1850, leaving William with an infant. Within a year, the child also died. William continued working in the Luelling & Meek enterprise, but in 1854 his partner moved to California, to start a nursery business there. The letters William received from Mr. Luelling must have praised his new location, because William himself moved to California in 1859. He spent the rest of his life there. An item in the *Oregonian*, December 29, 1880, reported the death of William Meek, at San Lorenzo, California.

Millard

Gideon Millard was born in New York state in 1818. In July 1849, in Clackamas County, Oregon, he married Elisabeth. As a married couple, they qualified for the maximum Donation Land Claim, one section. A month after their marriage, they settled on a 637-acre claim. The tract is now part of the Portland Airport. At that time, their farmstead was a weary way by wagon from the village of Portland.

The only other reference to Mr. Millard in all the archives we searched was the report of a marriage that took place in 1857 "at the residence of G. Millard." Except for these meager residua, his name on 637 acres of hinterland, as original owner, is the only evidence we have that Gideon Millard ever passed this way.

Miller

Seeking the life-story of Henry Miller, and ever eager to find dramatic incidents to enliven these pages, we were excited to discover that Henry Miller, a Portland baker, was drowned July 30, 1865 in the tragic wreck of the steamboat *Brother Jonathan*. But, it turned out, that was not our DLC settler. Potentially even more melodramatic was an item in the *Oregonian* of December 6, 1872, reporting that Henry Miller, a Portlander, was among eleven persons murdered near Klamath Falls by some rebellious Modoc Indians. That, too, was the wrong Henry. Our man — Henry G. Miller — died peacefully in bed at his comfortable home at 20th and S.W. Jefferson Street April 18, 1894, aged 79. He was Oregon's first florist.

Though lacking sensational details, Mr. Miller's life was adventurous enough. He was born in Hanover, Germany in 1814. When he was 19 years old, he crossed the Atlantic by sailing ship. His destination was Ohio, where he joined two brothers who had preceded him there. In 1837, when he was 23 years old, he married Mary Ann Shulte. The ceremony took place in Indiana, where, in 1840, he received his U.S. citizenship. Mr. Miller held several public offices in Indiana before migrating, with his wife and seven children, to Oregon. They arrived here in September 1853.

In July 1854, they settled on their Donation Land Claim, located near the claims of William Meek and the Luellings. The 301-acre Miller DLC is bounded today by S.E. 45th on the west and S.E. 62nd on the east. The south boundary is at the County Line. On the north, the boundary is approximately at Bybee, 52nd, and Flavel streets.

Henry's first job was at the Luelling & Meek nursery (see Henderson Luelling, above). In 1855, he started on his own, in the florist business. When William Meek left Portland for California in 1859, Henry Miller and J.H. Lambert bought out the Meek interest. They operated a nursery and orchard business under the name Miller & Lambert. In 1870, Mr. Miller sold all his interests in S.E. Portland and moved his operation to S.W. Jefferson, at 18th. There, on two city blocks, he built greenhouses and grew flowers commercially.

Mr. Miller was "an old and highly respected resident of Portland," according to his obituary. He was an active member of the Methodist Church. His son, Frank W. Miller, continued the floral business and added a seed store.

Mock

After the "Whitman massacre" and subsequent difficulties with the Cayuse Indians, volunteers went to eastern Washington intermittently during the years 1848 and 1849 to fight "wars" with the Cayuse. Among those serving was Joseph Pain, a private in Captain McKay's company. For that duty, Private Pain received a "Military Bounty" certificate good for 160 acres of government land. He sold his certificate to John Mock, who used it, May 10, 1864, to acquire 160 acres in what is today north Portland. The tract is bounded by Newman, Houghton, and Dana streets, and extends to the riverfront.

John Mock was born in Mechanicsburg, Pennsylvania in October 1838. He came with his parents to Oregon, arriving at Portland in October 1852. The family name was originally spelled "Muck." John's father and mother, Henry and Elizabeth, were born in Germany. "Muck" is a perfectly acceptable and euphonious word in German, but in English perhaps too suggestive of sludge, dung, and decayed organic matter. So John changed it to "Mock." The transmutation evidently occurred before 1864, since the title to his 160 acres was issued that year to "John Mock." John was 25 years old at the time.

When the family first arrived in Oregon, they settled, in January 1853, on a Donation Land Claim. Title to that land was issued to Henry A. Muck (John's father). Therefore, the Mucks became Mocks sometime between 1853 and 1864. Henry and his DLC are discussed a few pages later, under the name "Muck."

John Mock

Son John was only 13 years old when the family crossed the plains to Oregon, but he had a job on that six-months long trek: to drive a yoke of oxen pulling a wagon. At Portland, he worked on his father's DLC farm for four years. In 1856, when he was 13, he went to the mines in eastern Oregon and Idaho. He spent the next six years of his life looking for gold and running a pack-train business.

In 1864, he acquired his 160-acre claim (by the "military bounty" certificate mentioned earlier), and became a farmer. His land adjoined his father's 317-acre DLC. In 1868, father Henry sold his land to his son for $600. John thus expanded his tract to a total of 477 acres. One reason Henry transferred his farm to his son was that he was about to make an extended trip to Germany, to visit his relatives there.

On August 2, 1874, John married Mary Sunderland, daughter of another DLC settler. John was 35 years old and Mary 18.

John Mock's land includes the later real estate development known as "Mock's Addition." Also on his property, and still standing today on Willamette Boulevard, is "Mock's Mansion," an ornate Victorian residence John had built in 1894.

When the Methodist Church of Oregon was launching its Portland University and the accompanying residential real estate development in 1891, John Mock donated some land for the "University Park" subdivison. That university venture failed financially, and the campus, purchased by the Roman Catholic Church, eventually became today's University of Portland. The history of the Methodists' school and "University Park" is told in detail in our previous book, *Portland Names and Neighborhoods*, pp. 31-37.

In 1912, an interesting transaction occurred in the history of the title to John Mock's land. At that time, the Oregon-Washington Railroad and Navigation Company was building a railroad tunnel for a more direct link from Portland to its bridge across the Columbia River. The tunnel was dug beneath John Mock's land. The company bought from John the rights to a slice of earth 50 feet wide and extending down to the tunnel. This vertical slab ran the length of his property, and John received $2000 for the right to burrow through it. The tunnel is still in regular use today.

(A down-to-earth aside for legal sleuths: How far down does such a title extend? To the center of the earth? If so, this vertical slab must be slightly wedge-shaped, like the segments of an orange.)

John Mock died in 1916 and his wife Mary died in 1934. Father Henry died in 1884. All of these bodies are buried, as are also some other members of the family, in a small cemetery (Columbian Cemetery) near Columbia Boulevard. On John's tombstone is the Masonic emblem.

Moffett

Walter Moffett left Portland in March 1878 aboard his seagoing sailing vessel for a voyage to the South Pacific. He had given some thought to the risks involved — there were no radio navigational aids then, nor any air-rescue patrols — so, shortly before leaving, he made his will. His apprehension was justified; he died at sea, May 20, 1878. The cause of his death is unknown. It may have been due to the strains and stresses of life aboard a small sailing vessel on "a long and stormy passage." He was 47 years old. What details we have were reported in the *Oregonian*, July 29, 1878:

> Death of Walter Moffett
>
> A letter was received day before yesterday from Tahiti telling of the death of Mr. Walter Moffett, an old and well-known resident of Portland. Deceased left here...on his vessel, the *Edward James*, for the Sandwich Islands [Hawaii]. After a long and stormy passage, the bark reached Honolulu, remaining there a short time and then sailing for Tahiti. The voyage from Honolulu to Tahiti took 24 days, and it was during that long passage that Mr. Moffett died. The *Edward James* reached Tahiti on 8th June...Deceased was a resident of Portland for many years, and was a public spirited gentleman whose honesty and business integrity were above reproach. For some years past, Mr. Moffett has held interests in different vessels, and at the time of his death he owned the *Edward James*. He...leaves a wife and three children, all still residing in Portland.

The *Oregonian* of August 14, 1878 gave some additional information:

> Walter Moffett's Remains
>
> The steamer *Elder*...brought to Portland the mortal remains of Walter Moffett, who died aboard the bark *Edward James*. The funeral will take place from his residence, corner of Salmon and Seventh [now Broadway] streets, tomorrow. The funeral will be conducted by the I.O.O.F. lodge, of which deceased was a member. The members of Willamette Fire Engine Co. No. 1 [the volunteer fire brigade], of which Mr. Moffett was also a member, will also attend the funeral, in uniform.

We don't know when Walter came to Portland. He was probably born in England. An item in the *Oregonian*, April 12, 1876, reported that Peter Moffett, aged 76 and the father of Walter Moffett of Portland, had died, in Northumberland, England.

On April 12, 1860, Walter married Charlotte Terwilliger, daughter of DLC settler James Terwilliger. The ceremony was conducted by S.E. Barr, Esq., "at the home of the bride's father." Walter was then 29 years old.

In the early 1860s, Walter was owner of a saloon, on Front Street. In 1864, he bought 70 acres in what is now southwest Portland. He acquired the land under a Homestead Act, and paid $1.25 per acre. The tract is bounded today by S.W. 10th, 19th, Vermont Street, and Nevada Court. In 1865, he sold it to Michael McCavett for $550. Though he owned it for only about one year, Walter Moffett's name is on it indelibly as first owner.

By 1873, Mr. Moffett was a ship broker. His firm, Moffett & Co., was on Front Street. It was in this work that Walter developed a fatal interest in sailing ships.

Monaghan

The following item in the *Oregonian* of January 14, 1874 tells virtually everything we know about the life, and death, of Terence Monaghan:

> Paralytic Stroke
>
> A man named Terry Monaghan fell at Oak and First streets, from the effects of a paralytic stroke, yesterday afternoon. He was observed to reel and stagger for a moment and then fall helpless on the sidewalk. Temporary quarters were provided for the unfortunate man in the Eureka Saloon, hard by. A physician pronounced it paralysis. Later in the afternoon, a carriage was obtained and Monaghan conveyed to the residence of

Mrs. Dougherty, at Third and Alder. Monaghan owns a farm several miles northeast of this city, and is engaged in the wood business. He is an industrious, steady man, and has many friends in Portland.

P.S. Since the above was written, Monaghan died last evening, at the residence of Mrs. Dougherty. Deceased had only been married a few months at the time of his death. His wife was not apprised of the terrible intelligence until after he had died. The remains will probably be buried tomorrow.

The farm referred to was the 80 acres Terence Monaghan bought under the "Homestead Act of 1862" at $1.25 per acre. Final title was issued to him in November 1873, just two months before his death, but he had settled on it a few years before that. The Monaghan tract is bounded today by N.E. 47th, 52nd, Prescott, and Fremont streets.

Mr. Monaghan's wife, so recently wedded, was named Mary Ann. She was appointed adminstrator of the estate. Terence had left no will. Besides his real estate, he had 3 cows, 6 calves, 4 horses, 2 wagons, and a large quantity of cordwood. There were no children. Terence had one brother, "whose age and residence were unknown to Mary Ann."

Pursuing the history of the Monaghan tract, we find that the widow, Mary Ann, married a man named Pengally. She seems to have fallen on unprosperous times because, in 1878, she was the defendant in a case in circuit court brought by Nathaniel Miller for a claim against her. Mr. Miller won the judgment, and the sheriff was authorized to sell her property to pay Mr. Miller. The sheriff sold the 80 acres to the highest bidder, a Mr. James Thomson, who paid $304 for Monaghan's homestead. About a year later, 67 of those 80 acres were sold for $12,000, as Portland entered a period of booming residential development and proliferating subdivisions. Terence Monaghan had a good idea — he just ran out of luck. Poor old Monaghan.

Muck

We were introduced to Henry A. Muck in the biography of his son, John Mock. We saw that they changed the spelling of their family name from Muck to Mock. But they made that change after Henry had settled on his Donation Land Claim, which therefore bears the name "Henry A. Muck" as original owner.

Henry was born in Germany in 1793. There he married Elizabeth in 1829. The couple emigrated to Pennsylvania, where Henry was awarded U.S. citizenship in 1843. In 1844, the family moved to Missouri, where Henry bought a 40-acre farm. In 1852, they came across the plains to Oregon, reaching Portland that October. In January 1853, Henry took up a 317-acre Donation Land Claim, bounded today by North Dana, Lombard, and Wabash streets. The tract extends to the riverfront. It contains "Mock's Crest" (the bluff from which Willamette Boulevard offers a broad view of the harbor and city) and "Mock's Bottom" (the swampy flat near Swan Island which long remained the home of birds and frogs but is now covered with warehouses).

Henry died in 1884. More details about his life and land are given in the earlier article about John Mock.

Murray

Seldon Murray was among our earliest pioneers, crossing the plains to Oregon in 1844. In February 1851, he married Hiantha Caples, daughter of Dr. William Caples. The ceremony took place at the home of the bride's father, and was performed by Rev. James H. Wilbur, of the Methodist Church. Romance doubtless played its usual role in the marriage, but as an extra dividend, Seldon, now a married man, qualified for a full section of free land under the Donation Land Act. One month after their marriage, Seldon and Hiantha settled on a 642-acre claim. It is bounded today by S.E. 20th, 38th, Stark and Division streets.

The only other fact we know about Seldon Murray is that he died, February 23, 1883, without having made a will. The widow Hiantha was appointed administrator of his estate, which had a total value of $3,700. The couple had five children.

Naylor

William Naylor was a farmer, tilling the hilly terrain of his 320-acre Donation Land Claim, along what is now N.W. Barnes Road. The other boundaries of his claim are difficult to locate, even for a surveyor, but they are approximately where N.W. 35th, 30th, and Glisan streets would be if they were laid out on the ground. The tract includes the later subdivision "Hilltop Woods Addition."

William was born in Kentucky in 1800. There, in 1828, he married Levina. They arrived in Oregon in November 1852 and settled on their claim in October 1853.

William died January 21, 1879. His obituary stated that "Deceased was 72 years old," but if the birth date on his application for his DLC was correct, he must have been about 78. He died at his farmhouse on his claim. The obituary added, "He was a member of the Taylor Street Methodist Church, and was buried at Amen Chapel. He leaves an aged widow."

Five days before his death, Mr. Naylor made a will, in which it is noted that, at the time, he was "afflicted with sickness." He left everything to Levina. For the paperwork involved, Levina signed with "X," her mark. There were no children. Levina stated that William had two brothers, "somewhere in Missouri," but that they had not heard from them for 20 years. How different was inter-personal communication only a century ago! How great the distances! How infrequent, or non-existent, the news and ties.

Neff

If you own land in the "Blythswood" subdivision in northwest Portland, your property's Abstract of Title, which traces all ownership transactions back to the original holder, is a voluminous document. The reason is that, in its early ownership, the property was the subject of an involved legal imbroglio.

The original title is clear enough: "United States to Marcus Neff." Marcus was born in Ohio in 1826 and came to Portland when he was 22 years old. He settled on his 323-acre Donation Land Claim in September 1850. The tract extends northward from N.W. Raleigh Street for about a mile, and from about 45th to 55th, or where those streets would be if put through. Part of it is now in the city's "Forest Park," and part is in the neighborhood known as "Willamette Heights."

Early in the 1860s, Marcus and his wife Margaret and their children moved to California. Unfortunately, he left behind an unpaid bill. It was a fee for legal services rendered to him by John H. Mitchell, of the law firm "Mitchell & Dolph." The nature of those legal services doesn't appear, but Marcus should have known that it is not wise to ignore debts to lawyers. Attorney Mitchell brought suit against his erstwhile client for $341, which included the unpaid $253 fee plus accrued interest. The Circuit Court handed down a judgment for Mitchell, authorizing him to levy the charge against Neff's property. The only property Neff had in Portland was his Donation Land Claim. So the Sheriff took possession of the Neff DLC and, on August 7, 1866, sold the 323 acres to the highest bidder. The highest bidder happened to be attorney John Mitchell himself, who bought the tract for $341, exactly equal to the unpaid bill. Mitchel then submitted his bill to the sheriff, and received back his $341, thus, in effect, exchanging his bill for the property.

If it seems amazing that no one bid more than about $1 per acre for land which now includes some choice residential sites, we must remember that, at that time, it was remote and almost inaccessibly forested. But $1 per acre was remarkable even in 1866.

On August 10, 1866, three days after he had acquired possession of the Neff DLC, attorney Mitchell sold it to Sylvester Pennoyer for $341, precisely what he had paid for it. Perhaps Mitchell though he was doing a little favor for a friend, by selling him for about $1 per acre land which, as any person with foresight could see, would eventually be worth many times than amount.

Let us pause here to note some biographical facts about the protagonists in our little drama. John Mitchell and Sylvester Pennoyer were rather controversial characters who both came to Portland as ambitious young men. Mitchell arrived in 1860 when he was 25 years old. Within two years, he had been elected to the city council and the state legislature, and had formed a law partnership with Joseph Dolph. In 1873, he was elected U.S. Senator (at that time, U.S. Senators were chosen by state legislatures). Sylvester Pennoyer came to Portland in 1855 when he was 24 years old. He was a school teacher and then, from 1860-62, superintendent of Multnomah County schools. At the time he bought the Neff property he was in the lumber business. He later became mayor of Portland and governor of Oregon. A biographer says of him: "Shrewd investments in real estate made him a wealthy man." The Neff venture, as we shall see, was not one of his shrewd ones.

A few years after the aforementioned transactions, Marcus Neff, his wife Margaret, and a son and a daughter, returned to Portland. (Another daughter remained in California, where she married James H. Budd, who was governor of California 1895-1899.) Mr. Neff felt that his DLC had been taken from him unfairly. He engaged three attorneys (not one, but three!) to bring suit against Pennoyer to recover possession of his 323 acres.

"Neff vs. Pennoyer" came before the court in September 1874. Neff's battery of lawyers were J.W. Whalley, M.W. Fechheimer, and W.W. Page, whose offices were in "Glisan's Building" at First and Ash streets. Mr. Pennoyer's occupation, as shown in the City Directory, was now "accountant for Smith

Bros. & Co." and his residence was at West Park and Alder Street.

The case turned on two basic questions: (1) Was $341 a fair value for the Neff DLC, and (2) Did Mr. Neff have reasonable notice of the impending auctioning off of his land? Appraisers' testimony was introduced, placing the value of the tract at $15,000. Admittedly, eight years had passed, during which there had been much growth in the city. But the discrepancy between $15,000 and $341 was considerable. As to notification of the seizure and proposed sale of the land, the Sheriff asserted that he had given notice by advertising in four issues of the *Oregonian* and by posting notices in "four public places." Just where those four public places were was not disclosed. Mr. Neff testified that he had been unaware of the seizure and sale of his DLC. That seems believable. Even if he had been in Portland at the time, he might not have learned of it, since he could not read or write. In all the legal documents with which he became involved, Mr. Neff always signed for himself with "X," his mark. (His wife, however, could sign her name.) In any case, he was living in California at the time, where the *Oregonian* of 1866 had a very meager circulation, if any.

The arguments of Mr. Neff's triumvirate of attorneys prevailed and the court found for the plaintiff. Mr. Pennoyer appealed to the Oregon Supreme Court, where, on March 9, 1875, Matthew Deady, one of Oregon's most illustrious judges, upheld the lower court. Judge Deady declared that "Neff was then and still is owner of this property" and that Neff "is entitled to recover from Pennoyer the possession of the property plus costs and expenses." But Mr. Pennoyer was not yet ready to surrender. Perhaps he was not only shrewd but also stubborn. He actually took this superficially insignificant case to the United States Supreme Court. His determination suggests that he, too, was convinced that there was considerably more than $341 worth of value at stake. But the Supreme Court upheld Judge Deady. Thus, the property was Mr. Neff's as firmly as American law could make it so.

As for Mitchell and Pennoyer, the unsuccessful issue of their transaction does not appear to have caused ill-feeling between them. The records do not disclose how they settled up the matter of the $341 Pennoyer had paid Mitchell for what turned out to be nothing.

Subsequently, the 323 acres passed through many hands. The persuasive arguments of Mr. Neff's three attorneys had, it appears, convinced not only the court but also themselves that the property was worth a great deal more than $341. The three attorneys bought a one-third interest in the DLC for $6000. The remaining two-third were then transferred by Mr. and Mrs. Neff to their children. In a long series of complicated transactions, the property was little by little sold off. For example, the Neff son sold his interest, in 1883, for $14,000. By 1894, some of the property had come into the possession of a group of investors in Edinburgh, Scotland, called the "Scottish-American Investment Company." In 1907, that company platted and developed part of the Neff DLC as a residential real estate tract. Their agent in Portland was an attorney named Percy H. Blyth, and the subdivision was christened "Blythswood."

Nelson, David

David F. Nelson was born in South Carolina. In 1823, when he was 20 years old, he married a girl whose first name was Mehethalem. The marriage took place in Alabama. In October 1852, the couple arrived in Oregon, and they settled on their Donation Land Claim in May 1853, when David was 49 years old. The 320-acre tract is bounded today by these southwest streets: Vermont, Dolph Court, 45th, and 55th. The couple lived in a small log cabin located in a ravine about where 49th and Texas streets intersect today, but which was then a wilderness. There, they passed the remainder of their lives, in rustic peace but historic oblivion.

Dr. Samuel Nelson

Nelson, Samuel

The story of Samuel Nelson is an American family odyssey. These Nelsons were originally from England. Samuel's grandfather, Thomas Nelson, was a signer of the Declaration of Independence. He fought under Washington at Yorktown. Samuel was born in Ohio in 1805. In 1825, in Ohio, he married Mary Brooks. She died, and in 1839, in Illinois, he married Elizabeth Davis. In 1849, Samuel went to the California gold fields and spent a year there. Then, in 1852, he and Elizabeth came across the plains, starting from Hannibal, Missouri. They arrived at Portland in October 1852 and, one month later, settled on their 316-acre Donation Land Claim. It is bounded today by these southeast streets: Stark, Madison, 60th, and 80th. Within it is the north half of Mt. Tabor Park.

Samuel was a physician, and spent the rest of his life practicing in Portland. He died February 21, 1888, aged 83, leaving an estate valued at $13,000, his widow, and three children. He was a member of Grace Methodist Church.

Northrop
Thomas
Henry

Thomas E. Northrop was born in New York state in 1827 and arrived in Oregon in July 1852. He married Eliza Ann King on April 14, 1853, the ceremony being performed in Portland by the Methodist minister, Rev. P. G. Buchanan. In November 1853, Thomas and Eliza settled on their 320-acre Donation Land Claim. It is bounded today by these southwest streets: Nevada Court, Dolph Court, 10th, and 19th. Thomas died December 16, 1857, without having made a will. He was 30 years old. The widow Eliza was appointed administrator of his estate. For the paperwork involved, Eliza signed with "X," her mark.

Henry C. Northrop was born in New York state in 1832 and arrived in Oregon in October 1853. He settled on his Donation Land Claim in February 1854. He was unmarried and so qualified for only 160 acres. His tract adjoined that of Thomas Northrop, and is bounded today by these southwest streets: Dolph Court, Lucille, 8th, and 19th. Henry acted as "surety" for the widow Eliza when she was named administrator of Thomas's estate. It is very likely that Thomas and Henry were related. Probably, they were brothers, but we were unable to find proof of that.

Henry was a printer. He married Martha Quivey (known as "Mattie") on May 31, 1860. The ceremony took place at the home of the bride's father and was performed by Rev. Thomas H. Pearne, of the Methodist Church. Henry was 28 years old, and Mattie 19.

Henry died of tuberculosis June 27, 1870, aged 37. A few days earlier, he had made his will, leaving everything to his wife. They had three children, who, in 1870, ranged in age from nine to two years. Four years later, January 20, 1874, Mattie died, also of tuberculosis. The children were placed in guardianships.

Ogden

"Cupid's Capricious Capers" was the headline in the *Oregonian* of January 1, 1881, appearing over a list of all marriage licenses issued in Multnomah County during the year 1880. Despite the headline writer's flippant humor, the list is helpful in historical research. For example, we find that a license was issued October 21st for the marriage of "Hattie" Ogden, age 40, and B.F. Chase, age 54. The marriage took place on October 23rd, the full names of the couple being Harriett E. Ogden and Dr. Benjamin F. Chase. Rev. John Rosenberg, of St. Stephens Chapel, performed the ceremony, according to the rites of the Episcopal Church.

Harriett was the niece of Peter Skene Ogden, a famous early Oregonian. Peter arrived at Hudson's Bay Company's Fort George (Astoria) in 1818, when he was 24 years old. He spent the rest of his life working for "HBCo". In 1846, he succeeded John McLoughlin as Hudson's Bay Company's principal agent, when McLoughlin retired from Fort Vancouver to make his home at Oregon City. Peter had an older brother, Henry Ogden, living in New York City, to whom he wrote eulogistic letters about Oregon's climate and opportunities. This influenced Henry's son, William Seton Ogden, to come to Oregon in the 1840s. Then, about 1870, Harriett, who was William Seton Ogden's sister, came to Oregon to join her brother's family. She was one of the first kindergarten teachers in Portland.

Shortly after her marriage to Dr. Chase, he made a trip to California, during which he died. There were no children.

In 1882, Harriett received title to 20 acres in what is now southeast Portland. She acquired them under the Homestead Act, at $1.25 per acre. The 20-acre tract is bounded today by these southeast streets: Flavel, Crystal Springs Boulevard, 72nd, and 75th.

Harriett Ogden Chase lived the remaining years of her life on her homestead. She died August 7, 1911, aged 71. Her obituary noted that she had spent some time "in travel abroad" and was "a woman of culture."

Louis M. Parrish

Parrish

Louis Marion Parrish came across the plains to Oregon in 1852, arriving in September. He was 22 years old, single, and had 25 cents in his pocket — his total assets. Before the end of his life, in 1908, he had become a husband and owner of a profitable real estate business. His progressive steps up the ladder of achievement can be presented in tabular form:

1852-53: had a job sawing logs.

April 1853: settled on his 160-acre Donation Land Claim and became a farmer. The tract is located in the vicinity of S.W. Boones Ferry Road and Arnold Street.

1855-56: served as a private in a regiment of volunteers under Colonel J.W. Nesmith in the Yakima Indian "wars."

February 21, 1859: married Sarah Jane Watkins. The ceremony was performed by Rev. W.S. Lewis, a Methodist.

1856-1862: became, successively, a woodworker, nightwatchman, carpenter, and bricklayer.

1862: was distributor of the daily *Oregonian*, which, according to one historian, had about 170 subscribers in Portland at that time.

1863: opened his own real estate office. He was 33 years old. That was his vocation, and a profitable one, for the rest of his life.

Besides all those accomplishments, Louis was a deacon of the Congregational Church, a Republican, and "a strong temperance man." Taken altogether, his career, we suppose, would be called a "success," as measured by any reasonable expectation for this life.

Payne

William H. Payne was born in Virginia in 1824. In March 1852, he settled on his 320-acre Donation Land Claim. He was a single man at that time, and, since he qualified for 320 acres, he must have arrived in Oregon before December 1, 1850. Single men arriving after that date were eligible for only 160 acres. His tract is in northeast Portland along Columbia Slough and bounded by 18th, 24th, and Holman streets.

William did get married, on February 24, 1853, to Anna Smith. The ceremony was performed by a neighboring DLC settler, Lewis Love, who, as we saw in his biography, was a Justice of the Peace. William and Anna had five children. William was a merchant in East Portland in the 1880s, and, in 1890, he was proprietor of the Villard Hotel, in Albina. He died August 25, 1899, at the age of 75.

Pointer

The William Pointer Donation Land Claim includes some valuable view property along Scholls Ferry Road south of Sylvan. But William, sad to say, did not live to reap any substantial benefits himself. In fact, in 1873, his son Theodore was still trying to get title to the claim. Despite the arguments, there is no doubt that the Pointers were the original settlers on those 576 acres. This DLC extends into Washington County, down to about the "West Slope" district.

William was born in Virginia in 1810. In 1839, in Missouri, he married Martha. The family arrived in Oregon in October 1850, and settled on their DLC in May 1851. Within the next year or two, the family, which included four children, moved to California, where William died January 14, 1854. Martha died in 1857. The dispute about the title to the land arose because, though William clearly had a right in the property, he had not lived upon and cultivated it for the required length of time and had died before he received final title to it. Hence, the legal argle-bargle.

The only other thing we know about William is that he was a member of the Methodist Church.

Potter

Levi C. Potter (the "C" is for "Cincinnatus"!) was born in Chautauqua County, New York and was 21 years old when he arrived in Oregon, in December 1847. He settled on his Donation Land Claim in February 1850. Since he was unmarried at that time, but came to Oregon before 1850, he was eligible for 320 acres. His tract is in today's industrial area in the vicinity of N.W. Express Avenue, extending from the riverfront up the hillside to Leif Erickson Drive in Forest Park. The "Regent Heights" subdivision is in the Potter DLC.

Levi married Hannah Knox March 11, 1857. They lived for

many years in a house at what is now N.W. Broadway and Flanders Street. Levi was a carpenter. He was also a member of the Masonic order. He died December 15, 1898.

Powers

David Powers was born in New York state in 1801. In 1839, in Indiana, he married Julia Ann Tuley. The couple arrived in Oregon in November 1852 and settled on their 320-acre Donation Land Claim in February 1853. The tract is located in southwest Portland, bounded today by these streets: Lucille, Stephenson, 35th, and 45th.

David was a farmer. He died January 10, 1864 "after an illness of only eight hours," according to a newspaper report. That was the only time the newspapers mentioned him — from which we may suppose that his life was a peaceful one.

Prettyman
    Perry
    David

He seemed like such a pleasant man — kind, intelligent — and in many ways he was. And yet Dr. Perry Prettyman did this terrible thing. Of course, *he* thought he was doing "good." But that, probably, could be said of every perpetrator of evil — they always think they are doing the right thing. One wonders if Dr. Prettyman saw the awful results of his act before he died, and repented of his folly. He lived only 25 years after he introduced the first dandelions into Oregon. But that should have been long enough. As every householder knows, dandelions multiply very rapidly and it must have been apparent to him, by the time he died in 1872, that he had released a malevolent genie.

Dr. Prettyman, his wife (nee Elizabeth Vessels), and their children arrived in Oregon in December 1847. He was then 51 years old. They made the journey across the plains from Missouri, but they were originally from Delaware, where Perry Prettyman was born in 1796. Perry graduated from a school in Baltimore called the "Botanic Medical School," whence came his title "Doctor." That school taught the use of herbs, barks, and plants to make medicines. It was there that he acquired his unfortunate devotion to dandelions, which have long been used in Europe and Asia as a tonic — the leaves make "greens" and the flowers and roots make "tea." This prolific weed came to America from Europe. It was brought by the Colonists, who also brought smallpox. By the middle of the nineteenth century, dandelions had reached Missouri. It was from there that Dr. Prettyman brought the seeds to Oregon. Dandelions would have got here anyway (by seeds caught in the cuffs of pioneers' trousers, perhaps, or by birds or on the wings of the winds), but not so quickly or deliberately. If Dr. Prettyman had foreseen their fierce reproductivity, he might have kept them under lock in a guarded greenhouse.

Dr. Prettyman was a man of awesome energy (presumably a great advertisement for his herbs and tonics!). Upon reaching Oregon, he began exploring the Northwest to decide where to "settle." He visited many localities, including the Puget Sound area — all this on horseback. He chose Portland because he guessed, correctly, that it was at the head of ocean navigation and would become a large city. I suppose we are glad he settled here! The 621-acre claim he selected is on the west slope of Mt. Tabor. It is bounded today by 41st, 60th, Stark, and Division streets. The Prettyman family settled there in March 1850. The doctor built a log cabin at what later became the head of Hawthorne Boulevard. From there, he cut a three-mile trail to the Willamette River. His trail's route approximated the present-day line of Hawthorne Boulevard, and it ended at a point on the river bank from which a "ferry" made crossings to the village of Portland, on the opposite bank of the river. The ferry (it was a row-boat) was operated by "Uncle" Jimmy Stephens (as he was called). He was another of our original DLC settlers.

Perry and Elizabeth had 10 children, but six of them died while their parents were still living. The four surviving were sons David, Daniel, Henry, and William. David took up a Donation Land Claim adjoining his father's. David was born in Delaware in 1832. He settled on his claim in October 1851 when he was 19 years old. It contained 321 acres, and is bounded today by these southeast streets: 60th, 80th, Madison, and Division. The tract includes the south half of Mt. Tabor Park. Son David farmed his claim until 1861, when he moved to a farm near Salem. Father Perry sold off part of his DLC, at $250 per acre. The remainder of the claim was eventually divided among the four sons.

Dr. Perry Prettyman was, according to a biographer, "a devoted practitioner of his profession, occasionally riding as far as Roseburg on horseback to attend a patient." That shows not only praiseworthy solicitude for his patients, but also great confidence in the curative powers of his naturopathic medicines. And a house call of 180 miles on horseback makes, for today's office-bound physicians, an embarrassing and humbling contrast.

Dr. Prettyman died March 27, 1872, at his residence on his DLC, after an illness of six weeks. He was 76 years old. The obituaries noted that "Deceased was a man of great enterprise, and was always foremost in agricultural and horticultural matters... He will be buried on his farm, at his request... He has been a member of the Methodist Church for many years... he died of old age."

The *Oregonian* of March 30, 1872 reported:

> The funeral of Dr. Prettyman yesterday was largely attended. Among the number could be seen many of the old settlers of this vicinity, who sadly paid their last earthly respects to the deceased.

Proebstel
Wendel
Frederick

Vater und Mutter Proebstel, with their four sons, migrated from Germany to the U.S., to Missouri, in 1842. Here, more children were born, and the older son added grandchildren to the growing family. About 1850, the father died. Early in 1852, the sons were awarded U.S. citizenship. Later that spring, the mother and her little flock of sons, grandsons, and daughters-in-law started across the plains to Oregon. But the mother died en route, and was buried in a grave beside the Oregon Trail. Her saddened family pushed on, ever westward, reaching Oregon in late September 1852.

The oldest son, Jacob, and his wife Catherine and their young children settled near Vancouver, Washington. Jacob was born in Berlin, Germany in 1817.

The next oldest son, Wendel, born in Germany in 1821, chose a 281-acre Donation Land Claim in what is now north Portland. He settled there, with his wife, in November 1852. The tract is bounded today by Fremont, Williams, and Russell streets. On the west, it extends beyond Greeley Avenue to include part of the Union Pacific Railroad yards. Wendel died July 7, 1874.

Another of the sons, Frederick, born in Germany in 1829, took up a Donation Land Claim near that of brother Wendel. It included 159 acres. He settled there in April 1853, when he was 24 years old and not yet married. His tract is bounded by Killingsworth, Delaware, and Going streets, and extends to Swan Island. After a few years of farming his claim, he sold it and moved to Wallowa County, where he took up a homestead and, in 1870, married Mary Hall. In 1900, the family came back to Portland, where they lived on Peninsular Avenue near Columbia Slough. Frederick died in 1911, survived by his widow and three children.

The fourth Proebstel son who immigrated with the parents in 1842 was William, born in Germany in 1830. He settled near La Grande.

Protzman

One of Portland's first public accountants was Louis F. Protzman. He had arrived in town by the early 1860s. In April 1864, he bought 40 acres in what is now northeast Portland. He acquired the land under the Homestead Act, paying $1.25 per acre. The tract is bounded today by these northeast streets: 92nd, 97th, Siskiyou, and Brazee. It includes part of Rocky Butte. In April 1865, Louis sold his 40 acres to a relative, F.C. Protzman, for $100. In the 1870s, accountant Louis Protzman was living on West Park, near Morrison Street.

Pullen

"There was no man living along Columbia Slough better known and liked than Mr. Pullen... He came out to Oregon with the very early settlers, with Milton Sunderland and Tom Cully... He raised a large family and his children have married and scattered over all the state." Thus, in his obituary, was summarized the life of Andrew Pullen.

He was born in Virginia in 1820, and, in Illinois in 1843, married Martha Jane Reynolds. The family came across the plains to Oregon, arriving in September 1852. In September 1853, they settled on their Donation Land Claim, encompassing 309 acres located in what is now northeast Portland. It is bounded by these streets: 82nd, 99th, Killingsworth, and Skidmore-92nd-Prescott.

Andrew Pullen died February 16, 1897. The executor of his estate and his principal heir was the widow Martha Jane, who signed the paperwork with "X," her mark. Andrew's will was a long one because, though his estate was not large, he saw to it that he gave at least something to every one of his many children and grandchildren.

Quimby

Two men named Quimby were prominent in pioneer Portland. One we met in our earlier book, *Portland Names and Neighborhoods* (p. 192), because Quimby Street was named for him. That was L.P.W. Quimby (the initials stand for Lot Porter Woodruff). He came to Portland in February 1862 and operated a livery stable (where horses and carriages were kept for hire — an early "U-Drive" business). Later, he owned several hotels. He was a state legislator, a Republican, and a Baptist. He was not an original land claim owner, but we give some details about him here so as to overcome a confusion that exists between him and Ebenezer Lane Quimby, who *was* an original land claimant.

Ebenezer, his wife Elmira (nee Peck), and a two-year old daughter (Eunice Alice Jane) came across the plains to Oregon in 1849. By coincidence, both Lot Quimby and Ebenezer Quimby were born in Vermont, and one might have thought they were brothers. But that was not so. They may have been distant cousins, but even that is uncertain because, according to genealogical records, Lot's ancestors were Scottish and Ebenezer's were Welsh.

From 1849 to 1852, Ebenezer and his family lived at Milwaukie, where he worked in a sawmill. In October 1852, they settled on their 640-acre Donation Land Claim. It includes the Parkrose district, and extends from 99th to 115th, and from Prescott Street to the Columbia River. Ebenezer farmed his claim from 1852 to 1865, during which time several more children were added to the family, for a total of six (though four died before their father did).

Ebenezer Lane Quimby (the Lane is for the family name of his mother) was a County Commissioner in 1853, and a Justice of the Peace. He was active in politics as a Democrat, which was somewhat unusual for a Vermonter — most of Oregon's Democrats at that time were from the South. An item in the *Oregon Statesman*, May 12, 1857, noted that 28 delegates to a Democratic Convention were called to order by "E.L. Quimby, Esq.," chairman of the Multnomah County Democratic Committee.

In 1865, Ebenezer sold his land and moved to the near east side, which was then the town of East Portland. His wife Elmira (sometimes spelled Almira) died there May 9, 1876, aged 58. In 1885, Ebenezer moved to Woodburn, where he died February 7, 1891, aged 78.

Ebenezer (an Old Testament name) was, according to one biographer, "...of frugal nature and habits" but "public-spirited." Another writer characterized him in these somewhat ambivalent terms: "Though rough in exterior, he had a warm heart. To appreciate him best, one had to know him well, for it was to his friends rather than mere acquaintances that he gave the sunlight of his really genial nature." He seems to have been a personification of the rockbound and dour Vermonter, as portrayed in the clichés of folklore. The fact that he was elected to public office suggests that he was not quite so forbidding as that quotation might imply.

Quinn
John
Terrence

Ireland in the 1840s was an island of unemployment, poverty, and hunger, especially after the failure of the potato crop in 1845-46. As we noted in the earlier biography of Michael Kennedy, more than one million Irishmen emigrated from the Emerald Isle during the years 1845 to 1850. Among them were Terrence Quinn and his younger brother John. We don't know the exact year they left Ireland, but 1848 would be a good guess. Terrence would have been 30 years old and John 20. They went to Newfoundland. There, in 1850, Terrence married Mary Whelan, who had been born in St. Johns, Newfoundland. The

Quinns didn't remain there long — perhaps, after the gentle greenness of Ireland, Newfoundland seemed cold and barren. Early in 1851, they were in New York City.

In November 1851, Terrence, Mary, and John arrived in Oregon. That same month, Terrence settled on his Donation Land Claim. He qualified for 320 acres. The claim he chose is now the Laurelhurst neighborhood. His tract is bounded today by 32nd, 39th, Halsey, and Stark streets. Terrence was a farmer, but gradually sold off his land. A daughter, named Mary, was born to Terrence and Mary in December 1853. But, in March 1854, Mrs. Mary Quinn died, of "consumption." She was buried on her husband's DLC, with a Catholic priest performing the rites and John Quinn as witness.

John found a tract just north of his brother's, but he qualified for only 160 acres, being unmarried. The John Quinn DLC is bounded today by 36th, 50th, Halsey, and Brazee streets, and includes the Hollywood business district. John farmed his claim until about 1865, when he sold it and moved to Montana. There, on "Nevada Creek," he bought a ranch and built up a considerable herd of cattle. Unfortunately, a feud developed between John Quinn and one of his neighbors, a Mr. McArrison. We don't know how the feud started — a boundary dispute? — cattle wandering off and thought to have been "rustled"? In any case, one fine day in February, McArrison shot and killed our DLC pioneer. The sad event was reported in the *Oregonian* of March 11, 1873:

HOMICIDE

Mr. John Quinn was shot and instantly killed a few weeks ago at Nevada Creek, Montana Territory, by a man named McArrison. Quinn, unarmed, had ridden away from his cabin one morning and, that afternoon, his horse returned with the saddle empty but bloody. A friend went to search for him and found his body; it had been pierced by ten bullets. McArrison stated that he had shot Quinn, and he was held in lieu of bail set at $3,000. Mr. Quinn was about 45 years of age...

It appears there was a feud existing

> between the parties for some time, Quinn having shot at McArrison on one occasion, but no proceedings were ever taken in the matter.

Apparently, McArrison was a better marksman than our John.

Brother Terrence continued to live in Portland, where, on September 4, 1890, at the age of 77, he died peacefully, in bed.

Ramsey

January 2, 1895 was a cold day, and Frederick H. Ramsey, a 70-year old bachelor who lived with two dogs on a houseboat moored on Columbia Slough, built a roaring fire in his stove to keep warm. But the houseboat caught fire and Fred and his dogs died in the flames.

Fred had arrived in Oregon in October 1844, making him one of our earliest pioneers. He was born in Pennsylvania and was 20 years old when he came here. In 1848, he was a volunteer in the militia organized to control the Cayuse Indians. In March 1851, he settled on his 282-acre Donation Land Claim, located north of the St. Johns district where Columbia Slough flows into the Willamette River. He was also the first owner of about 200 acres in what is now East St. Johns, acquired under a Homestead Act. That tract is bounded approximately by these streets: Fessenden, Dana, Houghton, and, on the west, by Westanna-Hudson-Clarendon.

According to one bit of lore, Fred was a militiaman under Ulysses S. Grant, when Grant was a Lieutenant stationed at Fort Vancouver in 1852-53. The story, which seems plausible, is that Fred and Grant went on hunting trips together on Sauvie Island.

Except for his time in the militia, Fred spent his life farming his DLC. This is almost all the information we have from which to reconstruct the image of Fred Ramsey. Our only other detail is this: people who knew him recalled that Fred "always wore moccasins." That does give us a quite vivid portrait of Fred — from the ankles downward.

Rankin

John H. Rankin was born in New Hampshire in 1805. In 1841, in Missouri, he married Elizabeth. He came to Oregon in 1849, liked the opportunities he saw here, and returned East to bring his family to Portland. They settled on their 298-acre Donation Land Claim in April 1852, located in what is now north Portland. It is bounded by Peninsular, Minnesota, Newark (and the Columbia Slough), and Kilpatrick streets. Mr. Rankin died August 20, 1895, aged 90.

Rennison

A man on jury duty in 1879, Isaac Rennison, had been complaining to fellow jurors, saying that he did not feel well. Some might have thought he was merely inventing excuses, hoping to get off jury duty. But he was quite sincere. The next day, November 1, 1879, he died. He was 62 years old.

Mr. Rennison was born in England in 1817 and, when two years old, came to the U.S. with his parents. In 1838, Isaac was in Missouri where, at the age of 21, he married Mary Ann. They arrived in Oregon in November 1852 and settled on their Donation Land Claim in November 1855. It is bounded today by these northeast streets: 33rd, 60th, Holman, and Killingsworth.

Isaac's daughter Susan married Daniel Prettyman, son of another DLC settler, Dr. Perry Prettyman. Their marriage took place September 7, 1856. Susan must have been about 17 years old.

At Mr. Rennison's funeral, a sermon was preached by Rev. J. Exon, of the Methodist Church.

Solomon Richards

Richards

Solomon Richards was born in Ohio in 1820 and, at an early age, was left an orphan. We don't know anything about his childhood but, if his later years are a guide, it was energetic and adventurous. He must have spent some time in school, because he learned to read and write.

When he was 22 years old and a farmer, he married. But only two years later, his wife died. Perhaps to leave behind sad memories, he sold his farm and, in 1845, joined a wagon train coming to Oregon. That October, he reached Fort Vancouver — with six cents in his pocket. He got a job doing ploughing at $1 per day (which is not as meager as it sounds, since prices were about one-fifteenth what they are today).

In 1846, he staked out a 640-acre claim which, after the passage of the Donation Land Act in 1850, became his Donation Claim. It encompasses the present-day district of Linnton, and extends from the riverfront up the hillside into Forest Park. Also in 1846, Mr. Richards became one of the first subscribers to the Oregon City *Spectator*, the Oregon Country's first newspaper. And about this time, he served as a corporal in the militia organized to restrain the Cayuse Indians.

In 1848, he married again. This wife's name was Sarah. His claim was thickly timbered, and he cut trees and sold the logs to the small mills that were busy cutting lumber for the booming San Francisco market. It was relatively easy to move his logs to the mills because his claim was on the bank of the Willamette River — in those days, most things were moved by water.

Mr. Richards was elected a Justice of the Peace, and performed several early-day marriages. In 1854, his wife Sarah died. He married for the third time in 1856. In 1857, he started a dairy business, with 23 cows, and marketed butter. In 1879, his third wife died. His fourth marriage was in 1882. Mr. Richards died June 4, 1897, aged 77. Altogether, he had four children.

Robinson

Thomas Graham Robinson was born in Kentucky. He arrived in Oregon in 1844 when he was 37 years old, and single. In Portland, he met an Irish girl named Bridget Teresa Clarke and they decided to marry. Bridget was born in Dublin. Her wanderings and adventures in migrating from Ireland to Portland would surely make a good story, but, alas, we have none of the details. We do know that she was a Roman Catholic. Thomas was not Catholic, but after the necessary dispensations had been granted by Archbishop Blanchet, they were married at Portland on October 4, 1852 by Father James P. Croke, a Catholic Missionary Priest. The witnesses at the marriage ceremony included some well-known Portlanders: Benjamin Stark, another Donation Land Claim pioneer and later Oregon's

U.S. Senator: L.C. Broy; and Stephen I. McCormick.

Tom and Bridget chose a Donation Land Claim on Portland Heights, and settled there in May 1854. The tract was quite small, only 28 acres, and Tom would have qualified for a 320-acre grant. But to find such a piece of as yet unclaimed land would have required him to go farther out from the village of Portland. The 28 acres were a residual piece of land in among other larger claims, and Tom must have felt that the scenic location made the site so attractive that he preferred it to 320 acres of forested outlands. The Robinson claim is located just above what is today S.W. Broadway Drive, and extends approximately from Davenport to Chelmsford streets, and from about 10th to 13th, or where those streets would be if put through. From their claim, Tom and Bridget had (after they had cut down some trees) a spectacular view of the Willamette River, the little Portland townsite at their feet, and Mt. Hood and Mt. St. Helens in the distance. The site was known as "Robinson Hill." During the next few years, Tom sold off 22 of his acres.

But, sad to say, Tom lived to enjoy all this domestic and scenic bliss for only 13 years — he died in October 1867, aged 60. His estate, which passed to the widow Bridget, included six acres remaining unsold in the Robinson DLC, valued at $300. There was, Bridget testified at the probate hearing, "no issue living." Nor is there any record of Bridget's later life.

Roe

George C. Roe was a Methodist minister in the "Oregon Conference" of that church from 1854 to 1875. In 1855, he was appointed to the Board of Trustees of the Rainier Academy, one of many schools launched by the Methodist Church in Oregon's early days. That particular school lasted only four years, though others were much more enduring.

Rev. Roe was married July 13, 1857 to Miss Ann Campbell, of Portland. One of the few bits of information we have about them is a sad one: a newspaper item in 1865 reported that their six-year old son had been killed by a falling tree. The accident occurred "near Portland." The family were probably living at the time on their 46-acre homestead. The tract is located along what is today West Burnside Street, just west of the Kings Heights and Arlington Heights neighborhoods, and includes the present Pittock Mansion property.

Rev. and Mrs. Roe received the final title to their claim in May 1869. In 1872, they sold their 46 acres for $4600 to Arthur Johnson, for whom Johnson Street is named (see *Portland Names and Neighborhoods*, page 157).

Root

George Washington Root was born in Ohio December 2, 1837, and spent his childhood on his father's farm. The family moved to California in 1848. Later, George came to Portland, where, in August 1872, he began occupancy of his 30-acre homestead. He received final title to it in 1877. The very next year, he sold all 30 acres to E.L. Eastham, for $400. The tract is located north of Macleay Park, and borders N.W. Mountain View Park Road, about where N.W. 45th Avenue would be.

Mr. Root was still living in Portland in 1926, when, nearly 89 years old, he was the subject of an interview. Among his reminiscences were these:

When I was a boy, children were taught to respect and obey their parents, to observe the Sabbath, and to cultivate the habits of industry and thrift... When I was six years old, I rode the corn horse all day long. This horse was a steady slow-moving horse which father used to cultivate the corn, and it was my job to see he went straight down the middle of the row while father held the plow... We started for California in the spring of 1848, before news of the discovery of gold reached the East... My father opened a store, a hotel, and saloon near Sacramento. He also had a very profitable side-line — pasturing miners' horses while they went to Sacramento or San Francisco... I started to school when I was 17, and put in two terms. That was about the extent of my schooling.

In his later years, Mr. Root was an amateur musician. But he was not the George Root who, about the time of World War I, composed a sentimental popular song titled "Just Before the Battle, Mother"!

Ross, Darius M.

The first individual to own the 40-acre tract bounded today by S.W. 40th, 45th, Dolph Court, and Alice Street was Darius M. Ross. Mr. Ross seems to have led a quiet and blameless life — we found nothing in the archives about him. The 40 acres were "school land" he purchased from the State of Oregon. But he was also a Donation Land Claim settler elsewhere (he had a 315-acre DLC in Columbia County, west of Rainier), and from the Land Office records we know that Darius was born in Pennsylvania in 1825, married Eliza Jane in 1849 in Iowa, arrived in Oregon in September 1851, and settled on his Donation Land Claim in December 1854.

Ross, Sherry

The Donation Land Claim of Sherry Ross is easy to see and identify — it is Ross Island. Land Office records gave its area as 298 acres, but the size of the island varies widely with the seasonal high and low water levels in the Willamette River.

Sherry was born in Indiana in 1824, and settled on his island in December 1850. In November 1851, at the age of 27, he married Rebecca Deardorf, at Milwaukie, the ceremony being conducted by Rev. W.A. Willis, of the Methodist Church.

After having lived on their island for the requisite four years, the Ross family moved to the mainland. Sherry operated a livery stable at what was then 165 Second Street, and resided nearby, at 147 Second. He used his island to pasture cows — as many as 27 of them at one time. The island was a convenient location on which to let cows wander about and graze, because no fences were needed to keep the animals *in situ*. But the daily trips by rowboat, to bring over the milk, may have been a nuisance.

In 1866, Sherry was in poor health, and he went to California to recover. But he died there, January 4, 1867. Sherry had left no will, and the widow Rebecca was named administrator of the estate. Rebecca's report to the court was written in a neat, clear hand, and stated that there were on the island, besides the cows, a yoke of oxen and two boats. She decided, probably wisely, to sell the island and everything on it. The estate also included various other real estate and personal property, for a total value of about $17,000. The heirs were Rebecca and four children, aged (in 1867) 14, 11, 7, and 3.

Royal

The Rev. James Henry Bascom Royal was one of the early-day Methodist ministers in Oregon, as were his father and brother. James, as we shall call him for brevity, was born in Illinois in April 1830, of English-German ancestry according to genealogical records. He graduated from college in Illinois. In 1853, he came to Oregon with his family, which included his father (Rev. William Royal), his mother, an older brother (Rev. Thomas Fletcher Royal), another brother (Jason Lee Royal — named, of course, for the pioneer Methodist missionary), and a sister, Mary Elizabeth. The family started across the plains from Illinois March 17, 1853. James walked all the way, driving five yoke of oxen. They arrived at Jacksonville, in southern Oregon, October 27, 1853.

About that time, the Methodist Bishop of Oregon sent Rev. J.H. Wilbur to the Umpqua Valley to open a mission and school.

"Umpqua Academy," as the school was called, opened in April 1854, with our James Royal and his sister Mary Elizabeth as its faculty. The school, in the village that came to be known as Wilbur, met in a log house on the Donation Land Claim of Rev. Wilbur. James and Mary taught there until July 1855. This was the first school in southern Oregon. During those terms, more than 100 students attended the school at various times, many of whom later became prominent Oregonians.

In 1855, our James was assigned as minister for the Methodist Church's district that extended from St. Helens to Astoria. To reach the homes of his parishioners, James had to travel by boat (criss-crossing the river many times), and by horseback and on foot. Later, James was assigned to other districts.

On July 23, 1868, James, now 38, married Emma J. Cornell, of Portland, the ceremony being performed by a well-known Methodist minister, Rev. H.K. Hines. Shortly thereafter, James and Emma acquired the 33-acre homestead, as a result of which they come within the scope of this book. The tract is located in the vicinity of today's N.W. 53rd Drive, Blyths Road, and Forest Park. They received final title to it in 1876. In 1882, they sold all 33 acres to James Surman for $750.

Rev. James Royal had 21 years of active service in the ministry. He retired in 1875, on account of blindness. He died in 1910, at the age of 80, and his body was buried in Lone Fir Cemetery. Surviving were his widow Emma and four children. Also still living in 1910 were his brother, Rev. T.F. Royal (a Trustee of Willamette University), and his sister, who had married another prominent Methodist minister, Rev. John Flinn.

Schmeer

Peter and Caroline Schmeer came to Portland in 1861. Peter was 38 years old and Caroline was 32. Peter was a "laborer," according to the 1863 City Directory, and the family lived on First Street. The next year, they moved to the corner of what is today S.W. Broadway and Hall Street. In 1868, Peter bought the real estate that brings him within our horizon. It was a 44-acre tract of "school land" purchased from the State of Oregon for $830, and bounded today by S.E. 28th, 32nd, Burnside, and Stark streets.

Meanwhile, relations between Peter and Caroline were not as congenial as one might have wished, and, in January 1879, the court granted Caroline a divorce from Peter, who was required to give her a settlement of $1800. Perhaps to pay that obligation, Peter later that year sold 14 acres to John Gates for $2900.

Peter moved to East Portland, where he died January 22, 1889, aged 66. Caroline died in Portland May 19, 1899, aged 70. Their son, J.P. Schmeer, appears in the 1880 City Directory as a "saloonkeeper," residing on Broadway.

Schramm

The trip across the plains in covered wagons — six months of adventures, dangers, and frustrations — would give young people many opportunities to appraise each other. One who, under duress, showed courage, patience, and ingenuity would seem an admirable life partner. So it must have been with Charles and Melinda. Charles was hired as a wagon driver by a man named Squire Hawkins, who, with his family, came to Oregon from Missouri in 1852. In the Hawkins household were four boys and girls, the oldest being Melinda. They and their wagons, with Charles driving an ox team, reached Oregon in October 1852, and Melinda and Charles were married February 8, 1853. Melinda was then 18 years old and Charles 21.

Charles Gustav Schramm was born in Hanover, Germany. The records are conflicting as to the exact year, but 1832 is probably correct. He emigrated to the U.S. in 1850, when he was 18. How he spent the years from 1850 to 1852 we can only conjecture, but it seems fair to suppose that, among the immigrants in Philadelphia or New York, he tried various jobs and learned to speak English. In 1852, in company with three other young men, he started on foot for California. But in Missouri occurred his fortuitous meeting with Mr. Hawkins, whose need for a wagon driver altered Charles' plans and determined his destiny. On the covered wagon journey, he was a 20-year old youth, speaking English with a strong German accent, and Melinda (as we visualize her) was a teenage girl in homespun, with braided tresses.

In March 1854, Charles and Melinda settled on a 320-acre Donation Land Claim. It is bounded today by these N.E. streets: 82nd; Skidmore-92nd-Prescott; 102nd; and Fremont. There, in a log cabin at the foot of Rocky Butte, seven children were born to the Schramms. During the Indian "wars" of the 1850s, Charles served in a volunteer regiment. And he learned the bakery trade from Mr. Opitz, in whose "German Bakery" he worked for several years. Later, he was a clerk in the Multnomah County offices — thus ending his career in what would seem, after his adventurous beginnings, a rather sedentary mode.

Shattuck

It does seem an unusual honeymoon, at least to most of us in these modern days. But our pioneers were, by definition, adventurous. In 1852, E.D. Shattuck, having just been admitted to the bar in New York, married Sarah. A few months later, in 1853, they boarded a primitive steamship (propelled by paddle wheels) bound for Panama, crossed the Isthmus on mule-back, and came up the West Coast by a succession of small steamboats to Portland. When he arrived here, Erasmus Darwin Shattuck was 29 years old. He had graduated in 1844 from the University of Vermont, his native state.

From 1853 to 1856, Erasmus was a school teacher. From 1856 to 1858 he was a Probate Judge. He practiced law in Portland from 1858 to 1861, when he was appointed U.S. District Attorney. He was a Republican — his name appears in the Republican League Register for Oregon — and the appointment was made by President Lincoln, also a Republican, who took office that year. In 1862, Mr. Shattuck was elected Circuit Judge. Later, he was a member of the Oregon Supreme Court. Altogether, he sat on one judicial bench or another for 24 years.

In 1868, Judge Shattuck bought 40 acres of "school land" from the State of Oregon. He paid $80 for the tract, bounded today by these S.E. streets: 92nd, Woodstock, 97th, and Duke. In 1879, he sold the 40 acres to one Richard Drake for $1250.

Shattuck Road is named for the judge. A few additional facts about him are in *Portland Names and Neighborhoods*, page 203.

Judge Shattuck was a Unitarian. He died in 1900, aged 76. A biographer called him "A grand old man, loved by all."

Shaver

There are numerous references in the archives to "John Shaver" living in the Portland area in the latter half of the nineteenth century. But they need to be sifted carefully because they refer to at least three separate and unrelated individuals. *Our* John (the only one who was an original owner of any Portland real estate) took up a 120-acre Homestead Claim in the hills northwest of Portland. Today, the tract is bounded approximately by N.W. Thompson and Cornell roads, about where 68th Avenue would be. But at that time, John's property was quite remote. Most of his land was forested, but he had a clearing where he operated a small farm.

John was a kind, gentle man who kept bees and liked simple music. But he met a most tragic death. The sad affair was recounted in the *Oregonian* of October 18, 1872:

Four miles northwest of Portland, an old man named Shaver has resided for a number of years. Mr. Shaver carried on gardening as a means of livelihood. He peddled vegetables... through the city and consequently was well known in the community. His wife died some years ago, and he has since that time resided on his little farm all alone. About two weeks since, Shaver was missed from his house, but it was thought he had gone away somewhere on a visit. Several days more passed away, and still neighbors who called to see him found the house solitary and deserted. Shaver's continued absence at length excited some comment, ending in apprehensions that all was not right. Last Wednesday, several of his near neighbors met and after a consultation as to the possible whereabouts of the old gentleman, concluded to look for him. Search was instituted. After a diligent quest of several hours, the body of Shaver was found, crushed between two trees, about half a mile from his house. It appears that the unfortunate old man had gone out to chop timber. A tree about two feet in diameter was found lying directly across the middle of his body. He had chopped at the tree until it began to fall and failed to get out of the way... Deceased was aged about 53 years. He has a brother residing in Washington County, and a son, about 22, living near Hood River. Deceased was for several years a resident of Clackamas County, where he was well known. He was a quiet, peaceable citizen, industrious and well respected by all who knew him.

It is depressing to see that a 53-year old man was thrice called "old"! Today, it would be "early middle age."

Mr. Shaver had settled on his Homestead about 1865, and received final title to it in 1869. Between that time and his death in 1872, he sold off 40 acres. He had made no will, death coming to him unexpectedly. The court named Mr. Shaver's son

Frances administrator of the estate. Frances and his two married sisters were the heirs. The total value of all property, which included two stands of bees and 5000 shingles, was $1450. Frances proceeded to sell most of the homestead — 40 acres in 1872 for $250, and 20 acres in 1875 for $291. Among the father's personal possessions in his little farmhouse were two music boxes.

Slavin

Portland was a frontier village of 600 souls in 1850 when Mr. and Mrs. Andrew Skidmore, who arrived here that fall, opened a room-and-board business in their house. One of their first residents was John Addison Slavin, who reached Portland that same fall. He was from Missouri, and 24 years old. (Some details about that boarding house or "hotel", located on First Street, are given in our previous book, *Skidmore's Portland*, pp. 16-20.)

John Slavin's formal education was limited, but he did very well in early-day Portland, because he was hard-working and efficient. The town was growing rapidly, and his first job was in construction — building houses for new arrivals. At first, he made $2 a day. He was paying the Skidmores $12 a week (the usual rate at that time), which meant that at the end of a six-day week, he was just even! But soon he became so expert at preparing timber for construction of houses that his wages rose substantially. He then went to work on construction for Stephen Coffin, one of the Portland townsite proprietors, who paid him with deeds to real estate.

In February 1852, he took up a 312-acre Donation Land Claim in what is now southwest Portland. It is bounded today by Hamilton, 25th, and Vermont streets, and, on the east side, by an irregular line about at Cheltenham Street. The tract includes the Hillsdale district and Wilson High School. Slavin Road, named for this pioneer, is near but not quite in his DLC.

John A. Slavin, his wife Emma, and children, 1867

John built a small cabin on his claim and moved there from the Skidmore boarding house. A few months later, December 30, 1852, he married Emma Ross, who had come to Oregon from Ohio in 1847. John was 26 years old and Emma 16.

Because the Donation Land Act gave twice as much land to a married couple as to a single man, some crusty pioneers got married in a hurry, to double their "spread." But since our John married *after* taking up his claim, we infer that matrimony was the result of purer motives of romance and love. The inference is strengthened by the fact that they proceeded to have six children.

The Slavins farmed their claim actively. In 1884, they built a substantial house on the property.

Mr. Slavin was a Republican, active in school district affairs, and a County Commissioner. He died at his home in Hillsdale January 13, 1908, aged 81. Emma Slavin died in 1913, aged 77.

Smalley

In 1849, when he was 21 years old, James A. Smalley, born in Kentucky, went out to California to look for gold. Whether he found any we don't know. But he *did* find that which is, according to the Proverb, better than a barrel of rubies — namely, a good and virtuous wife. She was Martha Magan, who came across the plains with her parents in 1849. Perhaps she and James met on the westward migration. They were married in California in 1850. Whether Martha was one to "riseth while it is yet night and giveth meat to her household... planteth vineyards... layeth her hands to the spindle... speak wisdom... etc." it is unsafe to pronounce judgment at this distance in time. Certainly, there is no evidence to the contrary. We do know that she bore James seven children. And there is a strong presumption that she was a good sport about travelling — as we shall see.

James and Martha moved from California to Oregon in 1852, probably in response to the news about free land. They reached Portland in October 1852 and in April 1853 they settled on a 318-acre Donation Land Claim. The tract is bounded today by these southwest streets: Hamilton, Vermont, 54th, and 65th (the city and county boundary). They lived on their claim until they received final title. Then, in 1857, they went back to Missouri, which was Martha's original home.

The journey back was an interesting one — steamship to San Francisco, another to Panama, across the Isthmus by railroad, steamship to New York, and railroad from New York to the Mississippi River. These were early railroad rides. The railroad across the Isthmus had been completed in 1855 and the first railroad westward to the Mississippi River in 1854. On this long and arduous trip, Martha had two or three infants to manage and was also pregnant — or had just been or was about to be pregnant.

In 1865, the family came back to Oregon, again crossing the plains by ox-team. The motives for these peregrinations we can hardly imagine. But by now, on this half-year journey, Martha was shepherding six or seven little Smalleys, and continuing to earn high marks for patience — more rubies!

This time, the family spent a few years living near Portland and then moved to Rocky Point, Washington. There were several geographic features in Washington known as "Rocky Point," but the one best known and established in usage of the term was, and is, on Whidbey Island, in Puget Sound. It was named by the Wilkes expedition in 1841. That is probably the place — and it would be hard to visualize a more pleasant one — to which the Smalleys retired. There, James and Martha spent the rest of their lives, happily recalling, we suppose, their many adventures.

Smith, B.P.

(Five apparently unrelated men named "Smith" were among Portland's original land owners. There are bits of information in pioneer archives and old newspapers referring to many Smiths in the Portland area and in early-day Oregon, but to determine whether such items refer to one of our five original settlers is a perplexing and perilous business. How convenient it would be if everyone and everything about him were filed by social security number! That would be a boon for future historians, though the confusions of the past would remain unresolved. Here, we give, for our pioneer Smiths, only those facts of which we can be reasonably sure.)

In March 1871, the State of Oregon sold, to B.P.Smith and his wife Susan, 80 acres of "school land." The tract is located in the Lents district and is bounded today by these southeast streets: 97th, 102nd, Holgate, and Harold. The Smiths paid $240 for the 80 acres. Only two months later, they sold the entire tract for $300. It was a short ownership, but it was enough to get B.P. Smith's name attached forever to that land, as the first individual to own it.

Since this was not a DLC, there are no Land Office records to give us any statistics about Mr. Smith. In fact, the record of the preceding transaction is all we *know*. There was no requirement that Mr. Smith should live on his tract, and it is possible that he never resided near Portland. No "B.P. Smith" appears in early Portland records. But there are references to a B.P. Smith (probably also known as B. Pitzer Smith) who, in 1860, at the Umpqua Valley Agricultural Society Fair, received an award for his exhibit. This could be our man.

Smith, George W.

In 1864, George W. Smith acquired two 160-acre tracts by exercising Military Bounty Land warrants he had purchased. Both are in what is now northeast Portland. One tract is bounded by 82nd, 92nd, Brazee, and Clackamas streets; the other by 92nd, 102nd, Clackamas, and Glisan streets. For the warrants, he probably paid $1 or less per acre. In 1872, George and his wife Viola sold 160 acres to Henry Buckman for $1700.

Smith, George (no middle initial)

In 1866, this George Smith used a Military Bounty Land warrant to acquire 160 acres in north Portland. The tract is bounded today by Kerby, Union, and Killingsworth streets, and Portland Boulevard. In July 1870, Mr. Smith bought 80 additional acres, for $400, from Evander Howe, whose Homestead was just to the west. In August 1870, George and his wife Elizabeth sold all their land, now totalling 240 acres, for $2400. The buyers were H.F. Bloch and A.P. Dennison, both of whom, as original owners of other land, were discussed earlier in this book.

Smith, Peter

With Peter, we are on firmer ground because he acquired his 319 acres as a Donation Land Claim, and reliable Land Office records are available for DLCs. Peter was born in 1810 in Virginia (more precisely, in the part that separated from Virginia in 1861, because of a difference of opinion about the Civil War, and became the State of West Virginia in 1863). Peter came to Oregon in 1851. A year before, in Indiana, he had married Rachel, so he was entitled to 320 acres. Claimants often accepted a tract smaller than that for which they might have qualified, in order to get a desirable location amidst the claims that had already been taken. Peter's tract, upon which he settled in November 1851, is in what is now southwest Portland, in the vicinity of Patton and Scholls Ferry roads and extending southward to Hamilton Street. By 1868, Thomas Humphrey, probably related to H.M. Humphrey whose DLC was just to the north, had purchased most of Peter's land.

At least five Peter Smiths appear in various Portland and Oregon archives, but not one of them has a birth year or year of arrival in Oregon which corresponds with that of our subject. So, but for the bare facts just stated, Peter and Rachel must live and die in obscurity.

Smith, Philip T.

We are able to construct, from various sources, a rather complete dossier on Philip T. Smith, who was the first individual to own the 320-acre tract in north Portland bounded today by Wabash, Delaware, Lombard, and Killingsworth streets. Philip was born in eastern Tennessee in 1834, where he remained with his parents until he was about 18 years old. The family then moved to Missouri. There are some inconsistencies as to the dates of his subsequent movements, but the general outline is clear. About 1853, Philip decided to look for gold. He was 19 years old.

He joined a group of settlers headed for California, and earned his way driving cattle across the plains. He worked at gold mining in California for about three years, then went to British Columbia, where gold had been discovered. Prospects weren't encouraging, however, so he came to Portland.

Now aged 23, he found a job cutting wood. About 1857, he bought 150 acres from an earlier settler. This land bordered the Willamette River north of the village of St. Johns. Philip cut trees there and sold wood to steamboats for fuel. Eventually, he had a 400-foot dock on the riverbank.

In 1862, with his economic future more secure than it seems to have been while gold mining, Philip, now aged 28, married Mary Windle, daughter of John Windle, another pioneer Portland DLC settler. Mr. Smith died in 1901, aged 67. He was clerk of the School Board and a member of the United Evangelical Church.

Southmayd

Daniel S. Southmayd was born in Vermont and was 26 years old when he married Ailcy Caples, at Portland, July 5, 1851. The ceremony was performed by a prominent Methodist minister, Rev. James H. Wilbur. Ailcy was the daughter of DLC settler Dr. William Caples, whose claim, as we saw earlier, included part of the St. Johns district.

In September 1851, Daniel took up a Donation Land Claim of his own — 610 acres adjoining that of his father-in-law. Daniel was entitled to the maximum of 620 acres because he arrived in Oregon prior to December 1850 and also was now married. The Southmayd DLC includes the portion of St. Johns east of Central Street and north of Fessenden and extends northward beyond Columbia Boulevard.

Daniel was a printer. In the early 1850s, the biggest printing operation in the Portland area was the *Oregonian* — four tabloid-size pages (that is, one sheet folded) once a week. But

Daniel S. Southmayd

it required much work. The type was all hand-set and the little press was hand-operated, one copy at a time. Perhaps Daniel worked there. If so, he would have commuted between his home in St. Johns and the Portland townsite by boat. That was the best way to travel at that time, and there were little steamboats running on the Willamette River. It would have been a one-hour excursion by steamboat. Or, Daniel may have had a print shop in the village of St. Johns. But this is conjecture. We do know that in 1855 Daniel was a candidate for Multnomah County Probate Judge, as a member of the Whig party. He was defeated by a Democrat, A.L. Davis, who received 319 votes to Daniel's 246.

Ten years after his marriage, when he was only 36 years old, Daniel died, May 1861, of tuberculosis.

Benjamin Stark

Stark

Benjamin Stark was one of the original owners of the Portland townsite, and, as such, has been the subject of many articles and biographical reviews. For example, his early activities at Portland and his acquisition of a portion of the townsite are discussed in our previous book, *Early Portland: Stump-Town Triumphant,* pp. 34, 64, and 67. And Stark Street is named for him, so he appears in *Portland Names and Neighborhoods,* page 209, where his career is described in some detail. Since so much information is already available, we will give here only an outline of his *curriculum vitae.*

Born in New Orleans in 1820; first came to Portland in 1845; engaged in merchandising and shipping; went to the California gold mines in 1848; studied law and was admitted to the Oregon bar in 1850; married Elizabeth Molthrop; was one of the first trustees of the Congregational Church in Portland; elected to the Territorial Legislature, 1853; was active in

Democratic Party affairs as a Southern Democrat; was Aide-de-Camp to Governor Curry during an 1856 Indian revolt at Cascades.

During the 1850s, Mr. Stark made substantial sums by selling lots from his Donation Land Claim, a 49-acre triangular tract bounded by S.W. Stark Street, Burnside, and the riverfront. In an 1859 list of property valuations by the Multnomah County Assessor, Mr. Stark's real estate (assessed at $55,000) had a larger valuation than that of any other individual in town, though some companies owned real estate with a greater value than that. But Mr. Stark's DLC was obviously a desirable location.

In 1860, Mr. Stark was elected to the State Legislature as an "Opposition Democrat." In October 1861, Governor John Whiteaker appointed Mr. Stark to be Oregon's U.S. Senator, to fill a vacancy caused by the death of Colonel E.D. Baker, the incumbent, who had been killed in a Civil War battle. Since Mr. Stark was a Southerner and a supporter of the Confederacy, his appointment created a bit of a flap, particularly since Colonel Baker had died fighting on the Union side. It was no problem for Governor Whiteaker, however, because he was also a Southern Democrat. In fact, there were many Southern Democrats in Oregon, and considerable sympathy for the "South," as attested by the fact that both Whiteaker and Stark, despite their well-known views, were elected to office. Senator Stark represented Oregon until September 1862, when a replacement, B.F. Harding, was elected by the State legislature.

Mr. Stark was in Portland only occasionally after 1862. His home for the rest of his life was in Connecticut, where he died in 1898.

Starr

Benjamin F. Starr was born in Ohio in 1817. He was in Indiana in 1840 when he married Catherine. They came to Oregon in September 1852, and settled on their Donation Land Claim in October 1853. Since they arrived here after December 1850, but were a married couple, they qualified for 320 acres. The claim they found had 316 acres, and is bounded today by these southeast streets: Salmon, Lincoln, 80th, and 101st.

The Starrs lived on their claim until they had fulfilled the four-year residence and cultivation requirement, and then moved to the Portland townsite. Benjamin was a tinsmith and had a shop on Front Street. Their home was just a few doors away. In 1873, he still had his tinsmith business, but by then (according to the City Directory of that year), he was living at the Occidental Hotel. There is no mention of Catherine. Later in the 1870s, he moved to the Salem vicinity, where he died July 27, 1882, aged 65.

Stephens
James B.
Thomas F.

In the village of Oregon City in 1845, there lived a cooper named James B. Stephens. To support his wife and seven children, he made barrels for Hudson's Bay Company, for shipping wheat, flour, and dried salmon to Hawaii and California. Through his connection with the company, he learned that an interesting piece of property downstream was for sale. It was being offered by Dr. McLoughlin, the Hudson's Bay Company agent, who was administrator of the estate of a deceased Company employee (A. Davids) who had originally claimed it. The square-mile tract was on the Willamette riverfront opposite a little clearing which had just been christened "Portland." James, an enterprising fellow as we shall see, bought the claim for $200 — equivalent to something like $3000 at our 1989 wage-price level. That was a considerable sum, but James perceived the property's potential.

The boundaries of his 642-acre tract today are S.E. Stark and Division streets, extending from 20th to the river. In it is

James B. Stephens and his wife Elizabeth

"Ladd's Addition." But in 1845 it was "the forest primeval" and little more. The only civilization he could see was the Portland townsite, with two or three log cabins, a dock under construction, and an energetic owner-promoter, Francis Pettygrove, who was about to open a warehouse and store. Those amenities, though austere, attracted the few scattered pioneers on the "east side," and James Stephens saw the opportunity to start a ferry service to get them across the river. At first, it was simply a rowboat.

Meanwhile, three miles upstream, James' brother, Thomas F. Stephens, staked out a claim in what is now southwest Portland. He and his family settled there in November 1846. Both his claim and that of brother James were somewhat informal because the Donation Land Act had not yet been passed by Congress. But it was confidently expected that such a law would be passed, and, in the interim, claims could be registered with the Provisonal Government at Oregon City.

James and Thomas Stephens are among our earliest settlers. They arrived at Oregon City in December 1844, when James was 38 years old and Thomas 42. They came across the plains with their father, Emmons Stephens, and their wives and children. (Father Emmons was born in Maryland in 1777 and died near Portland in 1846.) James married Elizabeth Walker in Ohio in 1828. Thomas was married twice, first to Elizabeth Matthews, by whom he had two sons, and, after Elizabeth's death, to Phebe Atherton, by whom he had eight children. He married Phebe in Illinois in 1836.

The boundaries of the 634-acre "Thomas F. Stephens DLC" are at about S.W. Pendleton and Hume streets, extending from 10th to the riverfront. Today, the tract includes the North and South Burlingame districts. Thomas and his family lived on and farmed their land. The house they built there was shipped around Cape Horn from Maine, in the form of pre-fabricated modules, lumber cut to fit, and other parts and pieces — a giant "Tinker Toy" which must have been great fun to assemble, if the directions were clear!

Down-river, brother James was busy with several developments at his claim. As population grew, he enlarged his ferry business. He first had the "Jefferson Street Ferry," which crossed the river just south of today's Hawthorne Bridge. He added a second and more popular one, the "Stark Street Ferry." In 1855, James paid the first license fee to Multnomah County — $10, to operate his ferry service. The size of his vessels grew, so as to accomodate wagons, buggies, and cattle, as well as foot passengers. And he continued to work as a cooper, making barrels for the many frontier purposes and also exporting them to the Hawaiian Islands for use by the sugar plantations.

About 1860, James began to lay out and sell lots in "East Portland." All those new settlers on the lots he sold were, of course, potential ferry passengers. He expanded his real estate holdings by buying the south half of the Wheeler DLC and other land until he eventually owned about 1900 acres. He thus controlled all the sites on the east riverbank from which any ferry service to Portland could operate. In 1861, he sold the franchise for the "Stark Street Ferry" to A.J. Knott for $18,000.

In 1869, he laid out the Stephens Plat, in which he dedicated one of the streets as Stephens Street. His "East

Portland" was incorporated as a city in 1870. He was a City Councilman of East Portland. James was widely known as "old Uncle Jimmy."

In the 1860s, James built on his DLC a house which came to be a well-known landmark on the riverbank. It was a large three-story structure, with some elegance, near the foot of Stephens Street. It stood there until 1902, when it was moved to S.E. 12th and Stephens Street, where it can be seen to this day, although shorn of much of its original styling.

Thomas died April 13, 1885, aged 83, and James died March 22, 1889, also aged 83. Neither had made a will, and their estates became the targets of protracted and even sordid disputes in probate court.

Thomas was survived by widow Phebe (aged 70 in 1885), a son (aged 54) by Thomas' first wife, and four children (aged 40 to 28) by Phebe. One son, Emor, had been killed by Indians near the mouth of the Columbia River in 1850. Another son died in 1861 while prospecting along the John Day River. Phebe waived her right to administer the estate, signing that document with "X," her mark. One of Phebe's sons was named administrator. The probate records contain a tangle of claims. In 1892, Phebe petitioned for $300 from the estate, saying she was feeble and needed clothes and medicine. The administrator replied that she was incompetent from old age (she was 76 by then) and requested that a guardian be appointed for her. As evidence of her incompetence, the administrator said that Phebe had owned four city lots in her own name, but had given them, without any security, to a grandson (aged 23) who had mortgaged them and lost the money in a business venture. (All of these declarations in court were made, of course, by the various parties' lawyers.) Later, Phebe again petitioned for funds from the estate, saying she still had at home a son dependent upon her. The administrator said that son was addicted to morphine and Phebe gave him money "whenever he asks for it." As probate proceedings dragged on, Phebe objected to the attorneys' fees, which suggests she was more alert than her administrator son suspected. Probate of the estate was finally closed November 1, 1904, nineteen years after Thomas' death.

James' estate was much larger, and inheritance of it was contested. Six of his children had died before him. One, James Jr., had drowned in the Willamette River in 1869. His wife had died in 1887, aged 80. The only surviving child was a daughter, Elizabeth, married and living in Los Angeles. She claimed to be the only heir, and at her request a Mr. Gove was named administrator. The total value of the estate was somewhat uncertain but estimates suggest it may have been about $285,000 — equivalent to something like $4 million at today's wage-price level. Among the assets was $24,000 in cash, which James kept in a little personal safe — apparently he didn't trust banks!

But there then appeared two other claimants. One was James' granddaughter, Rosetta, daughter of India Stephens. Rosetta was married to one Henry Jones. The other claimant was James' nephew, Franklin, son of James' sister.

It was brought out that James had been ill for 17 months prior to his death, during which time he had been confined at the home of Rosetta and Henry, where he had died. Henry said he had known James for 15 years, and had acted as his business agent. Henry stated that he had received $33,000 from the sale of some of James' property, and also $10,000 which was a gift to himself from James. Henry added that James, two weeks before he died, had given him the key to the safe!

Franklin and Rosetta declared, through their attorneys, that Elizabeth had sold all her interest in the estate before she asked to have Mr. Gove appointed administrator, that Elizabeth was mentally incompetent, and that she and Gove were trying to defraud the rightful heirs, namely, themselves.

In reply, Elizabeth and Gove declared that Rosetta was an illegitimate child of India and therefore not a legal heir. Further, they said that James Stephens, as of March 1889, had owned real estate worth $250,000, which Henry and Rosetta had induced James, at a time when he was not mentally competent to act, to deed to Henry for $10. Elizabeth brought suit against Jones for $113,000.

In August 1890, the court decided for the defendants, thus leaving everything in the hands of Rosetta and Henry, and incidentally quashing innuendoes about illegitimacy. James' property eventually went to nephew Franklin, to Rosetta Jones, and to numerous other individuals. Some of those deeds had been drawn up before James had died.

The City Directory for East Portland in 1889 (the year of the probate brawl) shows Henry Jones, occupation "real estate," living on 9th Street. The Directory for 1890 shows Henry Jones, no occupation, living at "Stephens' Homestead," on the riverfront. That is, he and Rosetta had moved into the large house James Stephens had built in the 1860s.

The snarled affairs of the estates of the Stephens brothers are, altogether, further proof, if one needed it, of the truth of the Psalmist's lament:

> Surely, every man is as a breath
> And his endeavors are vanity.
> He heaps up riches
> But knows not who shall gather them.

Even so! But one can reduce the uncertainty to some extent with a well-drawn will.

Stephenson
John
Robert Edelin

In a long train of covered wagons, moving slowly across the plains, days were filled with chores and unexpected challenges, but there was time for some socializing, especially in the evenings. There would be camp fires, cooking, repairs, and the oxen and horses would be grazing. On such an occasion, in the summer of 1853, Robert Edelin Stephenson, aged 31 and single, discovered that someone else in their company had the same last name as his own. It turned out to be Ann Maria Stephenson.

They were not related, but having been brought to each other's notice by this coincidence, they became better acquainted. Evidently, they found they had more in common than a name, because a few months after they arrived at Portland, they were married.

Robert was crossing the plains with his father, John Stephenson, who was then 55 years old. John had been clerk and sheriff of Wood County, Virginia (in the portion of Virginia that later became West Virginia). John married Sarah Edelin, whence came Robert's middle name. Sometime after Robert's birth, Sarah died. John re-married, in December 1843, his second wife being Ann Steger.

As for Robert, he seems to have had a roving disposition even among pioneers, who are, by definition, somewhat restless. This was not his first trip across the continent. He had gone from Virginia to California in 1849, to look for gold. There, he became ill, so he returned to Virginia — by sailing ship around Cape Horn, which one would have thought might have made him even more ill! Then, in 1851, he went to Mexico, returning to Virginia in 1852. The next year, in response to news about free land in Oregon, he and his father undertook the covered-wagon journey during which he met Ann Maria.

The Stephensons arrived at Portland in October 1853, and, the next month, John settled on a claim. Being married, he qualified for 320 acres of donation land. The tract he chose, in what is now southwest Portland, is bounded today by Stephenson Street (named for him), the county line, Tryon Creek State Park, and S.W. 19th Avenue. John died at his residence in October 1871, aged 75 according to a newspaper obituary, but 73 if the birth date on his DLC application and in other archival material (March 1798) is correct.

Robert and Ann Maria Stephenson were married at Portland in April 1854, by Rev. George M. Berry, of the Methodist Church. Being married, they qualified for 320 acres of donation land. They settled on their claim in August 1854. The tract they found adjoined that of Robert's father, and is bounded today by Dickinson-25th-Palatine streets on the north,

Stephenson Street on the south, Tryon Creek State Park on the east, and S.W. 35th Avenue on the west.

Perhaps because of Ann's stabilizing influence (and the fact that she gave him five children to provide for), Robert would "no more a-roving go." He spent the rest of his life farming his DLC. He died in August 1903, aged 79 according to a newspaper obituary, but 81 if the date of his birth (1822) on his DLC application is correct.

Stevenson

Very little is known about Charles Stevenson, the first person to own a 264-acre tract along N.E. Marine Drive just east of Portland Airport. The only facts we have about him are those shown on the application he filed at the Land Office for his claim. There, we learn that he was born in Norway in 1815, arrived in Oregon in September 1850 (conveniently before the December 1, 1850 deadline after which he would have been entitled to only half as much land), was unmarried, and settled on his claim in January 1851. It is a triangular tract, extending along the Columbia River from about N.E. 102nd to 112th avenues, or where those streets would be if put through.

There is a strong presumption that, after selling his DLC, Charles left Portland. We found no obituary, no cemetery entry, nothing about him. Negatively, we know he was not the person for whom Stevenson, Washington was named. As no living memory can recall him and the archives are mute, we can only let the silence fall gently over our Norwegian-American pioneer, with an expression of frustration he would have appreciated: Uff Da!

Stewart

Eli Stewart was born in Ohio in 1813. When he was 25 years old and in Kentucky, he married Ann Christina. They came across the plains, with three children, in 1850, arriving at Portland in October. Later that year, a fourth child was born.

The family settled on their Donation Land Claim in April 1851. The tract contained 632 acres, and lies along today's Canyon Road, from the Zoo westward to Sylvan. On the north, it extends beyond Fairview Boulevard, thus including Hoyt Arboretum. The south boundary is near Humphrey Boulevard.

In 1856, Eli and Annie sold 190 acres for $1600 ($8.42 per acre). Three years later, they sold 20 acres at $10 per acre. In 1860, they sold 200 acres to Patrick Raleigh, also at $10 per acre. And in 1861, they sold 208 acres to Thomas Carter, a nearby DLC settler, at about $20 per acre.

The family then moved to Umatilla County. Eli died in 1900, aged 87, at Pilot Rock, where he and other members of his family are buried.

Street

Isaac F. Street was the initial owner of two tracts in what is now northeast Portland. One he bought under the Homestead Act, receiving title to it in 1866. It contained 80 acres, and he would have paid $1.25 per acre, a total of $100. This tract extends from 97th to 107th and from Siskiyou to Brazee streets, or where those streets would be if extended. Isaac sold those 80 acres in 1869 to George Buchanan for $350.

The other tract forever bearing Mr. Street's name as first owner contained 160 acres, bounded today by N.E. 112th, 132nd, Shaver, and Fremont streets. He acquired this land by using a Military Bounty Warrant. The warrant was originally issued to one Jacob Lebo, who was a private in a company of volunteers in the Cayuse Indian "war" of 1848-49. "Lebo" is probably a corruption of the French "Le Beau" ("the handsome one!"), and perhaps he was a French-Canadian who had been a fur trapper for Hudson's Bay Company. That is conjecture, but we do know that Lebo sold his warrant to a certain Irick T. Rollf, who sold it to Isaac Street. We don't know what Isaac paid for the warrant, but it was certainly very much less than the $720 he received when he sold those 160 acres in 1870 to Obed M. Barnard, a nearby DLC settler. Isaac was unmarried.

The archives contain no other reference to Isaac Street. But for his name on those deeds, he might be quite fictitious.

Streibig

Denmark, Ireland, Wisconsin, and the War of 1812 are the diverse strands brought together in the first ownership of a 160-acre tract in northeast Portland. Frank J. Streibig was born in Copenhagen in 1823. He emigrated to the U.S., settling in Portage County, Wisconsin. Then there was Mary, born in Ireland about 1840, who emigrated first to New York and then to the same Wisconsin county. Frank and Mary had different accents and different church backgrounds, but love knows no such barriers. Frank was received into Mary's Catholic Church, they were married, and came to Portland in 1858. Their home was at 7th and Alder Street, now S.W. Broadway and Alder and a very urban intersection, but then a residential area with chickens and picket fences.

Frank was a house painter. He and Mary had four sons. But Frank died in 1869, aged only 46. His ailment was diagnosed as "chronic dyspepsia." Next year, Mary had a worthy monument put up to Frank, described in the *Oregonian* of April 28, 1870:

> Mr. William Young, monument and tombstone manufacturer, of this city, yesterday put up another very handsome monument near East Portland, at the Catholic Cemetery, over the grave of Mr. F.J. Streibig, deceased. The monument is seven feet in

> height, of pure white Vermont marble, set on a base of Oregon granite. It is a fine memento to awaken the memory of a worthy citizen. It was erected by the widow of deceased, at a cost of $300.

Mary turned the family home into a boarding house, which she operated successfully for several years. She also engaged in a very profitable real estate investment. As we have already seen, there was a market for "Military Bounty" land warrants, and Mary bought one. She used it to acquire 160 acres bounded today by these N.E. streets: 72nd, 82nd, Tillamook, and Siskiyou. The warrant was issued originally to one Solomon Sparrow, a private in the Massachusetts militia in the War of 1812. We don't know what Mary paid for the warrant, but it was probably about $150, at most. Certainly, it was far less than the $25,000 for which she sold that tract in 1889 to Mr. B.A. Bowman.

Mary died November 17, 1897, aged 57. (Her age and birth date are somewhat uncertain. One source says she was born "about 1832," but the will she had drawn up in 1890 stated that she was 50 years old at that time. We are inclined to accept the statement in the will.) Her will provided for the division of her estate equally among her four sons. The estate's value was $61,000.

Stump

There were two distinct and apparently unrelated Stump families in early Oregon. One settled in the Monmouth area. The other came to Portland. Its patriarch was Cuthbert Stump, whom we met earlier because of his connection with the arrest and hanging of Danford Balch, another DLC pioneer. Here, we will give only a few additional details and vital statistics.

Cuthbert was born in Virginia (the part that later became West Virginia) in 1809. There, in 1829, he married Perlina Yocum. They were in Missouri in 1847, when Cuthbert, Jr. was born. The family arrived in Oregon in September 1851. They qualified for a 320-acre Donation Grant, and selected a tract along Columbia Slough, east of today's St. Johns district. Cuthbert was a farmer and blacksmith.

In 1858, Cuthbert was named administrator of the estate of his son Mortimer. Mortimer died intestate. He didn't have time to make a will — he was shot to death suddenly and unexpectedly by his father-in-law. The details of that sensational affair are given in the entry for Mr. Balch. We will only add here the accounting Cuthbert gave of his son's assets: 1 yoke of Red Oxen, $125; 1 watch; 1 pistol.

Cuthbert and wife Perlina sold all of their Donation Land Claim "except one acre used for burial purposes" to T.J. Stimson and S.P. Marsh for $4750. Cuthbert signed the deed with "X," his mark. That explains why his name is spelled several different ways: Cuthbert, Cuthbirth, Cuthbirt, etc. On such occasions as the signing of a deed or other record, the clerk would ask him his name and then spell phonetically what he thought he heard. But Perlina was literate. She possessed not only a rather lovely name but also the ability to write it!

Sullivan

"Sullivan's Gulch" is a term and locale well known to Old Portlanders but, for others, it should be explained that it is a ravine on the city's East Side wherein, many years ago, there ran a creek, but where now run the Union Pacific Railroad, a light-rail interurban train, and a freeway. It is named for Timothy Sullivan, who settled there on his Donation Land Claim.

Tim was born in County Cork, Ireland in 1805. In 1841, he was in Tasmania (!) where he married a girl named Margaret, probably also an emigrant from Ireland. The pattern is surprisingly similar to that of DLC settler Michael Kennedy, except that Tim Sullivan left Ireland *before* the Potato Famine. Perhaps he could see trouble coming. Or maybe he was just tired of potatoes.

According to Land Office records, Tim and Maggie arrived in Oregon in December 1850, but it must have been a few days after December 1st, because they qualified for only 320 acres. Perhaps he wasn't aware of the importance of that day. But even if he was aiming for it, the exact arrival date of a sailing ship from Australia would be hard to control.

In any case, it didn't take them long to find a claim — they settled on theirs in January 1851. The tract is bounded today by these streets: N.E. Halsey, S.E Stark, 18th, and 28th. There, on the south brow of the gulch about where 19th Avenue would be, Tim built a cabin for himself, Maggie, daughter Marie, and son John J.

A contemporary pioneer, reminiscing years later, said that the Sullivan cabin, in the 1850s, was surrounded by dense forest. "The woods were full of cougars and bears. They howled all night!" (This could be an instance of distance lending exaggeration.)

Tim received his U.S. citizenship in 1855. He would have applied for it when he took up his DLC. And he bought more land which he held in addition to his DLC. But Tim died in July 1865, aged 60. He willed all of his property to daughter Marie. Marie entered the Catholic order, Sisters of Providence, with the name Sister Mary Augustine, and lived at the convent in Vancouver, Washington. The widow Margaret moved to Vancouver, to be near her daughter, and died there in January 1890, aged 80. When Sister Mary Augustine died, she willed all of the Sullivan property to the Sisters of Providence. Son John died without leaving descendants.

Sullivan Street is named for Tim Sullivan, so he appears in *Portland Names and Neighborhood*, pp. 210-11, where more details about his property are given.

Benjamin Sunderland

Sunderland
Benjamin
Albert

    Benjamin Sunderland and his son Albert might represent the archtype of "The Pioneer" — successive migrations, work with the land, ending in comfortable attainment. Ben was born in Ohio in 1812. From childhood, he worked on his father's farm. But his father died when Ben was only 12 years old, so he was too busy to have any schooling. In December 1836, he married Marie Elizabeth Shaeffer. They moved to Illinois, and then were among the first to homestead "government land" in Iowa. A flood there in 1851 turned Ben's thoughts to some better place, and, in the spring of 1852, he, his wife, and their six children left for Oregon. They came across the plains in a train of 40 wagons, arriving at Portland in September 1852.

    They found a 323-acre tract they liked on Columbia Slough. An earlier arrival had claimed it, but Ben bought that man's rights for $750, and the title was subsequently issued as the "Benjamin Sunderland DLC." One might have expected Ben, having been flooded out back in Iowa, to be apprehensive about living on a riverbank, but access to water transportation was a big advantage at a time when there were no roads. Ben's DLC is bounded today by N.E. 24th, 33rd, and Portland Boulevard, and extends northward across Columbia Slough to, and including, Riverside Golf Course. There Ben engaged in dairying and stockraising, and had three more children.

One of Benjamin's sons, Albert, born in Illinois in 1840, was first owner of a 200-acre tract just northeast of his father's DLC. The Albert Sunderland claim is in the vicinity of N.E. Elrod Road and part of it is now in Portland Airport.

Albert's youth was a time of migration and work. He helped his father at farming and diarying from 1852 (he would have been 12 years old) until 1861, when he decided to try his luck at mining in eastern Oregon. He was quite successful and came back with sufficient capital to start out on his own. He acquired his claim, married Susan Fitzgerald in 1864, and became a farmer and dairyman. In 1870, he added a cattle-grazing business near Yakima. And in 1880, he bought 800 acres on Sauvie Island for stock raising.

Perhaps his most daring venture was in 1896 at the time of the Klondike gold rush. Albert loaded a ship to Alaska with several tons of food and supplies and some oxen to move his wares, and set up a restaurant and provision business. Albert knew something about mining — he had got his start that way — and he had observed that, while a few prospectors might find gold, they all had to eat. He was an enterprising man.

Father Benjamin died at his home on his original claim, in December 1896, aged 84. Up until a few months before that, he had never been ill. All nine of his children were still living. He could be proud of his two sons (Albert and Milton) and pleased that his seven daughters were happily married. Mary, for example, was the wife of John Mock, a nearby DLC settler.

His obituary reported that "last week he was taken with a chill and from then until his death, he was delirious most of the time". The writer added: "He was respected as a good neighbor and a man of integrity... honored by all."

Surely, it had been (except for a little trouble during the last week) a Good Life. He was buried in Columbia Slough Cemetery, services having been held at the Christian Church. He was of German and Scottish ancestry.

Son Albert retired and bought a magnificent residence on King's Heights, with beautiful grounds and a panoramic view. In the distance, he could see Columbia Slough, where he had spent many youthful years in hard work.

In September 1913, Albert and Susan celebrated 50 years of blissful marriage with a lavish reception. "At their large house at 1000 Melinda Avenue," 150 guests were entertained. "In the banquet room," as a newspaper reporter described it, "electric lights shaded in deep yellow cast a golden glow all over the happy scene."

Albert died in January 1925, aged 85. He was a long-time member of the Masonic Lodge, and a Presbyterian.

Swift

"The Shamrock Saloon," on Front Street in early-day Portland, was owned and named by an Irishman, Henry Swift. He was born in Ireland in 1827. It was probably during or shortly after the Potato Famine (1845-46) that Henry left Ireland (see the earlier biography of DLC settler Michael Kennedy).

In 1852, Henry, aged 25, arrived at Portland, a village of about 1200 inhabitants. In 1853, Henry married Jane McFarland. In July 1854, they settled on their Donation Land Claim. Being married but having arrived in Oregon after December 1, 1850, Henry qualified for a maximum of 320 acres. They found a 292-acre tract, bounded today by these N.E. streets: 62nd, 79th, Killingsworth, and Prescott.

During the years 1854-58, the Swifts would have been somewhat confined to their DLC tract, due to the commitment to live on and cultivate such claims for four consecutive years. So it was probably about 1859 that Henry opened "The Shamrock Saloon." Meanwhile, the Swifts first two children were born: Mary Anne in 1854 and James in 1856, according to baptismal records of the Catholic Church.

Expenses connected with the opening of his saloon may have put Henry in a financial squeeze. In 1860, he was sued for non-payment of a debt of $152. On March 30, 1861, the Sheriff auctioned off part of Henry's DLC to pay the debt — 240 acres were sold for $70! The record of the sale notes that the auction was held "at the Court House door" because the land being sold had no structures on it. In deeding the property sold, Jane signed with "X," her mark, but Henry wrote his name. In 1882, Henry deeded his remaining 52 acres to a son, Henry Jr., who, in 1885, sold them to one David Pardun for $3750. By then, Henry Sr. had moved to California.

Switzler
    John
    Joseph R.
    Jehu R.
    William

Before 1846, if you wanted to go from Oregon to Vancouver, Washington, you had to provide your own canoe. But in 1846, John Switzler began a ferry service. It was the first ferry operated on the Columbia River. "The Switzler Ferry," as it was widely and aptly known, ran from John's Donation Land Claim to a point near Hudson's Bay Company's Fort Vancouver. He operated his ferry — an important link in early-day communication — for ten years, until his death in 1856 at the age of 67. One of his sons continued the ferry service, later selling it to A.J. Knott, who was operating Portland's Stark Street Ferry.

John Switzler was born in Virginia in 1789 (or possibly 1779 — there is an inconsistency in the data). His father was from

Berlin, Germany. John married Elizabeth Lee in Virginia in 1811. He fought in the War of 1812. Elizabeth died in Virginia, leaving him with three young children. He moved, with them, to Missouri. There, in 1827, he married Maria Robinson, with whom he had six more children. The whole family came to Oregon in 1845. In September 1846, they settled on a square-mile claim, bounded today by Columbia Slough, the Columbia River, Williams Avenue (as extended) and N.E. 18th Avenue (as extended). It includes part of Columbia Edgewater Golf Course.

In the Columbia River just offshore from John's DLC lies Tomahawk Island. Between it and the Oregon riverbank is a branch of the river known today as Oregon Slough but called "Switzler Slough" in pioneer days. In this protected location was John's ferry landing.

John's first home was made of logs, but he soon built a more substantial and comfortable one. He also built a school on his property, and hired a teacher to instruct his children and grandchildren and some of the neighbors' children. In 1850, a post office was established at his ferry landing, with John Switzler post master. The post office was called "Slough, Oregon." It was discontinued in 1852, as settlement and communication began to center on the growing town of Portland.

John was a ready buyer of any cattle which newly-arrived immigrants wanted to sell. He maintained a large herd, grazing them where the golf course is today.

Among John's children, all nine of whom came with him to Oregon in 1845, were three sons who were also original owners of Portland-area land:

Joseph Robinson Switzler (his middle name was his mother's maiden name) was born in Missouri in 1830. He married Mary Wolf in 1848. They settled on a 412-acre Donation Land Claim just west of father John's claim. Joseph's tract today includes Portland Meadows Race Track, part of Delta Park, and extends from Columbia Slough to the Columbia River.

Jehu Robinson Switzler was born in Missouri in 1831 and settled on a 324-acre Donation Land Claim also along the

Columbia River and today taken up entirely by Portland Airport. He later moved to Umatilla County and became a stockman.

William Switzler, born in Missouri in 1834, bought a 21-acre Homestead adjacent to father John's claim. Title to William's tract was issued to him in 1863. He also moved to Umatilla County, where he was owner of a store. Both Jehu and William became prominent citizens of Pendleton.

Talbot

Council Crest, the highest spot in Portland (1073 feet, not counting TV towers) was known as Talbot Mountain in the 1850s and 1860s because John Talbot owned it. His 640-acre Donation Land Claim now includes a large part of "Portland Heights" — some of the city's most valuable residential view property — but when Mr. Talbot settled there, in December 1851, it was inaccessible wilderness.

John Beal Talbot was 54 years old when he, his wife, and four children came to Oregon in 1849. John was born in Massachusetts and served in the War of 1812 as a 17-year old volunteer. Before coming to Oregon, he had been a pioneer twice already — from Massachusetts to Kentucky and then to Illinois. There, in 1840, aged 45, he married Sarah Plumb, of the Virginia Plumbs. Sarah was 21 years old.

John was a County Commissioner in Illinois. He also acted as interpreter between U.S. troops and the Black Hawk Indians. How he acquired that skill is left to our imaginations.

The Talbots were apparently well established in Illinois, but for reasons unknown (free land? the chilly mid-western winters? the love or habit of pioneering?) they left for Oregon in March 1849. John had done well in Illinois and was able to prepare for their trek more adequately than many migrants. He spent $1300 (equivalent to nearly $20,000 today) for equipment, supplies, and livestock, including two wagons, five yoke of oxen, two teams of horses, and a saddle mare. There was also a milk cow, which, when the caravan was under way, was attached by a rope to the rear wagon. And they had provisions for six months and $350 in cash for expenses *en route*. But such journeys defy even the most carefully laid plans. Some of their animals died or were lost, and they had to abandon one wagon and squeeze everything into the remaining one. More serious was an epidemic, diagnosed as "cholera," which swept through their wagon train. The Talbots were very ill but survived; some people in the train died.

Wagon trains of settlers like the Talbots were troubled in the crossings of 1849 by the many single men on their way to the California mines. Those gold-seekers would attach themselves to the wagon trains, until they branched off on the Humboldt Trail through northern Nevada to Sacramento. Many of those men were rough characters, planning to live by their wits in California. Among them, there was a distressing amount of drinking, quarrels, and fights. Several unruly individuals had to be ejected from the Talbot train. In another train that year, one of these characters committed "so heinous a crime" that the men of the train sat in judgment on him, decided he was not worthy to live, and executed him by hanging. (The report omits mentioning the exact nature of his heinous act.)

At The Dalles, John Talbot and six other men from the wagon train built three flatboats, to transport their possessions down the Columbia River. For materials, they used parts from their now unneeded wagons. They also used boards which they salvaged from the ruins of the Methodist Mission house, which had been burned. They calked the seams of the flatboats with discarded clothing dipped in pitch. The men brought the flatboats down the river, and the women and children brought the animals across the Cascade Mountains, walking all the way. Mrs. Talbot and the other women quickly wore out their shoes on that rough terrain. They improvised by making a sort of slipper, using the hide of an ox. Here are the directions: place the foot in the middle of the hide; cut a large circle around the foot; gather the hide into a puckered sack around the ankle; and fasten it by wrapping a string of hide around the ankle. It was better, marginally, than going bare-footed. Such improvisations and discomforts were commonplace among our pioneers.

The Talbots all reached Portland in November 1849, eight months and ten days after leaving Illinois. Two more children were born here on the Talbot DLC, which is bounded approximately by these southwest streets: 18th, 45th, Humphrey, and Hamilton.

John Talbot died in April 1874, aged 79. The obituary noted that "Deceased was well known in and around Portland." His wife Sarah died in 1900, aged 80.

Terwilliger

This unusual name (not unusual if you happen to be a Dutchman) comes down from a distant ancestor who settled in New Amsterdam (now New York). In Dutch, "ter" means "at" or "by," and "willig" may come from "wilg," a willow tree. Thus, "Terwilliger" may mean "He who lives at or by the willows."

James Terwilliger was a prominent early Portland settler and biographical information about him has appeared in our previous books. In 1846, he established Portland's first blacksmith shop (see *Early Portland: Stump-Town Triumphant*, pp. 36-7). In 1878, he was one of six men appointed by the Governor to represent Oregon and Oregon products at the Paris World's Fair (see *Skidmore's Portland*, pp. 67-71, 73-75, and a photograph of him and of his first Portland cabin, p. 46). A street is named for Mr. Terwilliger, so additional information about him appears in *Portland Names and Neighborhoods*, p. 214. Here, we will add a few more bits of biography.

James Alexander Terwilliger left Illinois for Oregon in the spring of 1845. His wife was Sophronia Ann (nee Hurd), whom he had married in 1833. They had two children: Hiram and Charlotte. The family traveled across the plains with two wagons (each drawn by three pairs of oxen) and 13 cows! But Sophronia died on the trip. James and his two children reached Portland in the fall of 1845, and he took up a claim on 640 acres on the east side of the Willamette River, opposite the "Portland" townsite. Within a year or so, he traded that claim for one horse, a transaction which gives us a good idea of the relative value of animals and real estate when there is a great abundance of empty land. In 1848, James married a widow, Mrs. Philenda Lee Green. In 1850, he acquired the 630 acres which became his Donation Land Claim. It is bounded today by S.W. Lowell, 12th (as extended), and Pendleton streets, and the riverfront. James, Philenda, Hiram, and Charlotte settled there in October 1850.

James had a brother, Sol Terwilliger, who had also come to Oregon. In 1876, Sol was at Tillamook, where his nephew Hiram, now married, was living. That December, Sol decided to visit brother James and family in Portland. To go from Tillamook to Portland in 1876 was simple enough; you just got on your feet and started walking. At least, that is the way Sol tried it. Unfortunately, the exertion, and perhaps cold winter weather in the Coast Mountains, were too much, and Sol died on the way.

James's daughter Charlotte married Walter Moffett, in April 1860. Walter was another DLC pioneer who, as we saw in his earlier biography, died aboard a sailing ship in 1878. Charlotte later married Charles Cartwright.

James's second wife, Philenda, died at Portland in 1873, aged 61. James died at his residence in Portland in 1892, aged 83.

Thompson

James Thompson was born in Ohio in 1816 and there, in 1837, married a girl named Paulina or Perlina. They came to Oregon, settling on their Donation Land Claim in December 1850. It is bounded today by north and northeast Prescott and Fremont streets and extends from Union Avenue to the Willamette River. Because the river's edge varies with the seasons, the area of the tract is given as "about 595 acres" or "600 acres, more or less."

Title was issued to the Thompsons in March 1866. Six months later, they sold the entire DLC for $4800. The buyers were Daniel Abrams and Alonzo Knox, who, in 1882, sold 173 of the acres to the Oregon Railway and Navigation Company for $21,191, showing how land values in particular and the price level in general had appreciated.

We don't know what the future held for James and his wife. The inconsistency in the spelling of her name arose because she couldn't write it; she signed deeds with "X," her mark. The archives contain references (e.g., obituary notices) to several men named James Thompson, but not one has a birthplace or birth date corresponding to that of our DLC James. Probably, Jim and Perly took their money and left town. We do know he was not the person for whom Thompson Street was named; that was David P. Thompson.

Tibbetts

About the time Tom Sawyer and Huck Finn took their famous ride on a Mississippi River raft near Hannibal, Missouri (which occurred, according to Mark Twain's testimony, in the early 1840s), Gideon Tibbetts was working on flatboats, taking cargoes down the river to New Orleans. His home was probably in St. Louis, the great river port. There, his wife Mary and their young children would await his unpredictable return. Flatboats had no motive power; they floated down the river propelled by the current. Large oars were used principally to guide the barge-like vessel and keep it off sand bars. The boatmen would pass all the landmarks described so lovingly by Mark Twain in *Life on the Mississippi*.

At New Orleans they would deliver the cargo, and sell the boat itself for its wood and lumber. A flatboat was simply heavy logs lashed together and covered with a wooden deck, with a little tent-like shelter amidship. The crew would then come back upstream on a steamboat to St. Louis, and repeat the enterprise with another flatboat.

Gideon was born in Maine. In September 1833, he was living in Indiana, when he married Mary Fox. He was 25 years old. It was probably in the early 1840s that he had his flatboat job. In 1847, Gideon, Mary and family came to Oregon in an ox-propelled "prairie schooner" — perhaps easier to navigate than a flatboat.

At Portland, in 1849, Gideon discovered that a 640-acre claim on the east riverbank had been abandoned. It had belonged to a family named Dobbins, who had left to go to California to look for gold. The tract became the Tibbetts DLC, bounded today by S.E. Division and Holgate streets, and extending from 20th to the Willamette River. At that time, a stream, Brooklyn Creek, flowed where the Southern Pacific Railroad tracks are now. There, at what would be S.E. Taggart and 11th, Gideon built a flour mill, operated by the creek. It produced "Brooklyn Mills Flour," which, according to old timers, was "highly esteemed." Gideon later sold his flour mill to James Stephens, whose DLC was just to the north.

Gideon's address was "Brooklyn, Oregon." There, in 1859, one of his sons died. Gideon died August 5, 1887, aged 79.

Tice
Thomas
John M.

Thomas Tice and wife Polly arrived in Oregon in October 1850, thus qualifying for a full square mile of Donation Land. Thomas was born in Ohio in 1816 and married Polly in Missouri in 1846. They settled on their 640-acre claim in February 1852. The tract is bounded today by S.W. 19th, 40th, Nevada Court, and Alice Street, and includes the Multnomah community. Also in the spring of 1852, a relative back in Ohio decided to come west. This was John M. Tice, probably Thomas's younger brother. John was 25 years old and single when he reached Portland in October 1852. He took up a 160-acre Donation Land

Claim near Thomas's tract, bounded today by S.W. Kelly, 8th, Lobelia, and Lucille streets. It includes the "Collins View" subdivision.

John was probably motivated to come to Oregon by enthusiastic praise for the Willamette Valley he received from Thomas, although how Thomas communicated with John isn't clear, because Thomas could not write — he signed deeds with "X," his mark. Perhaps Polly was a better hand with a pencil and wrote for him. But apparently there were also other differences between Polly and Thomas; they were divorced in June 1858.

The Donation Land Act was worded in such a way that half of a claim granted to a couple belonged to the wife. Polly had, between 1852 and 1858, conveyed half of her half to Thomas, but she retained 160 acres, which the divorce court allowed to her. Shortly afterward, Polly married Edward Nottage, and in October 1858, Polly and Edward sold her 160 acres to Finice Carruthers, another DLC pioneer, for $1000.

Thomas also began selling parts of the 480 acres remaining in his name. In 1868, he sold 20 acres to Thomas Stephens, a nearby DLC settler, for $300. Thomas Tice signed by "X," his mark.

Meanwhile, John Tice had married Hannah. John and Hannah, in August 1873, sold 41 acres to Charles Rohr for $2000. John signed his name, but Hannah had to make an "X."

A John R. Tice, well-known as a pioneer in Southern Oregon, is apparently not related to our pioneer Portland Tices.

Tigard

Andrew J. Tigard married Sarah Jane in Missouri in 1848. They came across the plains to Oregon in 1852, arriving that October. In the same wagon train were Andrew's brother, Wilson M. Tigard, and their sister, Emily.

Andrew and his wife settled on a Donation Land Claim in April 1853. Their 320-acre tract is bounded today by these S.W. streets: Hamilton, Vermont, 45th, and 54th.

Wilson and his wife Mary Ann settled on a Donation Land Claim near present-day Tigard, Oregon, which is named for him. Wilson had a large family, including three sons (John, Charles, and Conrad) who lived on and farmed their father's original DLC.

This Tigard family's beginnings go back to the state of Georgia and to Hugh Tigard, who fought in the Revolutionary War. Hugh and his wife migrated to western Arkansas in the 1820s, settling at Fort Smith, which at that time must have been a remote dusty outpost on the frontier's leading edge. There, son Wilson was born in 1826 and son Andrew in 1828.

Their sister Emily married William Doblebower, and they, too, were Oregon DLC settlers, but not in Portland.

Toohill

One of our DLC settlers, Thomas Cully, was a private in a company of volunteer riflemen in the Cayuse Indian "war," for which he received a Military Bounty certificate good for 160 acres of government land. Perhaps because Tom already owned a square mile of Donation Land, he didn't want to take on any more, so he sold his certificate to John Toohill. John used it to acquire a 160-acre tract bounded today by these N.E. streets: Killingsworth, Prescott, 52nd, and 62nd. John received title to it in 1866.

Four years before that, in December 1862, he had married Rosa Jones, the ceremony having been performed by the County Recorder. In 1869, John and "Rosay" (as she signed her name) sold 80 acres to Joseph Ledlack for $350.

John died October 23, 1872. He had been quite ill for more than a month, and made his will that September, signing it in a very shaky hand. He left everything to "wife Rosanna" and their two children. His estate included the remaining 80 acres of his claim (valued at $500), a wagon, a horse, a cow, and some personal effects, with a total value of $1200.

Torrence

One of the pioneers active in Milwaukie's early days, as it challenged Portland for commercial supremacy, was William S. Torrence. He was from Massachusetts, arrived in the Portland area about 1847, and worked closely with Lot Whitcomb, the Milwaukie townsite owner (see *Early Portland: Stump-Town Triumphant*, pp. 61-63).

Bill Torrence married Lot Whitcomb's eldest daughter, Mary Jane, and in June 1849 they settled on a 632-acre Donation Land Claim, on the west bank of the Willamette River just opposite Milwaukie. Bill was 26 and Mary Jane 17.

Mr. Whitcomb had established a free ferry service across the river at that point, for the convenience, among others, of the Tualatin Valley farmers bringing grain to his flour mill. A road (now called Military Road) wound down the hillside through the Torrence DLC to a landing near "Elk Rock."

When the Milwaukie proprietors built the famous steamboat *Lot Whitcomb*, Bill became its purser.

The Torrence DLC is bounded today approximately by S.W. Riverdale Road, Greenwood Road, Palatine Hill Road, and the riverfront. Bill and Mary Jane had thirteen children.

Tryon

When Socrates Hotchkiss Tryon came to Oregon, he was unsure whether he would find his future here or in California. So he left his wife and one-year old son (Socrates Hotchkiss Tryon, Junior) in Iowa, while he looked over the territory. When he reached Portland in the fall of 1849, he was 33 years old. With him came his younger brother, Dorlon Dennis Tryon, 24 years old.

Socrates chose the relatively conservative social economy of Oregon, rather than the riotous and speculative California gold milieu. That tells us something about his character, but it would be wrong to conclude that he was not venturesome. He crowded much action and enterprise into the remaining six years of his lifespan.

Socrates (we know of no "nickname" but surely there must have been one?) was born in Vermont in 1816. He migrated to Illinois as a young man and there, in 1837, married Frances Safely. He was 21 and she was 20. Frances was from Edinburgh, Scotland, and was, as we shall see, an energetic, hard-working girl. They later moved to Iowa, where Junior was born in 1848. Before his birth, six other children had been born but had died.

At Portland. Socrates chose a Donation Land Claim on which he settled in February 1850. The 645-acre tract extends from today's S.W. Greenwood Road southward to about "D" Street in the suburban town of Lake Oswego, and from the river westward for about one mile. On his riverfront, he immediately built a sawmill. He also worked with Joseph Kellogg and J.C. Ainsworth, the Milwaukie steamboatmen, in river navigation, and was himself a steamboat captain.

Socrates was a prime mover in the organization of the first Masonic Lodge in Oregon. He, his brother Dorlon Dennis Tryon, Benjamin Stark (another DLC settler), and Berryman Jennings had all become Masons when they were still living in the East, and in May 1850, they called a meeting for all Masons in the Portland area, to form a lodge here. Fifteen Masons assembled June 24, 1850, and they chose Benjamin Stark and Socrates Tryon to go to San Francisco to obtain a charter for a lodge from the California "Grand Master." They sailed for San Francisco on the steamship *Carolina*. Among the members of that first Portland lodge were four other DLC settlers: W.W. Chapman, Captain John Couch, D.H. Lownsdale, and Eli Stewart.

In 1850, Mrs. Frances Tryon and their young son came from the midwest to San Francisco, by the ship-Isthmus-ship route. Perhaps they had already arrived by late June when Socrates went to San Francisco on Masonic Lodge business, although how they would have been able to coordinate their travelling in those days is difficult to imagine — no telegraph, no telephone, and letters taking many weeks for delivery. But Socrates made several other trips to San Francisco in 1850 and 1851 to see them, and for other Masonic Lodge business. It was decided that Frances and Junior would remain in San Francisco while Socrates organized his affairs in Portland. For about a year, Mrs. Tryon operated a boarding house in San Francisco. But one of the devastating fires that swept San Francisco during those years destroyed her boarding house. So, in 1852, Frances, Junior, and a baby girl who had been added to the family, came to Portland.

In May 1855, Socrates died, of an ailment diagnosed as "sciatic rheumatism." He was 39 years old. Socrates left some debts — he had died before his plans and ventures could mature. Evenso, he was able to leave a sum of money intended to give his two children an education. The widow Frances re-married. But apparently she did so without due care, because the deceitful fellow got his hands on the money and absconded — a melodramatic ending to the Life of Socrates! Frances went to work in a laundry to put the two children through school.

Ulery

For duty with U.S. troops in a "war" with the Creek Indians, a Military Bounty land warrant was issued to an individual named IT CHARS WAR CHEE! That's right; that's what appears in the real estate records. We suppose he was an Indian from some other tribe, hostile to the Creeks, who allied himself with the U.S. troops. In any case, CHEE (or IT?) sold his warrant to David Ulery, who used it to acquire 145 acres in what is now the "Woodlawn" neighborhood in northeast Portland. The tract is bounded by Portland Boulevard, Bryant Street, Michigan Avenue, and Union Avenue.

David Ulery received title to that land in 1864. In 1881, he and his wife Martha Jane sold 33 acres to Silas Jones for $1056.

Van Schuyver

Wesley Van Schuyver was born in Pennsylvania and came to Oregon about 1849. He settled on his Donation Land Claim in October 1850, when he was 30 years old and single. His 325-acre tract is in East St. Johns and extends eastward from N. Taft Avenue for about one-half mile, and northward from Cecelia Street across Colunbia Slough. In 1857, Wesley sold his 325 acres to Joseph Switzler, another DLC settler whose property was also along Columbia Slough, two miles to the east.

We found only one other reference to Wesley — an item in the *Oregonian* reporting that, on April 9, 1873, he married Mrs. Belinda Chittenden. The ceremony took place at the home of J.M. Stott, and was performed by Justice of the Peace Andrew Pullen, another DLC settler.

There was also in Portland a more prominent Van Schuyver, William James. He was born in Indiana in 1834 and came to Portland in 1860. We were not able to establish any connection between him and our Wesley.

Warren

One of the first entrepreneurs to exploit Columbia River salmon commercially was Francis Manly Warren. He was born in Maine in 1818 and came to Portland about 1850, leaving behind temporarily in Maine his wife and one son, Frank Warren, born in 1848. They came out to join him in 1855, via steamship and the Isthmus of Panama.

In 1867, Francis organized the Warren Packing Company. He used fish wheels to catch his salmon, which were shipped out dried at first, and later canned. The 1873 City Directory lists him as "Proprietor, Salmon Fishery" with his residence at the corner of West Park and (appropriately) Salmon Street. The 1883 City Directory lists him as "Canner." His cannery was near Cathlamet, Washington.

Francis Warren comes within our horizon because in 1871 he acquired 138 acres which bear his name as first owner. It was "school land" which he bought from the State of Oregon for $44. The tract is bounded today by 41st Avenue, Duke Street, 57th Avenue, and by Cooper-45th-Bybee-52nd-Flavel on the south. Francis died in 1900.

Son Frank married Anna Atkinson, daughter of Rev. George H. Atkinson, a Congregational Church minister. She was a niece of Josiah Atkinson, one of our pioneer landowners. The marriage took place in October 1872. Frank was 24 and Anna 21.

In 1912, Frank and Anna, now 64 and 61, were vacationing in Europe. They started back to America on the *Titanic*. When the ship struck the iceberg and passengers were ordered to take to the lifeboats, Frank helped his wife into a boat but then stepped aside to help some other women into it. Before he could get in, the boat was full and the sailors lowered it away. Anna recalled, "The last I saw of Frank, he was standing by the rail, waving to me and calling that he would be along on the next boat." But there wasn't any next boat, and Frank went down with the ship. It was a nice gesture, to step aside. Un Beau Geste.

Watts

George J. Watts was born in Maine in 1797. In 1838, he was in Missouri where he married Joan (also called Jane). He was 41 years old and she was 29. They came to Oregon in 1847 with two children, aged 8 and 3. A third child was born in 1847, probably in a covered wagon during their journey across the plains. In March 1850, the family settled on a 639-acre Donation Land Claim. It borders the Willamette River north of the St. Johns bridge, around N.W. Germantown Road, and extends from the river-front about one mile up the hillside.

In 1879, George and Joan sold a 100-foot-wide strip across their property to the North Pacific Railroad Company. They received $650 for that right-of-way. Also in 1879, they divided their DLC into three equal parts which they gave to each of their three children. Joan had to sign with "X," her mark.

George died at the house on his DLC in March 1883, aged 85. Joan died there in July 1896, aged 87.

Waud

Captain John Waud was master of several steamboats on the Columbia and Willamette rivers in the 1850s-1870s. He was born in England in 1822, and came to America with his parents when he was 14 years old. The family settled in Ohio. In his early 20s, John went "out west" to Missouri. There, in 1848, he married a girl named Nancy. The couple came to Oregon in 1850 and in March 1851 settled on a 638-acre claim which includes what is known as "Waud's Bluff" (where the University of Portland is located). The tract is bounded today by Westanna, Houghton, and Newman streets, and extends to the river.

John and Nancy sold two parcels of land in 1858: In January, 49 acres to Levi Potter (a DLC settler on the opposite riverbank) for $200; and in June, 150 acres to Peter Carlile for $1000. In July 1874, John and his wife sold 300 acres to D.W. Williams for $10,000.

Captain John died in 1895, aged 72. A news item in the *Oregonian* of March 15 gave the details:

> Capt. John Waud, the well-known steamboat man of former days, capitalist, and pioneer of Portland, dropped dead yesterday morning at the residence of his daughter, Mrs. Emma Ross, Portland. Capt. Waud had gone to the cellar to split some wood, and his daughter, hearing no noise, went to the cellar and found her father lying lifeless.

An obituary, printed March 17, 1895, gives us a picturesque portrait of John and his character:

> ...The suddenness of his death was a shock to his many friends, who have been accustomed for so many years to see his cheerful face and familiar form upon our streets... He took up a claim... embracing the beautiful spot now occupied by Portland University [the reference is to the Methodist school which preceded the present Catholic institution at that location]... Here he began to open up that home which in after years should be known to so many for its boundless hospitality... Although the lives of such men are obscure and unnoticed by the great world, their silent influence is a tremendous factor for the right in the endless struggle between good and evil.

Captain Waud was survived by three married daughters and one son, Orin S. Waud. The son carried on the nautical tradition; at the time of his father's death, he was mate aboard the steamboat *Dalles City*.

Wheeler

Jacob Wheeler, born in Tennessee, was one of our earliest pioneers. He arrived in Oregon in December 1845 when he was 17 years old. He found a square mile of land he liked and in 1848 put in some stakes to mark its boundaries. He registered his claim with the Provisional Government at Oregon City and it eventually became his Donation Land grant. The 627-acre tract is bounded today by N.E. Halsey Street and S.E. Stark Street, and extends from 18th Avenue to the riverfront. The Memorial Coliseum is located on the Wheeler DLC.

In 1849, Jacob, now 21, married a girl named Jemima. A fringe benefit of the marriage was that it qualified him for the maximum of 640 Donation Land acres.

In 1850, steamboats and steamships were first seen on the Willamette River. As their number increased, Jacob went into the business of selling cordwood to them for fuel. Also in the

1850s, he sold the south half of his claim to James Stephens, a DLC settler discussed earlier. Jacob received $1750 for those 320 acres. In 1864, Jacob traded 40 of his acres to the McMillen family for their 640-acre DLC near Aloha, Oregon. Those 40 acres eventually became "McMillen's Addition," a platted residential subdivision. In 1866, Ben Holladay bought most of the remainder of the Wheeler DLC. Jacob spent his later years in California.

Whitaker

Of our nine original Portland settlers born in Ireland, six were Catholics and three were Methodists. Anthony Whitaker was a Methodist, suggesting (though not proving) that he was an "Orange" Irishman from Ulster rather than a "Green" Irishman from Eire.

Anthony and his wife Isabella, living on their 644-acre Donation Land Claim along Columbia Slough, were known by friends and neighbors as "Uncle and Auntie Whitaker" because of their many kind acts. The first Methodist Church in that part of the county was established in their home. Rev. James H. Wilbur was their pastor from 1850 to 1854, when he was sent to the Umpqua Valley, as recounted in the biography of DLC settler Royal.

Anthony Whitaker was born in Ireland in 1802. He emigrated to Canada when he was 29 years old, and worked there as a carpenter until 1837, when he moved to New York. In 1842, he was in St. Louis, Missouri, where he married Isabella Patterson. Four years later, Anthony, Isabella, and their first child came across the plains in a wagon train with several other early Oregon settlers. The Whitakers selected a Donation Land Claim adjoining that of Tom Cully, and settled there in January 1850. The Whitaker DLC is bounded today by N.E. Cornfoot Road, Simpson Street, 42nd, and 66th.

The Whitakers sold their DLC in 1873 and moved to Portland, where they lived on Third Street. Isabella died in 1895 and Anthony died in 1900, aged 98. His body was buried in the Masonic Cemetery, located on the DLC of Andrew Pullen.

North Whitaker Road, Northeast Whitaker Way, and Whitaker School are named for this pioneer (see *Portland Names and Neighborhoods*, p. 227 and p. 242).

Williams, Isaac

Isaac Williams was born in Pennsylvania. In 1834, he was in Ohio, where he married Esther (sometimes spelled Hester). He was 20 years old and she was 25. They and their four children came across the plains to Oregon in 1852, arriving that October. They settled on their DLC in November 1855, just one month before the Donation Land Law expired. Their 320-acre tract is bounded today by these southeast streets: Harold, Flavel, 72nd, and 82nd. Also in 1855, one of their daughters, Dorcas, married Daniel Little.

Isaac and Esther sold 310 acres in March 1860 to a certain Ypsilanti Smith for $2000. They continued to live on and farm their remaining 10 acres. Isaac died in April 1874, aged 60. Probate of his estate showed that he owned a two-seated buggy, a bay horse, a chestnut mare, wagons, and farm tools. Esther died in 1877, aged 68. Her estate included seven acres, valued at $3166, a cow, and a heifer.

Williams, John A.

John A. Williams was born in Kentucky and there, in 1822 when he was 17 years old, he married Nancy Jameson. They arrived in Oregon in October 1852. That was the same month when Isaac Williams (see the preceding entry) arrived, and it is possible that they were related, but we found no proof of that. In February 1853, John and Nancy settled on their Donation Land Claim, comprising 165 acres along the Columbia River. It is now part of Portland Airport.

John was a State Senator from Multnomah County in 1860 when his wife died of "consumption." In 1863, John sold his 165-acre claim to Henry Holtgrieve, whose DLC was just to the west, for $700. John died in Polk County, near the Luckiamute River, in 1884, aged 79.

Wills
George
Jacob

George Wills was a farmer and pioneer sawmill operator. But he never allowed business activities to interfere with his primary concern, which was "saving souls." George was a "hard-shell" Baptist preacher. The word is somewhat comparable to "fundamentalist."

George was born in Kentucky. There, in 1820 when he was 19 years old, he married Sarah Jane Peacock. They had several children, including Jacob (born in Kentucky in 1826), Reuben, and Martha. The family moved to Iowa where, in 1846, Martha married Edward Long, another Portland DLC settler discussed earlier. In 1847, they all came across the plains to Oregon, arriving that October. Some description of their trip is given in the entry for Edward Long.

In the spring of 1848, George and his son Jacob, in partnership with Edward Long, built a sawmill on Johnson Creek. The location, between present-day Sellwood and Milwaukie, came to be known as "Willsburg." Rev. George Wills settled on his 641-acre Donation Land Claim in May 1849. It extends from about McLoughlin Boulevard eastward to S.E. 57th, and from about S.E. Harney Street southward across the county line into Milwaukie.

Rev. George Wills and his wife Sarah Jane

Jacob Wills married Lorana Bozarth in 1849 and, in December 1850, they settled on a 643-acre DLC just north of his father's claim. It is bounded today by about McLoughlin Boulevard, 45th, Bybee and Harney streets. The "Jacob Wills DLC" includes most of the "Eastmoreland" neighborhood.

Rev. George Wills died at Willsburg in March 1888, aged 86. Jacob and Lorana had eleven children, but six of them died before their father. Jacob kept his DLC intact until 1891, when he sold part of it and divided the remainder among his surviving children. He died in April 1891, aged 64.

Wilson

"Man is born to trouble as surely as sparks fly upward" — a lament in the Book of Job, which obviously has it right. There is no reason to doubt that the generic form "man" includes women. Certainly, the life of Sarah Switzler Logsdon Wilson Stoddard seems replete with trouble.

Sarah was the daughter of John Switzler (a Portland DLC settler discussed earlier) and his first wife, Elizabeth Lee. When Sarah was about 12 years old, in 1826, her mother died. Father John married a second wife (Maria Robinson) in 1827. In 1836, Sarah married William Logsdon, but he died the next year, leaving her with a baby daughter. In 1839, Sarah married Andrew Wilson.

In 1845, the Switzlers (including Sarah's father, step-mother and her eight brothers and sisters) and Sarah and her husband Andrew and *their* five children, all came across the plains to Oregon. It was a particularly difficult crossing; the best route for the Oregon Trail had not yet been delineated. A number of people in their wagon train died. But the Switzlers all made it.

Sarah and Andrew Wilson settled on a Donation Land Claim adjacent to, and just east of, that of her father. The Wilson DLC, 318 acres, is along the Columbia River in the vicinity of N.E. 33rd Drive. Today, parts of it are in Portland Airport and Columbia Edgewater Golf Course.

In September 1848, Andrew Wilson went on a trip to California to look for gold. He died there, at a place called "Hangtown," in February 1849. Sarah was left with five young children (Mary Logsdon by her first husband and four by Andrew Wilson). In April 1851, she married Thomas Stoddard. The wedding took place at her home on her DLC, and was performed by the Methodist minister, Rev. James H. Wilbur. But, alas, Sarah herself died one year later, in April 1852, probably in childbirth. She was about 38 years old. Mr. Stoddard and Sarah's children inherited the "Wilson DLC."

Windle

John Windle was born in Ohio. He married Isabel Dodson in 1842 in Missouri when he was 20 years old and she 18. They and their four children came across the plains to Oregon in 1852, arriving that October. They settled on a 314-acre Donation Land Claim in March 1853. It is bounded today by North Lombard, Dana, and Washburne streets, and Columbia Slough. Four more children were born to the Windles in Oregon. John was a farmer. He died at St. Johns in 1902, aged 80, and Isabel died in 1904, aged 80.

Witten

Joshua Ewing Witten was born in Tennessee in 1822. There, when he was 25 years old, he married Nancy. In 1852, Joshua and his wife and two children migrated to Oregon, arriving that September. Within two months, they had found and settled on their Donation Land Claim. The 323-acre tract is bounded today by these S.E. streets: Division, Powell, 52nd, and 72nd.

The family lived in a log cabin Joshua built on his claim. Three more children were born, but, of their five, only two lived beyond infancy. They were two daughters, named Tryphena and Tryphosa. Those are the names, mentioned in the Bible in the book of "Romans," of two women workers in the early Church. We suppose that, in daily affairs, the girls answered to nicknames — "Feeny" and "Fosey" perhaps? — or would that be too frivolous for names of such eminent origins?

Joshua became a blacksmith. To get started, he borrowed the necessary tools from the Rev. Clinton Kelly, who had brought them from Kentucky and whose DLC was nearby. The Wittens were members of Rev. Clinton Kelly's Methodist congregation. Joshua paid for the loan of the tools by shoeing the horse Clinton used to make his rounds as a clergyman.

The Wittens lived on their claim for 20 years, and then sold it and moved to Salem. Joshua died in 1882, aged 60.

David Wittenberg, his wife Caroline, and one of their eight children.

Wittenberg

David Wittenberg was born in Germany in 1826. When he was 27 years old, he emigrated to America, living first in Detroit, where he married a girl named Caroline. In 1856, they moved to Kansas. In 1862, David, Caroline, and their three children came across the plains to Oregon. David bought a "Military Bounty" land warrant which had originally been issued to William Hailey, a private in the Oregon militia in the Cayuse Indian "war." The warrant was good for 160 acres, and David used it to acquire title to a tract in what is now northeast Portland, bounded today by Union Avenue on the west, Bryant-8th-Holman on the north, 15th on the east, and Killingsworth on the south. There, David and Caroline had five more children.

David was in the wood business until he retired, in 1880. In 1882, David and Caroline sold their 160 acres to George J.

Ainsworth for $10,000. One of the Wittenberg sons, Herman, was part owner of the "German Bakery," located on Portland's Third Street for many years. Caroline died in 1904 and David died in 1911, aged 85. All eight of their children were still living in 1911.

Yates

The real estate records showing his purchase and sale of 160 acres in southeast Portland provide all the information we have about John Yates. His original claim is an L-shaped tract bounded today by 57th on the west, Duke-62nd-Ogden on the north, 72nd on the east, and Flavel on the south. John filed for the land under the Homestead Act, paying $1.25 per acre. He moved onto his claim about 1867. In August 1870, he sold it for $300. He was unmarried.

Whence he came and where he went are unrecorded. One J C. Yates, who came to Oregon in 1854, died in Lane County in 1890, aged 59. And a John D. Yates, a printer, was in Portland in 1857. But whether either of these was our John, we know not.

Index

A

Abbott, George	62
Abraham, James	1-2, 183
Abrams, Daniel	260
Abrams, W.P.	55
Ainsworth, George	182, 278
Allard, Alvin	2
Arrigoni, S.N.	68
Atkinson, Anna	268
Atkinson, George	ix, xv, 3
Atkinson, Josiah	3-4

B

Backenstos, Jacob	5-7
Baker, E.D.	237
Baker, Perry G.	7-9
Baker, William W.	7-8, 51
Balch, Anna	10
Balch Creek	9
Balch, Danford	9-15
Banks, Louis A.	83
Baptist Church	159
Barnard, Obed	15-16, 247
Barnes, Charles	16
Barnes, Isaac	16
Barnes, William	16
Barr Hotel	18
Barr, Samuel E.	17-18, 193
Battin, Thomas	18-19
Belle, riverboat	58
Berry, Rev. George	244
Beth Israel, synagogue	20, 164
Black Hawk, steamboat	119
Blackiston, William	19-20
Bloch, H.F.	20-21, 69, 232
Blyth, Percy H.	200
Bowering, William	21
Bowles, Jesse	22
Bowman, B.A.	248
Brother Jonathan, steamboat	188
Brown, Alexander	22, 83
Broy, L.C.	219
Buchanan, George	246
Buchanan, Rev. P.G.	184, 202
Buchtel, Joseph	182
Buckman, A.H.	79
Buckman, Henry	16, 232
Burrage, Charles	22-23
Bush, A., editor	57, 59, 64, 65, 66
Bybee, James F.	23
Bybee, William	23

C

Cahn & Co., grocers	21
Calliope, steamboat	163

Campbell, Ann 219
Campbell, Hector B. 24-25
Campbell, Hector P. 24
Campbell, Hiram T. 25
Campbell, William J. 25
Cann, Thomas H. 25-26
Caples, Hiantha 195
Caples, William 26-27, 234
Cardwell, B.C. 98
Carlile, Peter 269
Carolina, steamship 265
Carter, Julia, teacher 76
Carter, Thomas 27-28, 246
Cartwright, Charles 259
Caruthers, Finice 28-30, 71, 138, 142, 154, 262
Cason, A.J. 31
Cason, Hillery 31-32
Cason, William 31
Catholic Church 143
Catlin, Seth 158
Centenary Methodist Church 1
Chadwick, Stephen 89, 106, 110
Chapman, William W. 32-34, 49, 51-52, 265
Chase, Dr. Benjamin 203
Chase, Mrs. Nancy 158
Chenamus, brig 40
Chipman, Marshall 34
Chittenden, Lyman 18
Clark, Charles 35
Clary, John V. 35-36
Coe, N. 55
Coffin, Stephen 30, 32, 36-37, 51-52, 62, 228

Collins, William 38
Confer, John 15
Congregational Church 3, 116, 117
Constable, Brazilla 100
Corbett, Henry W. 166
Cornell, Emma J. 223
Cornell, William 38
Corwin, William 39
Couch, Capt. John 39-42, 149, 265
Creswell, Avis M. 158
Crimmins, Timothy 42-43
Croke, Rev. James 218
Cully, Thomas 43-44, 211, 263
Curry, Gov. George 53

D

Daly, Patrick 107-108
Dannals, Uriah 185
Darch, George W. 45-46
Davidson, Elijah 46-48
Davis, A.L. 235
Deardorf, Rebecca 221
Dekum, Frank 166
DeLashmutt, Van 74
Delay, Joshua 48-49
Democratic Party 56, 57
Denholm, William 110
Denlinger, Henry 117
Dennison, Ami P. 49-71, 232
DeVall, Christiana 99
Devee, John 71-72
Dickinson, Josiah S. 72-73
Dickson, Miss Elizabeth 119
Dillon, Rev. Isaac 73-75

Index 281

Disciples of Christ 46
Doane, Milton 75-77
Dolph, Joseph 89
Donation Land Act x
Donner, George 77
Donner, John 77, 178
Drake, Richard 226
Dryden, William 79
Dryer, T.J., editor 11-12, 13-14, 56-57, 59, 64
Dufur, E.B. 175
Dunning, John 108
Duvall, Nicholas 78

E

Eagle, riverboat 119
Eastham, E.L. 220
East, Hardman 78-79
E.D. Baker, steamboat 163
Elk Rock 264
Ellsworth, riverboat 86
Emerson, George 79
Estes, Levi 45
Exon, Rev. J. 216

F

Failing, Henry 166
Fair, first county 113
Fashion, riverboat 57
Fechheimer, M.W. 198
Finegan, Patrick 81
Finstamaker, John 80-81
Fisher, Adam 160
Fitch, Dr. Thomas 60, 82
Fitch, Thomas 81-82
Flanders, Caroline 40
Flanders, George H. 41, 42

Fleckenstein, Henry 156
Fleischner, Louis 89, 106, 110, 166
Flinn, Rev. John 223
Force, G.W. 82
Foster, John 83
Francis, Allen 109
Francis, Miss Huldah 109
Frush, James H. 81

G

Gates, Alonzo, 84
Gates, John 166, 224
Gates, Thomas W. 84
Gatton, William 84-85
Gault, D.M. 118
Gemmell, Alexander 76
Gerow, Jonathan 85-87
Gilfry, Henry 87-90
Gilham, Newton 90-91
Gill, J.K. 75
Glisan, Dr. Rodney 41
Gold Hunter, steamship 51
Goldsmith, Bernard 15, 36
Goldsmith & Lowenberg, merchants 166
Gove, I.H. 118
Gradon, Israel 91-92
Gray, George 92-94
Gray, Robert 92-94
Greenleaf, Robert 94-95
Grier, G.W. 73
Groom, Orson A. 95
Grover, Lafayette 28, 88, 89, 106, 110
Guild, Peter 95-97
Guntley, Anton 97-98

H

Haas, Jacob	106
Hailey, William	277
Hall, Capt. T.A.	52
Hall, William	98-100, 182
Hardie, Dennis	130
Hay, Clark	101-103
Hayden, Gay	104-105
Hendrickson, Lemuel	105
Hendrickson, William	105
Hildburgh, David	106
Hill, Rev. Edgar	150
Hill, Isaac	106-107
Hill, Laban	107
Hill, Lorenzo	107
Hill, Mrs. Lucinda Pickering	37
Hines, Rev. Harvey	35, 223
Holladay, Ben	271
Holland, Patrick	107-109
Holmes, Byron Z.	109-112
Holtgrieve, Henry	112-114, 160, 273
Holts, John	80
Hosford, Milton	25
Howe, Evander	114, 232
Hoyt, George W.	38
Hoyt, Richard	118
Humphrey, Homon	114-118, 130
Humphrey, Thomas	233

I

Irving, Robert	21, 69
Irving, William	118-120
Iris, steamboat	163

J

Jail, county	12, 14
Jefferson, Thomas, surveying	xvi
Jeffery, E.J.	150
Jennie Clark, steamboat	58
Jennings, Berryman	265
Johns, James	96, 120-123
Johnson, Arthur H.	166, 220
Johnson, William	123-24
Jones Cemetery	118
Jones, Henry	242-43
Jones, Nathan	124-32
Jones, Silas	266

K

Kelly, Albert	132-40, 142
Kelly, Archon	132-40, 158
Kelly, Clinton	31, 132-140, 144, 276
Kelly, Hampton	132-140, 158
Kelly, Penumbra	139, 178
Kelly, Plympton	132-140
Kelly, Thomas	132-140
Kennedy, Michael	140-143
Kern, William	143-45, 177
Kerns, Lois	32
Kerns, William	145
Kilgore, John	95
King, Amos	146-151
King, Edward	150
King, Eliza Ann	202
King, N.A.	150
King, Col. William	151
King, W.M.	17
Kingsley, Rev. Calvin	177

Index 283

Kittridge, George 151-53
Knapp, R.B. 166, 175
Knott, A.J. 240, 254
Know-Nothing Party 56, 143, 152
Knox, Alonzo 260
Knox, Hannah 206
Kyle, Samuel 153

L

Ladd, William S. 55, 166, 179
Lambert, J.H. 188
Lambert, Sarah 24
Lamerick, John 63
Lane, Senator Joseph 53, 60, 64
Lawrence, Charles 154
Leadbetter, Frederick 167
Ledlack, Joseph 263
Lemmons, Peter 154-55
Lemon Island 154
Lent, Fremont L. 156
Lent, Oliver P. 156, 175
Lewis, Cicero H. 41, 42, 166
Lewis, Julia 145
Lewis, Rev. W.S. 204
Limerick, L. 56
Little, Daniel 272
Long, Edward 156-59
Long, George M. 159-60
Loomis, James 8, 160-61
Loomis, Maria 8
Loring, J.L. 48-49
Lot Whitcomb,
  steamboat 55, 119
Love, Lewis 161-64, 205
Love, William 182

Lovejoy, Asa 32, 33
Lowenberg, Julius 164-68
Lownsdale, Daniel 32, 52, 148, 168-69, 178, 265
Luelling, Alfred 169-74
Luelling, Henderson 169-74
Lumsden, A. 150
Luther, Albert 174-75

M

Madonna, bark 41
Mann, P.J. 77
Marquam, Philip A. 62, 71, 77, 175-81
Marsh, S.P. 249
Martin, P.J. 120
Maryland, brig 39, 40
Masonic Lodge 42, 113, 131, 265, 272
Maxey, Robert 181-82
McCavett, Michael 193
McClung, William 182
McCormick, Stephen 219
McEntire, Henry 183
McKeown, James 184
McLean, Hugh 185
McMahan, Samuel 185
Meek, William 151, 171, 173, 186-87
Mendenhall, Ed
  and Bert 128
Menill, George 17
Metcalf, R.B. 63
Methodist Church 136, 191, 271
Millard, Gideon 187
Miller, Frank W. 189

Miller, Henry G.	188-89
Mitchell, John H.	15, 93, 197, 198
Mock, John	189-91
Moffett, Walter	191-93
Molthrop, Elizabeth	236
Monaghan, Terence	193-94
Monies, William	80
Monmouth University	47
Mormons	5
Mt. Tabor railway	1
Muck, Henry A.	195
Multnomah, steamboat	138
Murphy, Edward	158
Murray, Seldon	195-96

N

Naylor, William	196
Neff, Marcus	197-200
Nelson, David F.	142, 200
Nelson, Dr. Samuel	201
Newell, John	145
Nicholson, William	31
Nicolai, Lewis	155
Niebur, Francis	142, 143
Northerner, steamship	116
North Pacific Rural Spirit, publ.	8
Northrop, Henry C.	202
Northrop, Thomas E.	202
Norton, Capt. Zachariah	50
Nottage, Edward	262

O

Oatman, H.B.	110
Occidental Hotel	8
Odd Fellows lodge	88, 92
Ogden, Harriett E.	203
Ogden, Peter Skene	203
Ogden, William Seton	203
O'Neill, James	59
Opitz German Bakery	225
Oregonian, first issue	7, 51
Overton, William	32

P

Pacific Christian Advocate, publ.	13, 74, 117
Page, W.W.	198
Pain, Joseph	189
Panama, Isthmus railroad	230
Pardun, David	254
Parrish, Louis	204-205
Patton, Matthew	87
Payne, William	205
Pearly, J.N.	85
Pearne, Rev. Thomas	13, 38, 202
Pennoyer, Sylvester	198
Pettygrove, Francis	32, 43
Pittock, H.L.	65, 167
Plamondon, Marie Carissa	74
Pointer, William	206
Portland University	2
Potter, Levi	206-207, 269
Powell, David	99
Powers, David	207
Preston, John B.	xii-xiv, xix
Prettyman, Daniel	216
Prettyman, David	209
Prettyman, Dr. Perry	207-209
Proebstel, Frederick	210

Proebstel, Wendel 210
Protzman, Louis 211
Pullen, Andrew 211, 267, 272

Q
Quimby, Ebenezer L. 31, 212-13
Quimby, E.S. 99
Quimby, L.P.W. 212
Quinn, John 213-15
Quinn, Terrence 213-15
Quivey, Boyd 71
Quivey, Martha 202

R
Raleigh, Patrick 246
Ramsey, Frederick 215
Rankin, John 216
Reed, Simeon 166
Rennison, Isaac 216
Richards, Solomon 8, 217-18
Richardson, Thomas 166
Robinson, Thomas G. 218-19
Roe, Rev. George C. 219-20
Rohr, Charles 262
Root, George W. 220-21
Rosenberg, Rev. John 203
Rosenthal, Lewis 35
Ross, Darius M. 221
Ross, Emma 229
Ross, Sherry 221-22
Royal, Rev. James 222-23
Royal, Rev. Thomas 222-23
Royal, Rev. William 222
Ryan, Thomas 108

S
Schmeer, Peter 224
Schramm, Charles 224-25
Scott, James 78
Sea Gull, steamship 177
Seelye, Elizabeth 160
Sellwood, Dr. John 80
Sequin, brig 50
Shattuck, E.D. 175, 225-26
Shaver, George W. 163
Shaver, John 226-28
Sheldon, David 119
Sisters of Providence 250
Skidmore, Andrew 228
Slavin, John 142, 228-29
Smalley, James 230-31
Smith, B.P. 231-32
Smith, F.C. 166
Smith, George 232
Smith, George W. 232
Smith, Joseph 28
Smith, Peter 233
Smith, Philip T. 233-34
Smith, Seneca 94
Smith, W.K. 166
Smith, Ypsilanti 272
Southern Pacific RR 23
Southmayd, Daniel 27, 234-35
Soverans, Jesse 78
Spectator, publ. 40
Sperry, Thomas 34
Stallard, Thomas 160
Stark, Benjamin 32, 57, 92, 218, 236-37, 265

286 Index

Stark Street Ferry 11
Starr, Benjamin 237-38
Steinberger, Justus 63
Stephens, James 11, 238-43, 261, 271
Stephens, Thomas 238-42, 262
Stephenson, John 244
Stephenson, Robert 243-45
Stevens, Isaac 63
Stevenson, Charles 245
Stewart, Eli 246, 265
Stimson, David 45
Stimson, T.J. 249
Stoddard, Thomas 275
Stott, J.M. 267
Stout, Lansing 63
Street, Isaac 246
Streibig, Frank 247-48
Streibig, Mary 247-48
Stump, Cuthbert 248-49
Stump, Mortimer 10-11, 249
Success, brig 118
Sullivan, Timothy 249-50
Sunderland, Albert 251-53
Sunderland, Benjamin 251-53
Sunderland, Christina 138
Sunderland, Mary 190
Sunderland, Milton 211, 252
Surman, James 223
Swift, Henry 253-54
Switzler ferry 10
Switzler, Jehu 9, 255
Switzler, John 82, 182, 254-55, 275
Switzler, Joseph 22, 255, 267
Switzler, William 22, 104, 256

T

Talbot, John 256-58
Tanner's Creek 148
Tate, J.W. 76
Terwilliger, James 193, 258-59
Therkelsen, L. 166
Thomas, Joe 30
Thompson, D.P. 120, 149
Thompson, James 259-60
Thomson, James 194
Thoroughbred Stock Journal, publ. 8
Tibbetts, Gideon 260-61
Tice, John 261-62
Tice, Thomas 71, 261-62
Tigard, Andrew 262-63
Tigard, Wilson 262-63
Toohill, John 263
Torrence, William 264
Traveler, steamboat 163
Tryon, Dorlon D. 265
Tryon, Socrates 264-66
Tuttle, Hiram 103

U-V

Unitarian Church 23
Ulery, David 266
VanSchuyver, Wesley 267
Versteg, Nicholas 97
Volunteer Fire Dept. 9, 111, 192

W

Wade, Owen	21
Wadhams, William	184
Wait, Aaron	33
Wandell, William	76
Warren, Francis M.	267-68
Watson, E.B.	128
Watts, George	268-69
Waud, John	269-70
Welch, Joel	15
West Union Baptist Church	100
Whalley, J.W.	198
Wheeler, Jacob	270-71
Whig Party	152
Whitaker, Anthony	271-72
Whitcomb, Mary Jane	264
Whiteaker, Gov. John	53
Whitlock, Columbus	124
Wilbur, Rev. James	74, 195, 222, 234, 271, 275
Wilcox, Dr. Ralph	76
Willamette Stone State Park	xii
Willamette Survey	xii
Williams, D.W.	87, 269
Williams, Isaac	272
Williams, John A.	272-73
Williams, J.S.	145
Williams, Richard	118, 119
Willis, P.L.	97
Willis, Rev. W.A.	221
Willsburg community	157, 273
Wills, George	156, 157, 160, 186, 273-74
Wills, Jacob	273-74
Wilson, Dr. Robert	41, 42
Wilson, Sarah	275
Windle, John	83, 234, 276
Witten, Joshua	276
Wittenberg, David	277-78
Wittenberg, Herman	278
Wolf, Susan	82

XYZ

Yates, John	278
Young, William	247

Acknowledgments

Research for this book extended over several years. First, the original landowners had to be identified and the boundaries of their claims determined. This was done from maps at the Oregon Historical Society, maps and deeds at Title and Trust companies, legal descriptions of property at the County Assessor's office, and Donation Land Claim records. Summaries of DLC records compiled by the Genealogical Forum of Portland and available at the Oregon Historical Society library were helpful.

Then began the search for biographical material about these 212 first owners. Sources at the Oregon Historical Society library included biographical and pioneer files, indexes of the *Oregonian* and *Oregon Statesman*, old City Directories, and records (prepared by the Multnomah Chapter, Daughters of the American Revolution) of tombstone inscriptions and of wills and probate proceedings. Abstracts of Titles, available at Title and Trust companies, show the Deeds by which the original owners sold their land, and often contain interesting information about those individuals. Also helpful were the "newspaper files" at the county Public Library, which contain references to many individuals back into the 19th century.

The calligraphed maps were done by Katherine Cameron.

All the photographs are from the files of the Oregon Historical Society. The following list identifies them by page number, subject, and OHS negative number: 4, Atkinson, 25113; 5, Backenstos, 25110; 25, Cann, 25109; 27, Carter, Thomas, 25569; 27, Carter, Minerva, 25687; 40, Couch, 8354; 47, Davidson, 25121; 60, Dennison Building, 25112; 72, Dickinson, 25122; 88, Gilfry, 25166; 91, Gilham, 3512; 101, Hay's Wagon Factory, 12539;

104, Hayden, Gay, 25167; 104, Hayden, Mary Jane, 25165; 110, Holmes, 25172; 113, Holtgrieve, 25189, 115, Humphrey, 25188; 119, Irving, 25187; 121, Home of James Johns, 24082; 125, Jones, 25423; 133, Kelly, Clinton, 4504; 133, Kelly, Plympton, 25184; 157, Long, 25551; 170, Luelling, 25552; 176, Marquam, 25571; 186, Meek, 11286; 190, Mock, 25570; 201, Nelson, 25567; 204, Parrish, 25568; 217, Richards, 25601; 229, Slavin, 25657; 235, Southmayd, 25654; 236, Stark, 25659; 239, Stephens, James, 25655; 239, Stephens, Elizabeth, 25656; 251, Sunderland, 25721; 274, Wills, 25634; 277, Wittenberg, 25635.

The author gratefully acknowledges the help he received from the sources mentioned above, and also from the many individuals who provided other assistance, inspiration, and encouragement.